The First Book of

Lotus® 1-2-3® for Windows™

i

The First Book of

Lotus® 1-2-3® for Windows™

Peter Aitken

SAMS

A Division of Macmillan Computer Publishing

11711 North College, Carmel, Indiana 46032 USA

© 1991 by SAMS

FIRST EDITION
FIRST PRINTING—1991

International Standard Book Number: 0-672-27364-0
Library of Congress Catalog Card Number: 91-62204

Screen reproductions in this book were created by means of the program Collage Plus from Inner Media, Inc., Hollis, NH.

Printed in the United States of America

Trademarks

All terms mentioned in this book that are known to be trademarks or service marks are listed below. In addition, terms suspected of being trademarks or service marks have been appropriately capitalized. SAMS cannot attest to the accuracy of this information. Use of a term in this book should not be regarded as affecting the validity of any trademark or service mark.

Microsoft Windows is a registered trademark of Microsoft Corporation.

Lotus and 1-2-3 are registered trademarks of Lotus Development Corporation.

Quattro Pro is a registered trademark of Borland International.

Publisher
Richard K. Swadley

Publishing Manager and Acquisitions Editor
Marie Butler-Knight

Managing Editor
Marjorie Hopper

Development Editor
Lisa Bucki

Manuscript Editor
Faithe Wempen

Cover Design
Held & Diedrich Design

Indexer
Jill D. Bomaster

Production Team
Jeff Baker, Brad Chinn, Sandy Grieshop, Joelynn Gifford, Phil Kitchel,
Bob LaRoche, Matthew Morrill, Anne Owen, Julie Pavey, Howard Peirce,
Tad Ringo, Dennis Sheehan, Louise Shinault, Bruce Steed, JohnnaVanHoose,
Mary Beth Wakefield, Lisa Wilson, Christine Young

**Special thanks to Don Roche, Jr.
for assuring the technical accuracy of this book**

Contents

Introduction, xiii

1   Getting Started, 1

Using a Mouse, 1
Starting 1-2-3 for Windows, 2
A Brief Demonstration, 5
What You Have Learned, 8

2   The Screen, 9

Menus and Dialog Boxes, 9
Using the Icon Palette, 16
Windows, 17
The Main 1-2-3 Window, 29
Exiting 1-2-3 for Windows, 31
1-2-3 Classic Menus, 31
The Help System, 32
What You Have Learned, 37

3 Moving Around 1-2-3 for Windows, 39

Worksheet Structure, 39
Using Multiple Worksheets, 41
Displaying Different Parts of the Same Worksheet, 44
Synchronizing Worksheets, 46
Navigating in a Worksheet File, 47
What You Have Learned, 51

4 Working with Ranges, 53

Basic Concepts of Ranges, 53
Using Range Names, 60
What You Have Learned, 67

5 Working with Data, 69

Entering Data, 69
Copying Data, 76
Moving Data, 80
Erasing Data, 84
Editing Data, 90
Finding and Replacing Entries, 91
The Undo Command, 95
What You Have Learned, 95

6 Formulas and Functions, 97

Writing Formulas, 97
Formula Operators and Operator Precedence, 99
Using Built-in Formulas, 103
Worksheet Recalculation, 111
The ERR Indicator, 111
What You Have Learned, 112

7   *Worksheet Format and Style, 113*

Format and Style—What are They?, 113
Formatting Numbers, 114
Changing Row and Column Size, 119
Changing Styles, 125
Adding Background Shading, 134
Using Style Names, 136
Group Mode, 139
The Indicator Line, 140
Removing Styles from a Range, 141
Screen Display, Printed Output, and Draft Mode, 142
Using the Worksheet Titles Command, 143
What You Have Learned, 144

8   *Writing Macros to Automate Worksheet Tasks, 147*

Macro Basics, 147
Keystroke Macros, 151
The Macro Commands, 154
Autoexecute Macros, 155
Recording Keystrokes with the Transcript Window, 156
Macro Errors, 162
Debugging Macros, 162
Some Example Macros, 165
What You Have Learned, 166

9   *Printing Reports, 167*

Printing a Report, 167
Previewing a Print Job, 169
Changing Page Setup, 171
Printing a Graph, 176
Controlling Page Breaks, 176
What You Have Learned, 178

10   Graphs — the Basics, 179

Graph Basics, 179
Graph Types, 185
Selecting Graph Type, 194
Dual Y Axes, 197
Selecting Data Ranges, 198
Viewing and Saving Graphs, 202
Inserting a Graph in the Worksheet, 203
What You Have Learned, 206

11   Graph Enhancements, 207

Graph Enhancements, 207
Adding Titles and Footnotes, 208
Adding a Legend, 210
Data Labels, 213
Graph Axes, 216
Controlling Borders and Grids, 222
Setting Chart Options, 224
Clearing Chart Settings, 231
What You Have Learned, 232

12   Adding Text and Drawings to Graphs, 235

Adding Objects to a Graph, 235
Selecting Graph Objects, 240
Rearranging Graph Objects, 242
Changing Object Style, 244
The Layout Commands, 251
Changing Graph Window Display, 252
What You Have Learned, 256

X

13 *File Operations, 257*

Worksheet Files, 257
Using Multiple Worksheet Files, 261
Extracting and Combining Portions of Worksheets, 267
Importing Data from Other Programs, 272
What You Have Learned, 274

14 *Database Operations, 277*

Database Fundamentals, 277
Creating a Database Table, 279
Sorting a Database, 280
Setting Up Criteria, 282
Data Query Operations, 287
Performing Database Calculations, 292
Data Fill, 295
What You Have Learned, 297

15 *Worksheet Settings, 299*

Global versus User Settings, 299
Worksheet Global Settings, 300
User Settings, 302
Worksheet Protection, 305
What You Have Learned, 306

16 *The Solver Utility, 307*

Solver Basics, 307
Using Solver, 311
Activating Solver, 312
Reviewing Solver's Results, 314

xi

Solver Reports, 315
Types of Reports, 318
Using @functions in Solver Problems, 326
A Warning, 326
What You Have Learned, 327

17   *Using the Icon Palette, 329*

What are SmartIcons?, 329
Moving and Hiding the Icon Palette, 330
Adding and Removing Standard SmartIcons, 332
Attaching Macros to SmartIcons, 333
What You Have Learned, 335

xii

Index, 337

Introduction

It's finally here—1-2-3 for Windows, the long-awaited Lotus spreadsheet for the Microsoft Windows operating environment. Unlike earlier 1-2-3 versions, 1-2-3 for Windows uses a *graphical user interface*, or *GUI*, to interact with the user. A GUI screen makes use of windows, icons, pull-down menus, and other visual tools to simplify the interactions between the user and the program. The goal is greater productivity, faster results, and less wasted time.

1-2-3 for Windows is a very powerful program. Given this power, it is unavoidable that, despite the intuitive nature of the GUI, the program is very complex. You, the user, want to get started doing productive work with 1-2-3 for Windows *now*. You can't set aside several days to learn the program. And that's where this book comes in; *The First Book of 1-2-3 for Windows* presents the basic information that a busy person needs to start using the program for real-world tasks. It is not intended to be a complete reference to every detail of 1-2-3 for Windows.

This book is appropriate for readers at all levels of spreadsheet experience:

> ▶ If you have used another Lotus spreadsheet, you have a head start. However, you still need this book because 1-2-3 for Windows differs in many significant ways from earlier versions.

> ▶ If you have used a non-Lotus spreadsheet program, such as Excel or Quattro Pro, don't worry. This book assumes no previous knowledge of Lotus spreadsheet programs.

> ▶ If you have never used a computer spreadsheet program before, that's okay. Basic concepts are explained as needed throughout the book.

Features

Several features of this book are designed to speed the learning process.

- ▶ New terms in the text are printed in *italics* when first introduced.
- ▶ *Screen shots* show you the appearance of your 1-2-3 for Windows screen as you perform different tasks.
- ▶ Information appearing on the screen appears in computer font—for example, `File not found`.
- ▶ Text that the user should type in appears in color computer font—for example, `+B2>=20`.

 Quick Steps provide the exact sequence of actions needed to perform common worksheet tasks.

xiv

 Notes and **Tips** are brief summaries of important information.

 Cautions tell you what to watch out for.

Like all Windows programs, 1-2-3 for Windows makes extensive use of the mouse. Where appropriate, the book explains how to perform tasks using either the keyboard or the mouse. Key combinations are separated by a hyphen. For example, Alt-F4 means to hold down the Alt key, press the F4 key, then release both keys.

Acknowledgments

I am indebted to my editors, Lisa Bucki and Marie Butler Knight, for their assistance and guidance. I also thank the beta support staff at Lotus Development Corporation, particularly Karen Precourt, for their help.

Getting Started

In This Chapter

▶ *Using a mouse*
▶ *Starting 1-2-3 for Windows and entering some data*
▶ *Displaying a graph of your data*
▶ *Exiting 1-2-3 for Windows*

Using a Mouse

Like all Windows programs, 1-2-3 for Windows makes extensive use of a *mouse*. You can use 1-2-3 for Windows without a mouse, but having one makes most operations much faster and easier (and there are a few operations that require a mouse). If you don't have a mouse, I strongly recommend buying one—the relatively small investment will be well worth it. This book describes how to use 1-2-3 with either the mouse or the keyboard. If you are familiar with using a mouse, you can skip ahead to the section "Starting 1-2-3 for Windows." Otherwise, you should read the rest of this section, which explains mouse basics.

The *mouse pointer* is an arrow or other symbol that is displayed on the screen and moves as you move the mouse on your desk. The mouse pointer shape varies depending on what 1-2-3 is doing at the moment. I'll describe the different mouse pointer shapes and their meanings as needed throughout the book. For now you need to know only two of them:

▶ An *arrow* is the default pointer shape and means that you can perform normal operations.

▶ An *hourglass* means that 1-2-3 is busy and you must wait. The hourglass pointer will move in response to mouse movement, but you cannot take any action or enter any commands while the hourglass pointer is displayed.

Here are the most important actions that you make with the mouse:

Point	Position the mouse pointer at a specific screen location.
Click	Quickly press and release the left mouse button.
Double-click	Quickly press and release the left mouse button twice.
Drag	Move the mouse while holding the left button down.
Grab	Position the pointer on a specific screen region so that the pointer changes shape.

Starting 1-2-3 for Windows

To run 1-2-3 for Windows, you must have Microsoft Windows Version 3.0 installed on your computer, and must also have installed 1-2-3 for Windows according to the instructions in the 1-2-3 documentation. All Windows programs, including 1-2-3, are started from the Program Manager. The Program Manager is displayed when you first start Windows. If you are running another application, you can display the Program Manager by pressing Alt-Esc one or more times.

2

> ▶ **Tip:** To install 1-2-3 for Windows, start at the Windows Program Manager screen. Place the 1-2-3 for Windows INSTALL disk in drive A. Select File Run, and type `A:INSTALL.EXE` in the dialog box that appears. Press Enter, and then follow the on-screen prompt.

> ▶ **Note:** Alt-Esc means to hold down the Alt key, press the Esc key, and then release both keys.

The Program Manager contains one or more *windows*, or program groups, each containing *icons* (small pictures) for various programs and utilities. If 1-2-3 for Windows has been installed, one of the windows that appears will be titled Lotus Applications.

> ▶ **Note:** While Windows and 1-2-3 for Windows can display multiple windows at one time, only one of these windows can be *current*. The current window is indicated by being displayed on top of all other windows, and by having its title bar and border darkened. (This may not be obvious in the figures, but you'll see it on the screen.) Make a window the active window by clicking anywhere on it or by pressing Ctrl-F6 one or more times. You'll learn more about windows in Chapter 2.

3

The Program Manager is shown in Figure 1.1. Your Program Manager may appear different from this figure, but it should include the Lotus Applications program group.

To start 1-2-3 for Windows, you must select the icon labeled 1-2-3 for Windows. You can do this with either the mouse or the keyboard.

 Starting 1-2-3 for Windows

1. If the Lotus Applications window is not the topmost window in the Program Manager, bring it to the top by clicking anywhere on the window with the mouse or by pressing Ctrl-F6 one or more times.

The Lotus Applications window moves to the top of the visible windows in the Program Manager.

2. Select the 1-2-3 for Windows icon. With the mouse, double-click on the icon. With the keyboard, use the arrow keys to highlight the icon title, and then press Enter.

1-2-3 starts and displays its opening screen.

□

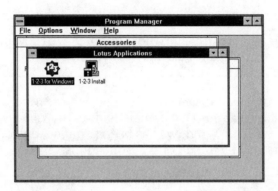

Figure 1.1   The Windows Program Manager.

4

When it first starts, a 1-2-3 for Windows logo appears briefly, followed by the opening screen, shown in Figure 1.2. This screen contains a blank worksheet and many other components that will be covered in detail in Chapter 2. For now, look at the components labeled in Figure 1.2.

► The entire screen displays the *1-2-3 window*.

► The *title bar* shows the name of the program being run.

► The *menu bar* displays program commands.

► The *control line* is used to display and enter data.

► The *worksheet window* displays a worksheet. In this figure the worksheet is blank (contains no data).

► The *cell pointer* is a rectangle that indicates the current worksheet cell.

► The *icon palette* displays icons that can be used for performing commonly needed tasks. You must have a mouse to use the icons.

► The *status line* displays information about the status of 1-2-3.

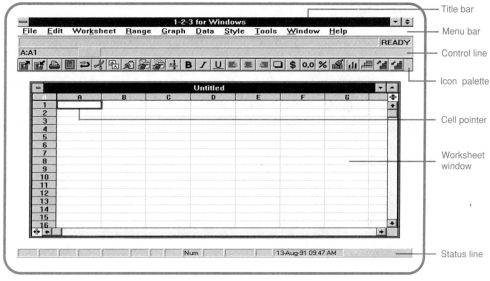

Figure 1.2   The 1-2-3 for Windows opening screen.

5

If you have any experience with spreadsheet programs, you will notice that the contents of the worksheet window in Figure 1.2 have the familiar worksheet structure: a matrix of cells with the rows identified by numbers and the columns identified by letters. You'll learn more about worksheet structure in Chapter 3. The remainder of this chapter takes you though a demonstration of a few of 1-2-3 for Windows' features. If you do not wish to continue, press Alt-F4 to end your 1-2-3 session and return to the Program Manager. If 1-2-3 prompts you Save All Files?, respond No. You can then go on to other tasks, go to Chapter 2, or turn your computer off.

A Brief Demonstration

The quickest way to start learning a new program is to actually use it. What follows is a brief demonstration in which you will enter some data into a worksheet, display the data as a graph, and then exit 1-2-3. This is only a brief demonstration, and you shouldn't worry if you don't understand everything. The details will come in later chapters. To work through this demonstration, you must have 1-2-3 for Windows on-screen with an untitled, blank worksheet.

Entering Some Worksheet Data

Before you can learn to manipulate data and display graphs, you must enter some data. For this example, use the following steps.

1. If it is not already there, position the cell pointer in cell A1. Either click cell A1, or press the Home key.

2. Type **January** and press the down arrow key. 1-2-3 enters January in cell A1 and moves the cell pointer to cell A2.

3. Type **February** and press the down arrow key. Type **March** and **April** into cells A3 and A4 following the same procedure.

4. Move the cell pointer to cell B1. Either click cell B1 or press Home followed by the right arrow.

5. Type **75** followed by the down arrow to enter 75 into cell B1. Enter **35**, **40**, and **55** into cells B2 through B4, respectively.

6. Return the cell pointer to cell A1 by clicking cell A1 or pressing Home. At this point your screen should look like Figure 1.3.

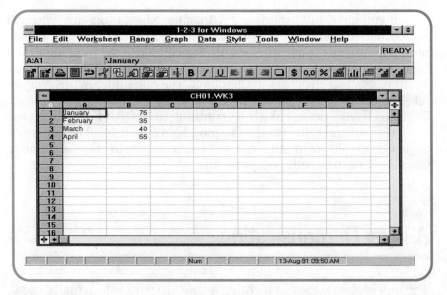

Figure 1.3   The 1-2-3 for Windows screen after entering some data.

Displaying a Graph

After you enter worksheet data, 1-2-3 can display it as a graph. There are two steps involved in displaying a graph. You must first tell 1-2-3 which data to graph, and then tell it to display the graph. The instructions to display a graph are as follows.

Using the Mouse:

1. Select the data with the mouse by pointing at cell A1, pressing and holding the left mouse button, and dragging the pointer to cell B4. Release the mouse button when the rectangle from A1 to B4 is highlighted. A darkened rectangle expands to cover cells A1 to B4.

2. Click the graph icon in the icon palette to display a graph of these cells. This is the icon with a small bar chart on it; it's just to the left of the icon with 0,0 on it. The graph is displayed in a new window, as shown in Figure 1.4.

Using the Keyboard:

1. Press Home to ensure that the cell pointer is in cell A1. Then press F4 and use the down arrow and right arrow keys to move the cell pointer to cell B4. A darkened rectangle expands to cover cells A1 to B4.

2. Press Alt-G, then N (for New), then Enter. A new window opens and displays a graph of your data, as shown in Figure 1.4.

Note that the graph window overlaps most of the worksheet window. To make the worksheet window current ("on top") again, click anywhere in the visible portion of the worksheet window, or press Ctrl-F6. The worksheet window will now be displayed on top of the graph window.

We're finished for now, so exit 1-2-3 by pressing Alt-F4. A small box will open on the screen asking if you want to save files. Since you don't need this demonstration data, select No by clicking No or by typing N. Your 1-2-3 session will end and you will be returned to the Program Manager.

This concludes the demonstration. I hope that this brief tour has whetted your appetite to learn more about 1-2-3 for Windows' power and flexibility.

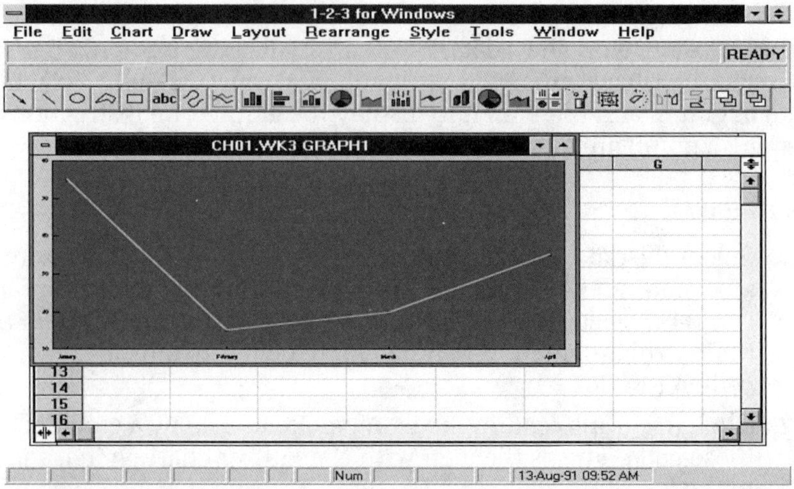

Figure 1.4   The demonstration graph.

8

What You Have Learned

▶ You can execute 1-2-3 for Windows commands with the mouse or the keyboard, but the mouse is faster in most cases.

▶ You start 1-2-3 for Windows by selecting its icon from the Windows Program Manager.

▶ A 1-2-3 worksheet holds data in a row and column format and is contained in a window.

▶ Data in a 1-2-3 worksheet can be displayed in a graph.

▶ You can exit 1-2-3 for Windows by pressing Alt-F4.

The Screen

In This Chapter

- ► *Using menus and dialog boxes*
- ► *The Icon Palette*
- ► *Controlling screen windows*
- ► *1-2-3 classic menus*
- ► *The Help system*

Menus and Dialog Boxes

When you work with 1-2-3 for Windows, you must give it commands and information to instruct the program to carry out the desired tasks. Commands are often entered by means of menus, and information is usually entered in dialog boxes. You must understand how to use menus and dialog boxes in order to use 1-2-3 for Windows efficiently.

The Structure of Menus

Menus are so named because they are analogous to restaurant menus, a list of choices from which you make a single selection. There are three types of menus in 1-2-3 for Windows:

▶ The *menu bar* displays the main menu on the second line of the screen. The menu bar contains the first level of menu choices.

▶ A *pulldown menu* is associated with each choice on the main menu. When you choose a command on the main menu, its pulldown menu is displayed. Each pulldown menu contains related commands.

▶ A *cascade menu* is associated with some (but not all) pulldown menu commands. The cascade menu is displayed when you choose the pulldown menu command.

The three types of menus are illustrated in Figure 2.1. When the menu system is active, the top line of the screen displays a brief description of the currently highlighted menu command. In Figure 2.1, the File Import From Text command is highlighted.

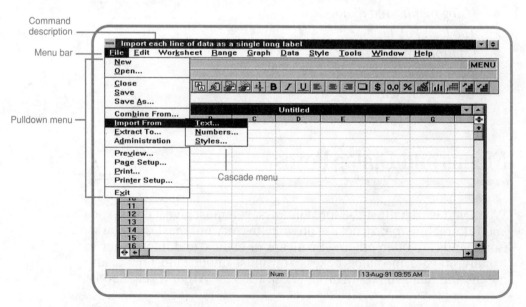

Figure 2.1   1-2-3 for Windows' three types of menus.

The 1-2-3 menus use several conventions to provide additional information about the menu commands. These are illustrated in Figure 2.2.

A description of the highlighted menu command appears in the title bar.

Menu pointer

Accelerator keys

Grayed text

Underlined letter

Ellipses

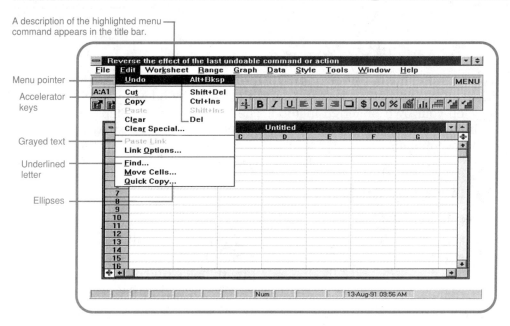

Figure 2.2   The conventions used in 1-2-3 menus.

11

Grayed text indicates that the menu item is not currently available.

Accelerator keys execute the menu command directly without using the menu system. Accelerator keys are provided for the most frequently used commands. When the shortcut includes two keys, as in Shift-Del, press and hold the first key, then press the second key.

Ellipses indicate that the menu command leads to a dialog box.

An arrowhead (not shown in Figure 2.2) indicates that the menu command leads to a cascade menu.

An underlined letter denotes the key that can be pressed to select the menu command when the menu is displayed. This is usually the first letter of the command name.

The moveable highlight bar, called the *menu pointer*, indicates the command that will be executed by pressing Enter.

If a command on a pulldown or cascade menu is not followed by ellipses or an arrowhead, that command is executed immediately when you select it.

Selecting Menu Commands

You can select menu commands using the mouse, the keyboard, or the two used in combination. As you work with 1-2-3 for Windows, you will develop your own preferred method. The following Quick Steps explain how to select a command from the main menu and display its pulldown menu.

Displaying a Pulldown Menu

Using the Mouse:

1. Click on the desired command

The command's pulldown menu is displayed and a description of the menu appears in the title bar.

Using the Keyboard:

1. Press Alt or F10 to activate the main menu.

The menu's first command is highlighted and a description of that command appears in the title bar.

2. Press the letter corresponding to the desired command (the underlined letter), or move the menu pointer to the desired command using the right and left arrow keys. Then press Enter.

The command's pulldown menu is displayed.

☐

Once you have opened the pulldown menu, you can select a command from it, using the Quick Steps below. (The steps below also work for cascade menus.)

Selecting a Command from a Pulldown or Cascade Menu

Using the Mouse:

1. Click on the desired command.

12

Using the Keyboard:

1. Press the letter corresponding to the desired command (the underlined letter), or move the menu pointer to the desired command using the up and down arrow keys. Then press Enter. □

When choosing commands from a menu, you can "back up" one step at a time by pressing Esc. To cancel an entire command sequence, click anywhere outside the menu box.

For the remainder of this book, menu command sequences will be condensed. For example, if the book says "select File Import From Text" you should select File from the main menu, select Import From from the pulldown menu, and then select Text from the cascade menu.

13

Dialog Boxes

Some menu commands lead to dialog boxes, which are used to enter additional information that 1-2-3 needs to carry out the command. Dialog boxes contain a number of components, which are illustrated in Figure 2.3. Some dialog boxes contain only a subset of these components. At any moment, one of the components in a dialog box is current.

A *dotted outline* indicates the currently selected dialog box item (not visible in the figure, but it will be visible on your monitor).

The *title bar* gives the name of the dialog box. Each dialog box's name is the command sequence used to display the dialog box.

A *text box* is used to enter and edit text information, such as the name of a file or a worksheet range.

A *list box* displays a list of items from which you can choose. If the list is too big to display at one time, a vertical scroll bar lets you scroll up and down the list (more on scroll bars soon).

A *drop-down box* is similar to a list box, but displays only a single item unless it is opened.

An *information box* displays information about the item selected in the list box.

Check boxes turn options on or off. An X in a check box indicates that the option is on. One or more check box options can be on at a time.

Option buttons also turn options on or off. Only one option button in a group may be on at a time.

The *command buttons* either confirm or cancel the dialog box.

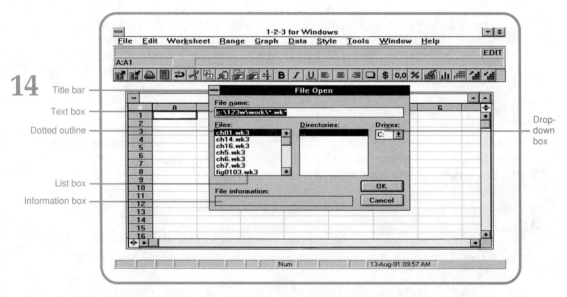

14

Title bar

Text box

Dotted outline

List box

Information box

Drop-down box

Figure 2.3a   Components of a dialog box.

When a dialog box is displayed, you can perform the following actions with the keyboard:

▶ To move forward and backward between items and groups of items, press Tab and Shift-Tab.

▶ To move directly to a dialog box item, press Alt-letter where letter is the letter underlined in the item's name.

▶ To select an item within a group, use the arrow keys.

▶ To select an item in a drop-down box, use the Arrow, Home, End, PgUp, and PgDn keys to scroll among the items in the box. You cannot open a drop-down box with the keyboard.

▶ To select an item within a list box, use the Home, End, PgUp, PgDn, and arrow keys.

▶ To toggle a check box or option button between on and off, select it then press the space bar.

▶ To cancel the dialog box without executing the command, select the Cancel button and press Enter, or press Esc or Ctrl-Break.

▶ To confirm the dialog box and execute the command, press Enter.

15

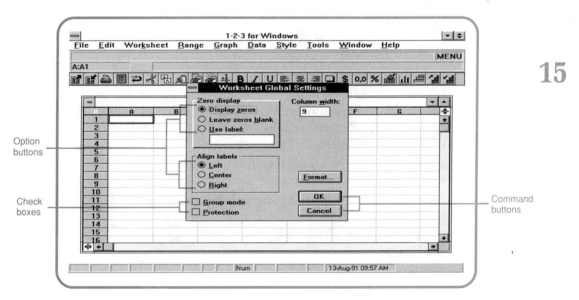

Option buttons

Check boxes

Command buttons

Figure 2.3b   Components of a dialog box.

When a dialog box is displayed, you can perform the following actions with the mouse:

▶ To select an item or a list entry, click it.

▶ To open a drop-down box, click the adjacent arrow. Then, select an item in the box by clicking it.

▶ To toggle a check box or option button between on and off, click the box, button, or adjoining label.

▶ To cancel the dialog box, click Cancel.

▶ To confirm the dialog box and execute the command, click OK.

When a text box is selected, the editing position is indicated by a blinking vertical cursor. When a text box is selected using the keyboard, the editing cursor appears at the right end of whatever text is in the box. When a text box is selected by clicking it with the mouse, the editing cursor appears at the place the mouse was clicked. Any new text you type will be inserted at the cursor position. You edit information in a text box as follows:

▶ To move the cursor one character at a time, press the left and right arrow keys.

▶ To move the cursor to the beginning or end of the text, press Home or End.

▶ To highlight one character to the right or left of the cursor, press Shift-left arrow or Shift-right arrow.

▶ To highlight all characters between the cursor and the beginning or end of the text, press Shift-Home or Shift-End.

▶ To highlight characters with the mouse, move the pointer to the first character, press and hold the left button, and drag the highlight over the desired characters.

▶ To highlight all the characters, double-click the left mouse button with the pointer within the characters.

▶ To delete all highlighted characters or one character to the right of the cursor, press Del.

▶ To delete the character to the left of the cursor, press Backspace.

Using the Icon Palette

The Icon Palette is one of 1-2-3 for Windows' unique features. On the Icon Palette you'll find a selection of *SmartIcons*. Each SmartIcon is a small, graphical button that you can click with the mouse to perform a specific worksheet task. The picture on each SmartIcon represents its function; SmartIcons are provided for the tasks that are needed most frequently. For example, the SmartIcon that shows a diskette with an arrow pointing toward it represents the command that saves data on disk.

> ▶ **Note:** You cannot use SmartIcons with the keyboard; you
> must use a mouse.

To determine what a SmartIcon does, point at it and hold down the
right mouse button. A description of the SmartIcon is displayed at the
top of the 1-2-3 window. You can also refer to the inside back cover of
this book, which gives descriptions of the most frequently used
SmartIcons.

You may notice that the Icon Palette on your screen appears
different from the figures in this book. This is nothing to worry about
and is caused by the fact that the Icon Palette can be customized. You'll
learn how to do this in Chapter 17.

Windows   17

Like other programs that run under Microsoft Windows, 1-2-3 displays
all screen information in *windows*. The 1-2-3 program itself runs in a
window (which usually occupies the entire screen). Worksheets, graphs,
dialog boxes, and all other program components also appear in windows that occupy a portion of the screen. While the contents of
windows can vary, the windows themselves and the ways you can
control them are standardized. You must understand how to manipulate windows if you are to use 1-2-3 efficiently.

The Main 1-2-3 Window

The window in which the 1-2-3 program runs usually occupies the
entire screen. The 1-2-3 window is shown in Figure 2.4 with its main
components labeled (you were introduced to some of these components
in Chapter 1).

The *window control menu box* is used to display the Window
Control Menu.
The *title bar* gives the name of the program.
The *maximize and minimize boxes* are used to control win-
dow size.

The *menu bar* lists the main menu commands.

The *address box* gives the address of the cell pointer.

The *contents box* is used for entering and editing data.

The *status indicator* indicates the current status, or mode, of 1-2-3.

The *indicator line* displays information about the current worksheet cell.

The *Icon Palette* contains icons that you can click with the mouse to perform commonly needed tasks.

The *work area* is where 1-2-3 displays windows containing worksheets, graphs, and other program components.

The *status line* displays additional information about the status of 1-2-3.

18

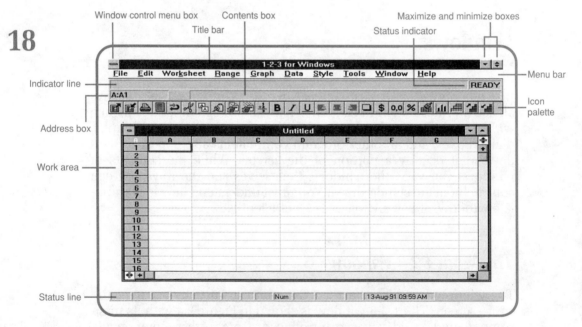

Figure 2.4   The main 1-2-3 window.

Worksheet Windows

Within its work area, 1-2-3 can display one or more windows that contain worksheet data, graphs, and so on. The worksheet window is the one you'll be working with most frequently. Its most important components are shown in Figure 2.5 and explained briefly here. More detailed information on their function is given later in the chapter.

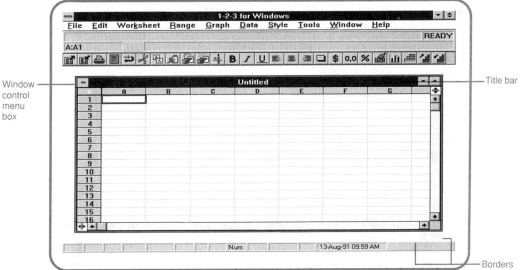

Figure 2.5   *The components of a worksheet window.*

The *window control menu box* is used to display the Window Control Menu.

The *title bar* gives the name of the worksheet in the window (that is, the file name).

> ▶ **Note:** A worksheet named Untitled automatically appears when 1-2-3 is started. New worksheets also are given the name Untitled.

The *border* surrounds the window. When the window is current, the border is darkened.

The *scroll bars* allow you to move around your worksheet. They are present even if a worksheet contains no data. You use the scroll bars to scroll vertically or horizontally in the window.

The *maximize and minimize boxes* are used to control window size.

19

The Window Control Menu

Every window has a window control menu, which is displayed by clicking the window control menu box. The window control menu for the main 1-2-3 window is shown in Figure 2.6. The commands on this menu provide an alternate way of performing certain window control tasks that are usually, and more quickly, performed with the mouse. Use of the Window Control menu commands is described in the following sections. To display the Window Control menu for the current worksheet or graph window, press Alt- – (Alt plus the keypad minus key). To display the Window Control menu for the main 1-2-3 window, press Alt-space bar.

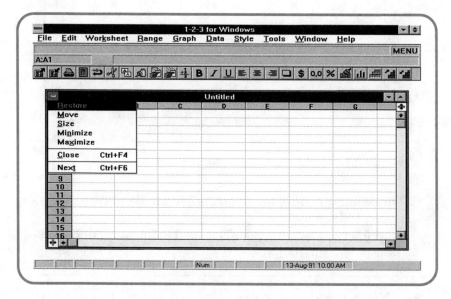

Figure 2.6   The Window Control menu.

Maximizing and Minimizing Windows

When a window is first created by 1-2-3, it has an intermediate size that occupies a portion of the work area. Any window can be maximized to occupy the entire work area, or minimized to an icon. A maximized window offers the largest possible view of its contents. Figure 2.7 shows a maximized worksheet window. You can easily switch a window between minimized, maximized, and intermediate sizes.

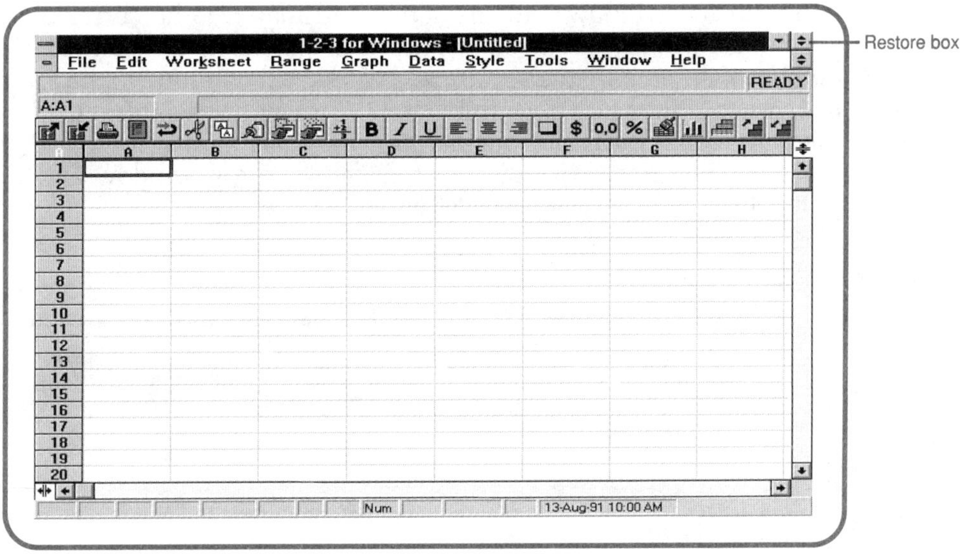

Figure 2.7   A maximized worksheet window.

21

Follow the steps below to maximize a window.

Maximizing a Window

Using the Mouse:

1. Click the window's
   maximize button.

Using the Keyboard:

1. Press Alt- – to display the
   Window Control Menu,
   and then select Maximize. □

When a window is maximized, the maximize box becomes the restore box and displays a pair of arrows, one pointing up and one pointing down (see Figure 2.7). Clicking this box will *restore* the window, returning it to the intermediate size it had before it was maximized. You can also restore a window by selecting Restore from the Window Control Menu.

A minimized window is represented on the screen by a small symbol, or icon, with the title of the window displayed below the icon. The icon may not be visible if it is covered by a maximized window.

A minimized window remains active and may also be current. If a minimized window is current, its title is displayed highlighted. Figure 2.8 shows the icons of two minimized worksheet windows in the lower left corner of the work area. In Figure 2.8, the window represented by the right icon is current. Note that the type of window is indicated by the icon. The left icon in Figure 2.8 represents a graph window, and the right icon represents a worksheet window.

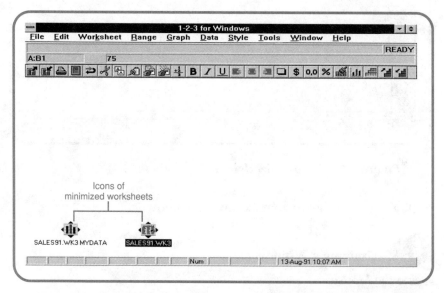

Figure 2.8   A 1-2-3 work area with two minimized windows.

Controlling Minimized Windows

You can manipulate a minimized window with the mouse or by means of its Window Control menu. When you display a the Window Control Menu for a minimized window, the Size and Minimize menu selections are grayed because they are not available. The Restore command returns a minimized window to the size and position it had before it was minimized. Figure 2.9 shows a minimized window with its Window Control Menu displayed.

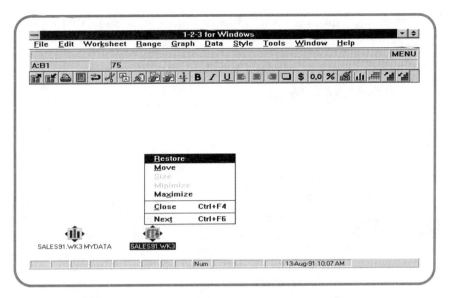

Figure 2.9   A minimized window with its Window Control menu displayed.

To display a minimized window's Window Control menu, follow the steps below.

Using the Mouse:

Click the window's icon.

Using the Keyboard:

Make the minimized window current by pressing Ctrl-F6 until the icon title is highlighted. Then, press Alt- –.

To restore a minimized window, follow these steps.

Using the Mouse:

Double-click the window's icon or name.

Using the Keyboard:

Display the Window Control Menu, and then select Restore.

To maximize a minimized window, use the Quick Steps that follow.

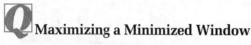 **Maximizing a Minimized Window**

Using either Keyboard or Mouse:

1. Display the Window
   control menu.
2. Select Maximize.   The window expands to
                                     maximum size.   ☐

   The icons of minimized windows are normally placed in a
"parking lot" in the bottom left corner of the screen. You can move icons
if you wish. With the mouse, point at the icon, hold down the left mouse
button, and drag the icon to the new location. With the keyboard,
display the Window Control Menu, select Move, use the arrow keys to
move the icon to the new location, and press Enter. Moving icons is
much easier with a mouse. The Close option on the Window Control
Menu will be discussed later in this chapter.

Resizing and Moving Windows

Most of the time you'll be working with windows that are intermediate
in size—neither maximized or minimized. You can change the size and
position of these windows to suit your preferences. Resizing and
moving windows can be done with either the mouse or the keyboard,
but is definitely faster and easier with the mouse.

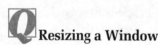 **Resizing a Window**

Using the Mouse:

1. Move the mouse pointer to   The mouse pointer changes
   grab a border or corner of   into a double-headed arrow
   the window.   (Figure 2.10).
2. Drag the window border to   As you drag, an outline of the
   the desired size.   new size is displayed.
3. Release the mouse button at   The window fills in the new
   the desired size.   outline (Figure 2.11).

24

Using the Keyboard:

1. Press Alt- –.	The Window Control Menu is displayed.
2. Select Size, and then use the arrow keys to expand or contract the window outline.	When you select Size, the arrow changes to a four-headed arrow. When you press one of the arrow keys, the four-headed arrow moves to that border (for example, press the right arrow key and the arrow moves to the right border) and changes to a two-headed arrow.
3. At the desired size, press Enter.	The window fills in the new outline. ☐

A window may be repositioned anywhere within the work area. You can even position a window so that part of it extends past the screen boundaries and is not visible. When working with multiple windows, you can reposition them so the data you need is visible.

25

 Repositioning a Window

Using the Mouse:

1. Move the mouse pointer to the window's title bar (Figure 2.12).	
2. Press the left button and drag the window.	An outline of the window moves to show the new location.
3. At the desired position, release the mouse button.	The window moves to the new position (Figure 2.13).

Using the Keyboard:

1. Press Alt- –.	The Window Control Menu is displayed.
2. Select Move.	
3. Use the arrow keys to move the window outline.	
4. At the desired position, press Enter.	The window moves to the new position. ☐

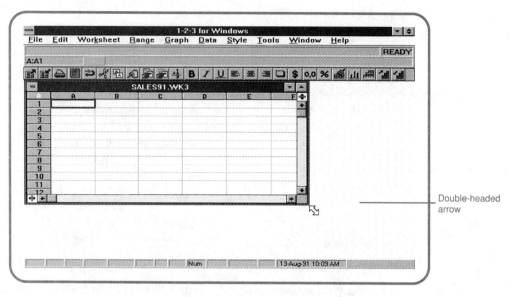

Double-headed
arrow

Figure 2.10   *When you grab a window border, the mouse pointer changes to a double-headed arrow.*

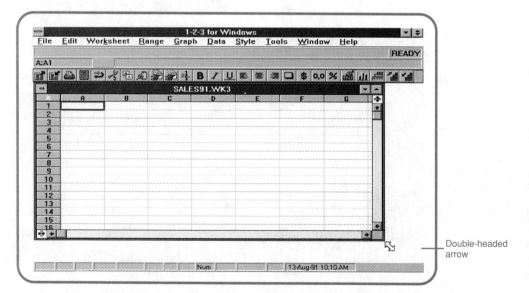

Double-headed
arrow

Figure 2.11   *When you reach the desired size, release the mouse button and the window changes size to fill the outline.*

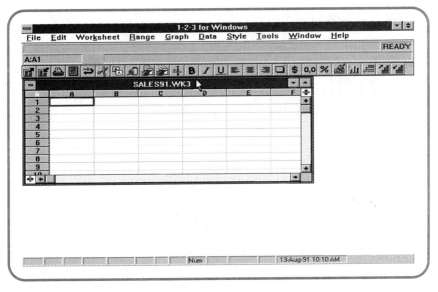

Figure 2.12 To move a window, first point at the window's title bar.

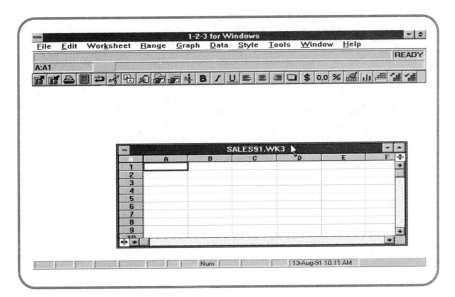

Figure 2.13 Release the mouse button and the window moves to the new position.

Closing a Window

When you are finished working with a window, you can close it with the File Close or Window Close commands. Closing a window means to remove it from the work area. If a window contains data, you must save the data to a disk file if you wish to use the data again. You can always reopen a closed window. There are several ways to close the current window:

▶ Double-click the Window Control Menu Box.
▶ Open the Window Control Menu, then select Close.
▶ Press Ctrl-F4.
▶ Select File Close from the main 1-2-3 menu.

If you try to close a window that contains unsaved data, 1-2-3 displays a dialog box asking if you want to save the window to a disk file before closing it. This dialog box is shown in Figure 2.14. The three dialog box choices are:

Yes saves the window, using the name that was in the window's title bar, then closes the window. If the file was a new file, and therefore named Untitled, 1-2-3 saves the file as Noname.wk3. It is a good idea to use File Save As to save a new file so you can give the file a meaningful name.

No closes the window without saving it. If you select No, you lose any changes in the window's data that were made since the last time it was saved.

Cancel cancels the Close Window command and brings you back to READY mode.

The Main 1-2-3 Window

As was mentioned earlier in the chapter, the 1-2-3 for Windows program itself runs within a window. The default is for 1-2-3 to start in full-screen (maximized) mode. You can control the size of the main 1-2-3 window in the same manner as described earlier for worksheet windows. When it is not maximized, 1-2-3 can share the screen with other Windows applications. For example, Figure 2.15 shows 1-2-3 for Windows sharing the screen with the word processing program Word for Windows.

The 1-2-3 window can also be minimized to an icon. When this is done, the program remains in memory, and all worksheet data, graphs, and other information is retained. You control the 1-2-3 icon in the same way as the icon for a minimized worksheet window, as you learned earlier in this chapter. Figure 2.16 shows 1-2-3 minimized to an icon on the Program Manager screen.

29

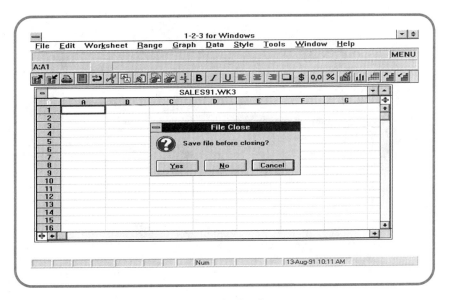

Figure 2.14   The File Close dialog box.

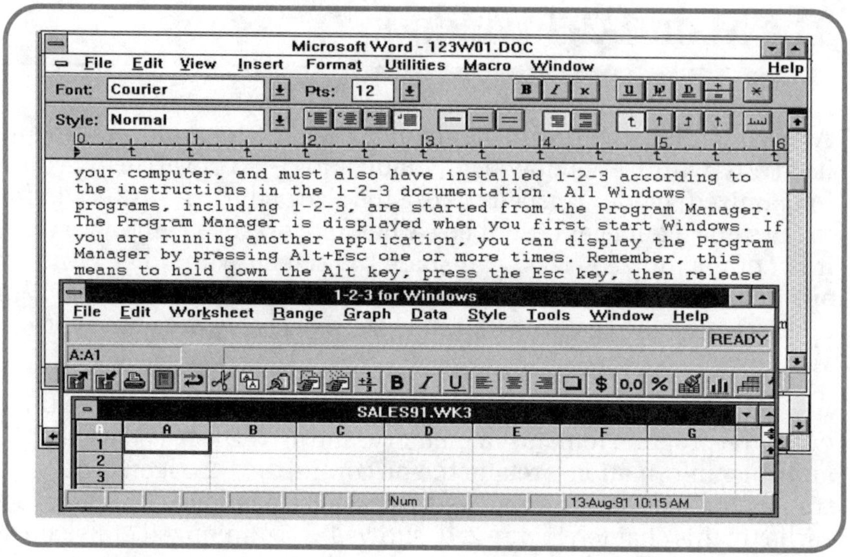

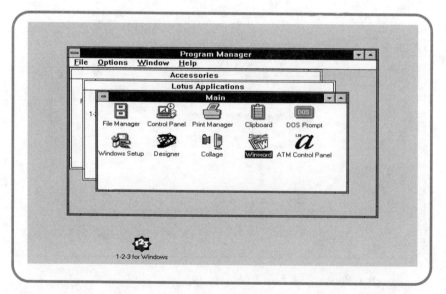

Figure 2.15   The main 1-2-3 window can share the screen with other applications.

Figure 2.16   The main 1-2-3 window can be reduced to an icon.

For more detailed information on running multiple Windows applications, please refer to your Windows documentation.

Exiting 1-2-3 for Windows

When you are finished with your 1-2-3 for Windows session you must exit 1-2-3 by issuing the File Exit command. There are several ways you can do this (these commands refer to the main 1-2-3 window, not to a worksheet window):

▶ Double-click the Window Control Menu Box.
▶ Display the Window Control Menu, then select Close.
▶ Press Alt-F4.
▶ Select File Exit from the main 1-2-3 menu.

If you try to exit 1-2-3 when it contains unsaved data, a dialog box is displayed asking if you want to save all files before exiting. Your three choices are:

Select *Yes* to save all unsaved data.
Select *No* to exit 1-2-3 without saving. If you select No, you will lose any unsaved data.
Select *Cancel* to cancel the File Exit command.

1-2-3 Classic Menus

If you are familiar with 1-2-3 Release 3.1, you may want to use the 1-2-3 Classic menu system, at least initially. The 1-2-3 Classic menus duplicate the menu system found on this earlier, non-Windows version of 1-2-3, including the menus for the WYSIWYG graphics add-in. The 1-2-3 Classic commands provide access to most of the features of 1-2-3 for Windows. You cannot select 1-2-3 Classic commands with the mouse.

To display the 1-2-3 Classic menu, press / or < when 1-2-3 is in Ready mode. To display the WYSIWYG menu, press : (colon). Figure 2.17 shows the 1-2-3 screen with the 1-2-3 Classic menu displayed near the top of the screen.

> **Note:** The Classic menu can be disabled when 1-2-3 for
> Windows is installed, and therefore may not appear when
> / or < is pressed. If the Classic menu is disabled and you wish
> to use it, run the 1-2-3 for Windows installation program and
> specify when prompted that Classic menus should be enabled.

32

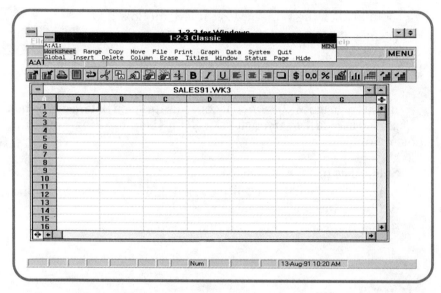

Figure 2.17   The 1-2-3 Classic menu.

The Help System

1-2-3 for Windows includes a sophisticated Help system that provides
detailed information on all aspects of program operation. The Help
system provides some information that is not included in the 1-2-3 for
Windows documentation and makes it very easy to access the needed
information. When you are using 1-2-3, the Help system should be the
first place you turn for assistance (after this book, of course!).

The 1-2-3 Help system is displayed in a screen window. This
window is like any other window in that it can be resized, moved,
maximized, and so on. You can leave the Help window displayed on the
screen while you continue to work in 1-2-3, providing reference for the
task you are doing.

Context-Sensitive Help

If you press F1, 1-2-3 displays context-sensitive help. Context-sensitive means that 1-2-3 displays Help information related to what you were doing when you pressed F1. For example, if you have opened the File Open dialog box, pressing F1 displays help on the File Open command, as shown in Figure 2.18.

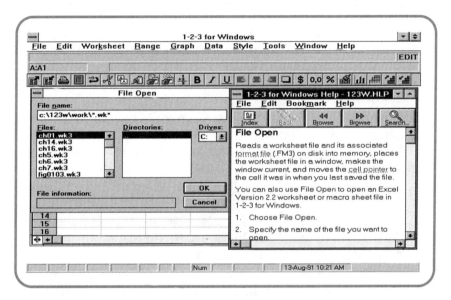

Figure 2.18   Pressing F1 displays context-sensitive help.

33

If you press F1 when you are not performing a specific task, the Help Index is displayed. The Help Index will be described below.

The Help Window

As has been mentioned, the Help window is like all other windows. It does have some special features, however, as can be seen in Figure 2.18. One of these features is the Help window menu, displayed just below the Help window title bar. There are four selections on this menu:

Select *File* to open another Help file, or to print a copy of the current Help topic. To print, you must have a printer installed.

Select *Edit* to copy the Help information to the Windows clipboard for pasting into another application, or to add annotations to the Help window.

Select *Bookmark* to place a bookmark in Help topics you refer to frequently.

Select *Help* to obtain information on using the Help system.

Another special feature of the Help window is the Help buttons, displayed immediately below the Help menu at the top of the dialog box. These buttons are selected by clicking with the mouse or pressing the underlined letter for each button command. The button commands are:

Select *Index* to display the main Help index (described below).

Select *Back* to display the last Help topic you viewed. You can move back through all previously viewed topics one at time. When you reach the first topic, the button is dimmed.

Select *Browse Backward* to browse backward through a predefined set of related Help topics. If you reach the beginning of the predefined sequence, the button is dimmed.

Select *Browse Forward* to browse forward through a predefined set of related Help topics. If you reach the end of the predefined sequence, the button is dimmed.

Select *Search* to search through Help for a specific topic. When you select Search, a list of Help keywords is displayed. You can select a Search term from this list, or enter your own.

The Help Index

At the heart of the 1-2-3 Help system is the Help Index, a logically-organized summary of all of the available Help subjects. You can use the Index to access any and all of the information in the Help system. Figure 2.19 shows the first Help Index screen displayed in a maximized Help window.

In the Index you will find two special types of entries:

An item displayed in green with a solid underline is a *cross reference*. A cross reference is a term or phrase for which the Help system has an entry. Select a cross reference anywhere in the Help window to go directly to the corresponding Help entry.

34

An item displayed in green with a dotted underline is a term or phrase for which the Help system has a brief *definition* or *example*. Select the item to display the definition or example in a pop-up window.

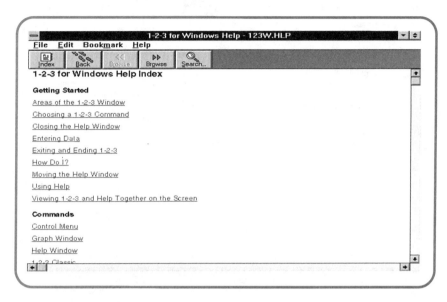

Figure 2.19   The first Help Index screen in a maximized Help window.

You select a special entry by clicking, or by pressing Tab or Shift-Tab to move the highlight to the desired one, and then pressing Enter. If you have selected a cross-reference (with a solid underline), the Help window displays the Help information for the selected word or phrase. If you have selected a word or phrase with a dotted underline, the definition or example is displayed in a pop-up window as long as you hold down the mouse button or the Enter key. Figure 2.20 shows a Help window with the definition of "pulldown menu" displayed in a pop-up window.

The Help Menu

You can also access the Help system by selecting Help from the main 1-2-3 menu. When you do so, the pulldown menu in Figure 2.21 is displayed.

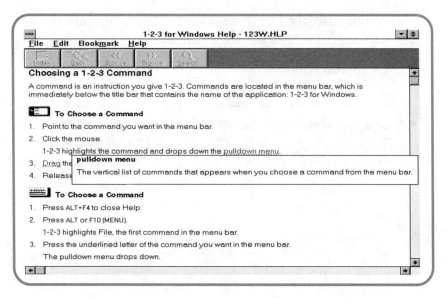

Figure 2.20   A definition displayed in a pop-up window.

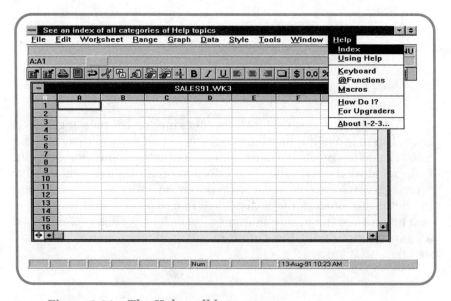

Figure 2.21   The Help pulldown menu.

This menu offers the following commands:

Index displays the Help Index.

Using Help displays information about using the Help system.

Keyboard displays help on using the keyboard with 1-2-3.

@functions displays information on 1-2-3's built-in @functions (described in Chapter 7).

Macros displays information on creating and using Macros (described in Chapter 9).

How Do I? provides "how-to" information on common 1-2-3 tasks.

For Upgraders displays tables that relate 1-2-3 for Windows commands to 1-2-3 Release 3.1 commands.

About 1-2-3 provides information about 1-2-3 for Windows, including the current version number and memory and disk space.

37

What You Have Learned

▶ The menu system provides commands that control the operation of 1-2-3 for Windows.

▶ You can select commands from the menu using either the keyboard or the mouse.

▶ When 1-2-3 for Windows needs additional information from you, it displays a dialog box.

▶ 1-2-3 windows can be moved and resized.

▶ The Icon Palette provides buttons that let you quickly perform commonly needed tasks with the mouse.

▶ The 1-2-3 Classic menus provide command compatibility with Lotus 1-2-3 Release 3.1.

▶ The 1-2-3 Help system provides information about operation of the program.

Chapter 3

Moving Around 1-2-3 for Windows

In This Chapter

▶ *The structure of worksheets and worksheet files*
▶ *Displaying multiple worksheets*
▶ *Navigating in a two-dimensional worksheet*
▶ *Navigating in a three-dimensional worksheet file*

Worksheet Structure

A 1-2-3 for Windows *worksheet* is analogous to a single page in an accountant's ledger book, ruled into rows and columns. A worksheet is much larger than any book page, however, containing 256 columns and 8192 rows. The columns are identified from left to right by letters A through Z, AA through AZ, BA through BZ, and so on up to IV. The rows are numbered top to bottom, 1 though 8192. Column letters and row numbers are shown in the *worksheet frame*, at the left and top edges of every worksheet window.

A 1-2-3 for Windows *worksheet file* is analogous to an entire ledger book that contains as many as 256 pages. Each new worksheet file starts with a single worksheet. You can add additional worksheets, up to a total of 256. The worksheets in a worksheet file are labelled

A: through IV:. The worksheet label is at the top left corner of the worksheet window. A worksheet window contains a single worksheet file. A worksheet file is sometimes called a *three dimensional (3-D)* worksheet.

Every cell in a worksheet file has a unique position in a particular worksheet, a particular column, and a particular row. A cell's position is given by its cell address that specifies its worksheet, column, and row position, as follows:

A:B2   Worksheet A, column B, row 2.

D:F21   Worksheet D, column F, row 21.

Every worksheet file has a single current cell, indicated by the cell pointer. The cell pointer is moveable (you'll see how soon), and the address of the current cell is displayed in the main 1-2-3 window's address box. Figure 3.1 illustrates cell addresses.

40

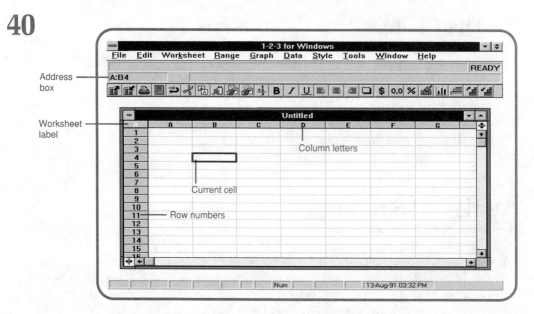

Figure 3.1   Cell addresses in a worksheet file.

Using Multiple Worksheets

A worksheet file starts off containing only a single worksheet, worksheet A. For many applications a single worksheet is all you'll need. To use additional worksheets, you must add them to the file.

Adding New Worksheets to a Worksheet File

One or more additional worksheets are inserted into a worksheet file with the Worksheet Insert command. The following Quick Steps describe how to insert one or more additional worksheets into a worksheet file.

Inserting Worksheets

41

1. Select Worksheet Insert.

   The Worksheet Insert dialog box is displayed (Figure 3.2).

2. Select the Sheet option button.

3. Select the Before or After option button to determine where the new sheet(s) will be inserted.

4. To insert more than one new sheet, enter the desired number in the Quantity text box.

5. Select OK.

   The specified sheet or sheets is inserted into the worksheet file. □

If you select After, the new sheet(s) will be inserted "behind" the current worksheet. If you select Before, they will be inserted "in front of" the current worksheet. For example, if the current worksheet is A: and you insert one new worksheet by choosing After, the original worksheet will remain A: and the new worksheet will be B:. If you insert by choosing Before, the original worksheet will become B: and the new worksheet will be A:.

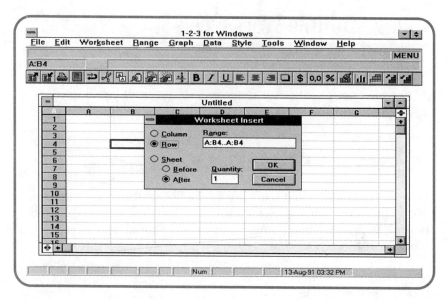

Figure 3.2   The Worksheet Insert dialog box.

42

Displaying Multiple Worksheets

A worksheet window normally displays only one worksheet of a multiple worksheet file. This is the *current worksheet*, the one containing the cell pointer. You can display other worksheets in the file by moving the cell pointer to them (as will be explained soon). You can also display three worksheets in a single window by selecting perspective view. Figure 3.3 shows a maximized worksheet window displaying three worksheets in perspective view. The following Quick Steps explain how to select perspective view.

 Displaying Multiple Worksheets in Perspective View

1. Select Window Split.	The Window Split dialog box is displayed (Figure 3.4).
2. Select Perspective, then select OK.	The worksheet window switches to perspective view. □

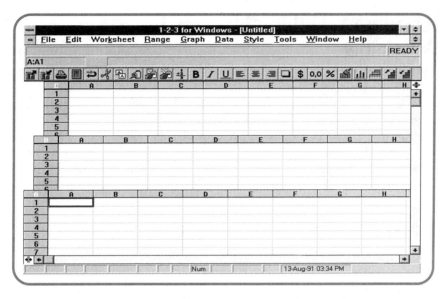

Figure 3.3   Perspective view lets you view three worksheets in a single window.

43

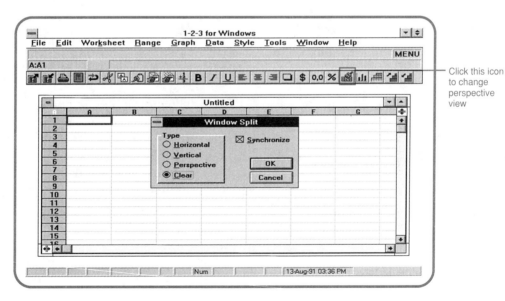

Click this icon to change perspective view

Figure 3.4   The Window Split dialog box.

To cancel perspective view and return to a single worksheet display, display the Window Split dialog box, then select Clear and OK.

Displaying Different Parts of the Same Worksheet

You can divide a worksheet window into two panes that allow you to view different parts of the same worksheet at the same time. Panes can be divided either vertically or horizontally. Figure 3.5 shows a worksheet window divided into horizontal panes, and Figure 3.6 shows a worksheet window split into vertical panes. The following are Quick Steps for splitting a window into panes.

 Splitting a Window into Panes

Using the Keyboard:

1. Position the cell pointer at the row or column where you want the split placed.

2. Select Window Split.   The Window Split dialog box is displayed.

3. Under Type, select either Horizontal or Vertical, then select OK.   The window splits into two panes at the location of the cell pointer.

Using the Mouse:

1. Grab the window's vertical splitter or horizontal splitter (see Figure 3.7).   The mouse pointer changes to a black double-headed arrow.

2. Drag the splitter to the desired split location.   A dividing lines moves in the window as you move the splitter.

3. At the desired location, release the mouse button.   The window splits at the dividing line.   □

For example, in Figure 3.5 the cell pointer was in cell A9, and we chose Horizontal. In Figure 3.6 the cell pointer was in cell E1, and we chose Vertical.

To move the cell pointer between panes, press F6 or click any cell in the destination pane. To unsplit a window, Display the Window Split dialog box, select Clear, then select OK. With the mouse, drag the splitter back to the top or left edge of the window.

44

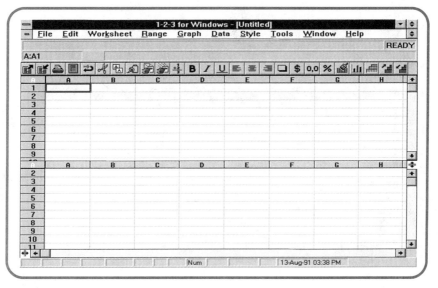

Figure 3.5   A worksheet window split into horizontal panes.

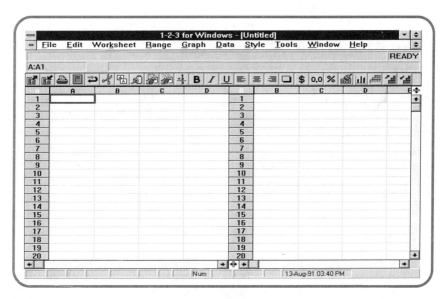

Figure 3.6   A worksheet window split into vertical panes.

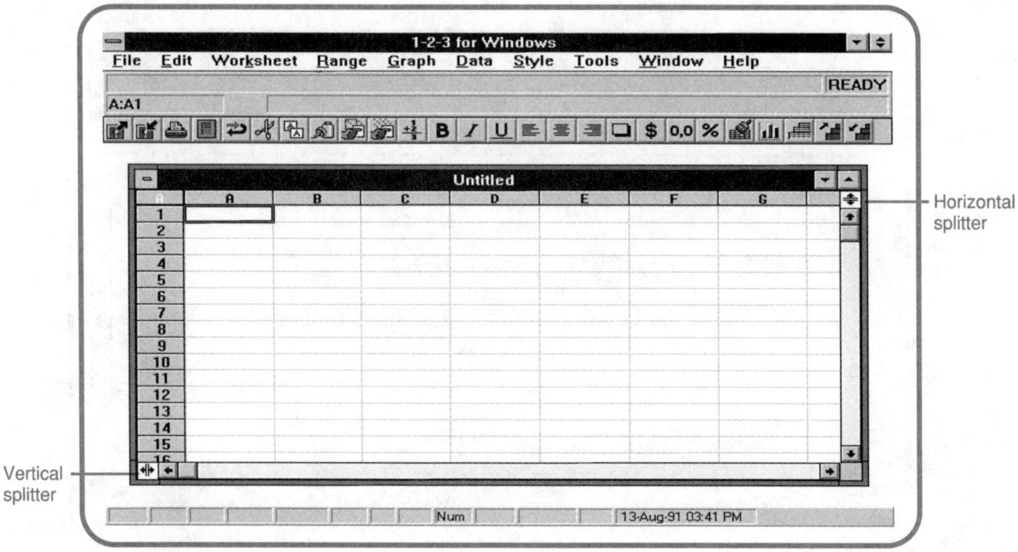

Figure 3.7   To split a window with the mouse, grab one of the splitters.

46

Synchronizing Worksheets

When a window is in either perspective or split pane mode, you have the option of turning *Synchronization* on or off. Synchronization is controlled by the Synchronization option button in the Window Split dialog box (see Figure 3.4). When synchronization is off, movement of the cell pointer in one pane or worksheet has no effect on other worksheets or panes. You can view two completely different portions of the spreadsheet with Synchronization off. In many situations, however, having Synchronization on is very helpful. Synchronization operates differently depending on the type of worksheet view you are using:

In *Perspective View*, all displayed worksheets are synchronized both vertically and horizontally. This means that scrolling in the active worksheet results in identical scrolling in the other visible worksheets; the identical row and column area will always be visible in all three.

In *Horizontal Pane* mode, the two panes are synchronized horizontally but not vertically. The same columns, but not necessarily the same rows, will be visible in both panes.

In *Vertical Pane* mode, the two panes are synchronized vertically but not horizontally. The same rows, but not necessarily the same columns, will be visible in both panes.

With *Synchronization* off, you can have two panes that show neither the same columns nor the same rows.

Navigating in a Worksheet File

A worksheet will usually contain more information than can be viewed at once in the worksheet window. You can scroll the contents of a worksheet to bring different regions in view. When you scroll, you are actually moving the cell pointer. When the cell pointer reaches the edge of the window, the worksheet scrolls so the cell pointer always remains visible in the window.

You can scroll using the keyboard or using the mouse and the scroll bars. The vertical scroll bar (the one at the right edge of the window) is used to scroll up and down through the window contents. The horizontal scroll bar is used to scroll left and right. The components of a scroll bar are shown in Figure 3.8.

47

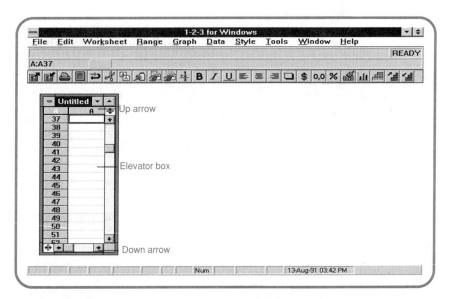

Figure 3.8   The components of a scroll bar.

Between the arrows at the ends of a scroll bar is a shaded bar containing a white or gray *elevator box*. The position of the elevator box in the shaded bar corresponds to the current window view relative to the entire worksheet. When the elevator box is at the top of the scroll bar the window is displaying the top portion of the worksheet. When the elevator box is at the bottom of the bar the window is displaying the bottom portion of the worksheet.

To move the cell pointer within a worksheet:

Using the Mouse:

Location	Action
To a visible cell	Click the cell.
Up or down one row	Click the up or down arrow on the vertical scroll bar.
Left or right one column	Click the left or right arrow on the horizontal scroll bar.
Up or down one page	Click the vertical scroll bar between the up or down arrow and the elevator box.
Left or right one page	Click the horizontal scroll bar between the left or right arrow and the elevator box.
To the top or bottom row	Drag the elevator box to the top or bottom of the vertical scroll bar.
To the leftmost or rightmost column	Drag the elevator box to the left or right end of the horizontal scroll bar.
Variable (vertical or horizontal)	Drag the elevator box to the desired position.

Using the Keyboard:

Location	Action
Up or down one row	Press the up or down arrow key.
Up or down one page	Press PgUp or PgDn.
Right or left one column	Press the right or left arrow key.
Right one page	Press Ctrl-right arrow or Tab.

Left one page	Press Ctrl-left arrow or Shift-Tab.
To cell A1	Press the Home key.
To any cell	Press F5 (GoTo), enter the destination cell address in the dialog box, and press Enter.

 Note: If you turn on your keyboard Scroll Lock before scrolling with the keyboard, the cell pointer moves only when scrolling brings it to the edge of the window.

The End key can be used in conjunction with the navigation keys for rapid movement of the cell pointer. Press End followed by an arrow key, and the pointer moves in the indicated direction until it reaches the first boundary between an empty cell and a nonempty cell. If the row or column is empty, the pointer moves to the edge of the worksheet. Press End followed by Home to move to the lower right corner of the worksheet region that contains data.

Navigating Between Worksheets

When your worksheet file contains more than one worksheet, you can move the cell pointer between worksheets. Following are the keyboard commands used to accomplish various movements.

 Note: "End Ctrl-Home" means to press and release the End key, then press Ctrl and Home together.

Press:	To Move:
Ctrl-Home	To cell A1 in worksheet A:.
Ctrl-PgDn	To the previous worksheet (for example, from B: to A:).
Ctrl-PgUp	To the next worksheet (for example, from A: to B:).

49

End Ctrl-Home	To the cell in the lower right corner and the last worksheet in the file's data-containing area.
End Ctrl-PgDn	Forward through worksheets, staying in the same row and column, to the first boundary between an empty and non-empty cell. If no nonempty cells are encountered, moves to the first worksheet in the file.
End Ctrl-PgUp	Backward through worksheets, staying in the same row and column, to the first boundary between an empty and nonempty cell. If no nonempty cells are encountered, moves to the last worksheet in the file.

You can also use F5 (GoTo) to move the pointer between worksheets. Press F5 to display the Range GoTo dialog box, and enter the address in the text box. To move to the same row and column in a different worksheet, enter only the destination worksheet letter followed by a colon (for example, C:). To move to any cell in any worksheet, enter the full worksheet-row-column address (for example, C:A2).

To move between worksheets using the mouse, click the Next Sheet or Previous Sheet SmartIcon. If you have multiple worksheets displayed in perspective view, you can move the cell pointer to any visible cell by clicking on it.

What You Have Learned

▶ A worksheet contains cells in a grid of 256 columns and 8192 rows.

▶ A worksheet file contains between 1 and 256 worksheets. (The workspace cannot contain more than 256 worksheets.)

▶ Every cell in a worksheet file is identified by its address, which gives its location in a worksheet, row, and column.

▶ A worksheet file has one current cell, indicated by the cell pointer. You can move the cell pointer using the mouse or the keyboard.

▶ The Worksheet Split command can be used to display different worksheets, or different parts of the same worksheet, in a window.

Working with Ranges

In This Chapter

- ► *What is a range?*
- ► *Defining a two-dimensional range*
- ► *Defining a three-dimensional range*
- ► *Assigning range names*
- ► *Using worksheet labels as range names*

Basic Concepts of Ranges

Many 1-2-3 for Windows commands affect worksheet cells. For example, you can erase, copy, or move the data in worksheet cells. The *current selection* is the group of cells your next command will affect. The default current selection is the single cell indicated by the cell pointer. More frequently, you will work with multi-cell selections, or *ranges*, as we will discuss in this chapter. With most 1-2-3 commands, you can specify the range to be affected either before or after selecting the command.

Note: The current selection is the current cell.

A window's current selection is highlighted when the window is active. In Figure 4.1 the group of cells extending from B3 to C14 is the current selection. A nonactive window can contain a current selection, but it is not highlighted. Remember that the default current selection is the current cell. This chapter will deal mostly with multi-cell ranges.

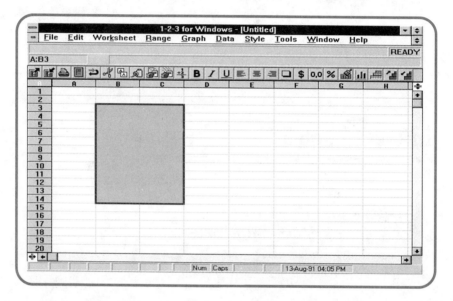

Figure 4.1   The current selection in the active window is highlighted.

If you select a range before choosing a command, the range remains selected after the command executes. This is useful when you need to use several commands on the same worksheet range. If you do not select a range before selecting a command that requires it, you will be required to specify the range in the command's dialog box.

Two-Dimensional Ranges

A two-dimensional range is a rectangular block of one or more cells contained in a single worksheet. It is defined by the cells in its upper left and lower right corners. For example, the range highlighted in Figure 4.1

is A:B3..A:C14. The following Quick Steps explain how to select a range before entering a command (in other words, when 1-2-3 is in READY mode).

Q Selecting a Range Before Entering a Command (from READY mode)

Using the Keyboard:

1. Move the cell pointer to one corner of the range.

2. Press F4. — The corner of the range is now anchored.

3. Use the navigation keys to move the pointer to the diagonally opposite corner of the range. — The highlighted rectangle expands as you move the pointer.

4. Press Enter when the desired range is highlighted. — You can now select a command to affect the range.

Using the Mouse:

1. Point at one corner of the range.

2. Press and hold the mouse button, and drag to the diagonally opposite corner of the range. — The highlight expands as you move the mouse.

3. When the desired range is highlighted, release the mouse button. — You can now select a command to affect the range. □

55

Whether using a mouse or the keyboard to define a range, you can cancel the range by pressing Esc.

Selecting a range after entering a command is similar to selecting it beforehand. In this case, you are selecting in POINT mode rather than in READY mode (remember, the worksheet mode is shown by the mode indicator near the upper right corner of the main 1-2-3 window). For the following examples, I'll use the Range Name Create command. You'll learn the details of this command later in the chapter. For now, concentrate on the methods of specifying a range detailed in the following two sets of Quick Steps.

Q Selecting a Range After Entering a Command (from POINT mode)

Using the Keyboard:

1. Enter the desired command.

   The command's dialog box is displayed (as in Figure 4.2).

2. Press Tab one or more times to select the Range text box in the dialog box (if it is not already selected).

   A dotted outline surrounds the Range text box.

3. Press the . (period) key.

   The dialog box is temporarily hidden, and the cell pointer is anchored at its current location.

4. If the cell pointer is not already located at one corner of the desired range, press Esc to unanchor it, use the navigation keys to move it to one corner of the range, then press . to anchor it.

5. Use the navigation keys to move the cell pointer to the diagonally opposite corner of the range.

   A highlighted rectangle expands to show the range, and the range address is displayed to the right of the 1-2-3 window's address box (Figure 4.3).

6. When the desired range is highlighted, press Enter.

   The dialog box is redisplayed with the selected range address entered in the Range text box (Figure 4.4).

7. Continue with the command.

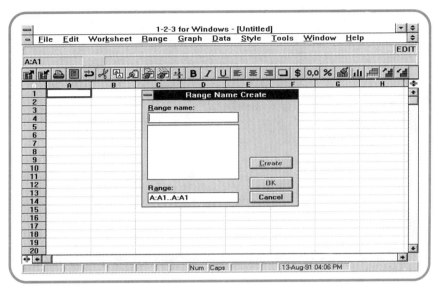

Figure 4.2   When a command requires a range, its dialog box contains a Range text box.

57

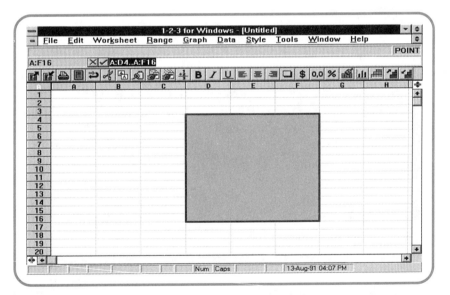

Figure 4.3   As you point to a range, the dialog box is hidden and the address of the highlighted range is displayed in the contents box.

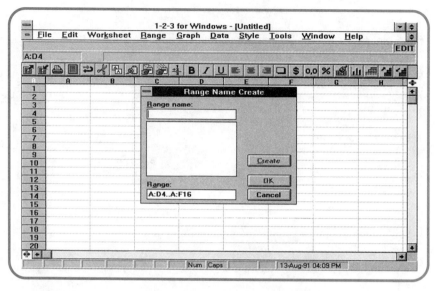

Figure 4.4 *Press Enter, and the dialog box is redisplayed with the selected range address in the Range text box.*

58

Using the Mouse:

1. Enter the desired command.	The command's dialog box is displayed.
2. Click the Range text box to select it.	A dotted outline surrounds the Range text box.
3. Point at one corner of the range, and press and hold the mouse button.	The dialog box is temporarily hidden.
4. Drag with the mouse to the diagonally opposite corner of the range.	The highlighted rectangle expands to cover the desired range, and the range address is displayed to the right of the 1-2-3 window's address box.
5. Release the mouse button.	The dialog box is redisplayed with the selected range entered in the Range text box.
6. Continue with the command.	□

After Step 2 in either of the preceding procedures, you could type the address of the desired range into the Range text box. It's usually easier, however, to indicate the range by pointing with either the mouse or keyboard. You could also type in the name that you have assigned to a range. You'll learn how to assign range names later in this chapter.

When using the keyboard to highlight a range in either READY or POINT mode, a cursor (_) is displayed in the corner of the highlighted range that you are moving with the navigation keys (the free cell). You can switch the free cell to a different corner of the highlighted area by pressing . (period) one or more times. This gives you greater control when defining the range, and lets you check the boundaries of a highlighted area that extends beyond the window borders.

Three-Dimensional Ranges

A three-dimensional, or 3-D, range is a range that spans two or more contiguous worksheets. A 3-D range always contains the same rows and columns in each worksheet. For example, a 3-D range could contain cells B2, B3, C2, and C3 in worksheets A:, B:, and C:. This range would be indicated by the address A:B2..C:C3. This range is shown highlighted in perspective view in Figure 4.5. Note, however, that perspective view is not required to specify a 3-D range.

59

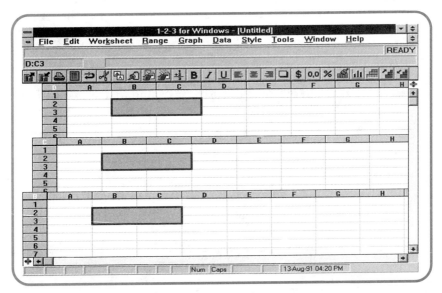

Figure 4.5   The 3-D range A:B2..C:C3 is highlighted.

You can specify a 3-D range anywhere a range is required, either before or after entering a command. You can type a 3-D range's address into a Range text box, or highlight it with the mouse or keyboard. The following steps describe how to specify a 3-D range.

1. Move the cell pointer to the first or last worksheet that will be included in the range.
2. Using the techniques described earlier, highlight the desired row and column range in the worksheet.
3. Press Ctrl-PgUp or Ctrl-PgDn to expand the range to other worksheets, and then press Enter.

For the remainder of this book, procedures will specify a range before entering a command. Remember, however, that you also have the option of specifying the range after entering a command.

60

Using Range Names

Some ranges are used only once—for example, to erase or reformat a group of cells. Other ranges are used over and over again. 1-2-3 for Windows lets you assign a name to a range, then refer to the range by name rather than by address or by pointing. Range names you have assigned are saved with each worksheet file.

 Tip: You can assign a descriptive name to a single cell or to a multiple cell range.

 Tip: When you press F5, you get a list of range names to choose among. This is an easy way to move quickly to the top cell of a range, or in the case of a single cell range name, directly to that cell.

Assigning a New Name

Assigning a name to a range is done with the Range Name Create command and requires two steps: select the range, then specify the name. As with other commands, you can specify the range either before or after entering the command. The following Quick Steps describe how to assign a range name.

 Assigning a Range Name

1. Specify the range to be named.

   The range is highlighted in the worksheet.

2. Select Range Name Create.

   The Range Name Create dialog box is displayed (Figure 4.6). Existing range names, if any, are displayed in the list box.

3. Type the desired range name into the Range Name text box. A range name may be up to 15 characters long.

4. Select Create to assign the name and leave the dialog box open. Select OK to assign the name and close the dialog box.

   The name is assigned to the specified range.

   □

61

▶ **Tip:** Select Create when you want to assign two different names to the same range.

⊘ **Caution:** 1-2-3 for Windows accepts more than the limit of 15 characters when you type in the range name. 1-2-3 will only remember and use the first 15 as the range name.

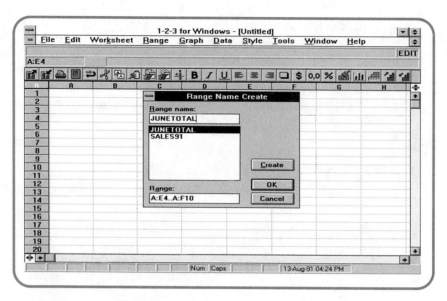

Figure 4.6   The Range Name Create dialog box.

62

Assigning Worksheet Labels as Range Names

A worksheet label is text data entered in a worksheet cell. 1-2-3 can automatically assign worksheet labels as range names for adjacent single cells. This can be very useful, particularly when the labels provide a description of the cell contents, as is the case in the worksheet in Figure 4.7.

You can assign labels as range names in four ways:

Up assigns the range name to the cell immediately above each label.

Down assigns the range name to the cell immediately below each label.

Left assigns the range name to the cells immediately to the left of each label.

Right assigns the range name to the cells immediately to the right of each label.

The following Quick Steps describe how to assign worksheet labels as range names.

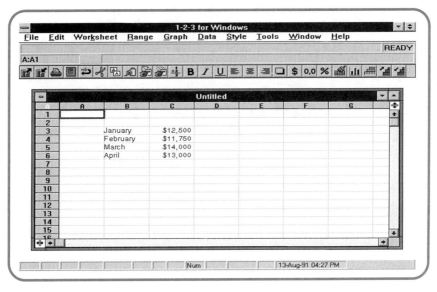

Figure 4.7   The labels in cells B3..B6 can be assigned as range names for adjacent cells.

 Assigning Worksheet Labels as Range Names

1. Be sure the labels are immediately adjacent to the cells you want to name.

2. Select (that is, highlight) the labels.

3. Select Range Name Label Create.

   The Range Name Label Create dialog box is displayed (as in Figure 4.8).

4. Select Right, Left, Up, or Down. For the labels in Figure 4.7, you would select Right.

   In Figure 4.7, cell C3 would be assigned the range name January, cell C4 would be assigned the name February, and so on.

5. Select OK.

   The selected labels are assigned as range names for the adjacent cells.   □

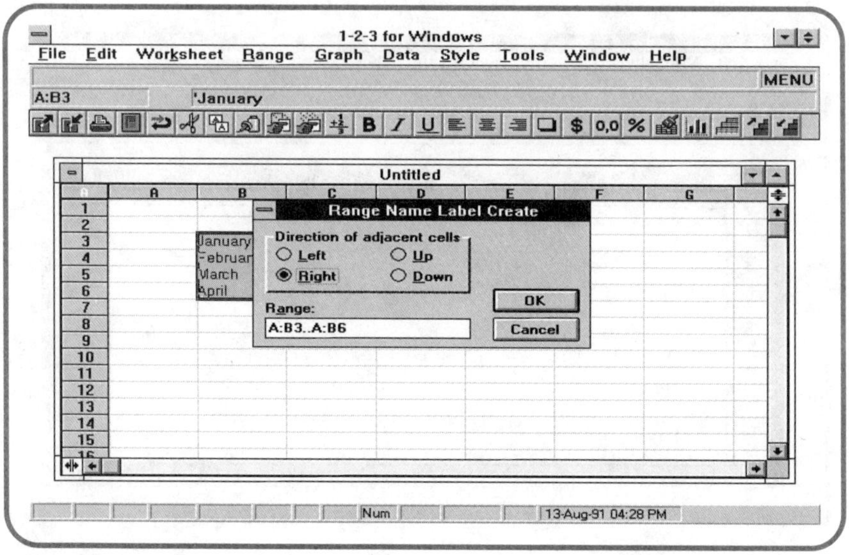

Figure 4.8   The Range Name Label Create dialog box.

Some Cautions

A duplicated range name is not allowed in a single worksheet file but can exist in two or more separate worksheet files. When assigning a new range name, be careful not to use a range name that already exists in that worksheet. The old name will then refer to the new range of cells, and mistakes may result. To avoid confusion, follow these guidelines when assigning range names:

▶ Use range names that are descriptive of the range's contents (for example, SALESTOTAL1991).

▶ Do not include spaces, commas, semicolons, or the characters # @ > < & / * + – in your range names.

▶ Do not use anything that could be interpreted as a cell address, column letter, or row number (X1, 110, BA).

▶ Do not use @function names, macro keywords, or 1-2-3 keywords.

▶ Do not begin a range name with a number, and do not use all numbers.

Other Range Name Commands

The Range Name Delete command is used to delete or undefine existing range names. To *delete* means to erase a range name from the worksheet. To *undefine* means to disassociate a name from its address range while retaining the name in the worksheet. In both cases, the data contained in the range is not deleted.

When you delete a range name, the name is deleted from any formulas that use it and replaced with the name's address. When you undefine a range name, the name is not removed from formulas. While a range name is undefined, any formulas that contain it will evaluate as ERR. If you later redefine the range name, its new range will be used in those formulas. Use Undefine when you plan to redefine the name later and want the name to remain in formulas. The Quick Steps which follow tell how to delete or undefine a range name.

 Deleting or Undefining a Range Name

1. Select Range Name Delete.

   The Range Name Delete dialog box is displayed (as in Figure 4.9).

2. Type in the range name to delete or undefine, or select it from the list box. To delete all range names, select Delete All.

   It is possible to undo this command, but be very careful!

3. Select Delete or Undefine.

   The specified range name is deleted or undefined. Selecting OK without choosing either Delete or Undefine is the same as selecting Delete.

4. To delete or undefine another range name, repeat steps 2 and 3.

5. Select OK.

   The dialog box is removed. □

65

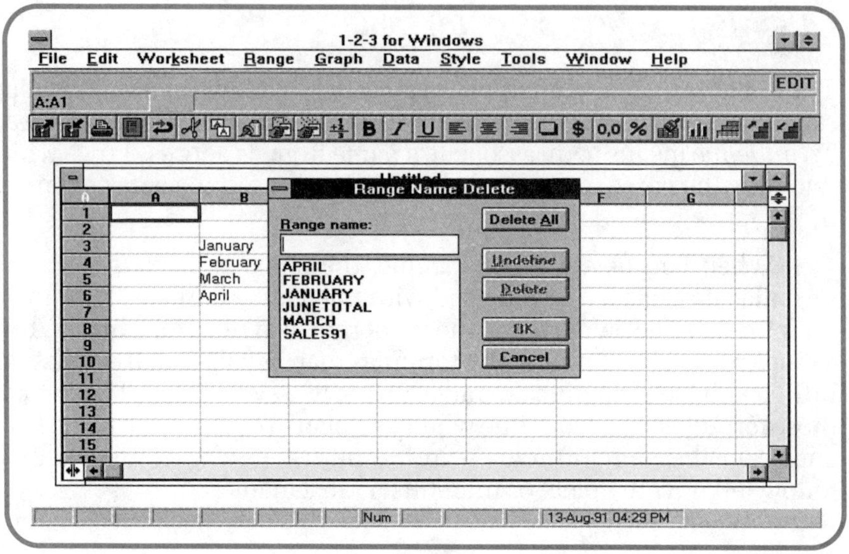

Figure 4.9   The Range Name Delete dialog box.

66

The Range Name Paste Table command creates an alphabetical list of all defined range names and their associated addresses. The list, or table, is pasted into your worksheet and will overwrite existing data, so you must be sure to place the list in an empty location. The list will consist of two columns and one more row than there are defined range names in the current worksheet file. Figure 4.10 shows a table of range names pasted into a worksheet, and the Quick Steps which follow describe how to create such a table.

 Creating a Table of Range Names and Addresses

1. Move the cell pointer to the cell where you want the top left corner of the table placed.

2. Select Range Name Paste Table. The Range Name Paste Table dialog box is displayed.

3. Press Enter or click OK. The table is pasted into the worksheet at the selected position. □

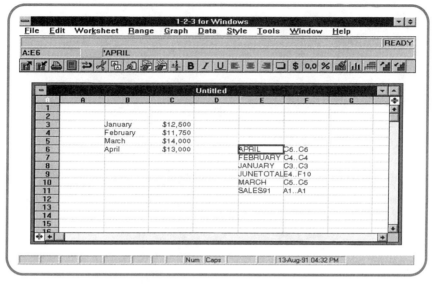

Figure 4.10   Cells E6..F11 contain a table of range names and addresses created with Range Name Paste Table.

67

What You Have Learned

▶ The current selection is the cell or group of cells that will be affected by your next action. The default current selection is the current cell.

▶ A range is a group of cells that is treated as a single entity. When you highlight a range in the worksheet, it becomes the current selection.

▶ A range can be either two- or three-dimensional, and is limited to a single worksheet file. You can specify a range with the keyboard or the mouse, either before or after entering a command that will affect the range.

▶ You can assign descriptive names to ranges, then refer to the ranges by name.

▶ 1-2-3 for Windows can automatically assign worksheet labels as range names for adjacent cells.

Working with Data

In This Chapter

- ▶ *Data types*
- ▶ *Entering data*
- ▶ *Copying and moving data*
- ▶ *Erasing data*
- ▶ *Editing data*
- ▶ *Finding and replacing data*

Entering Data

This section shows you how to enter data into a 1-2-3 for Windows worksheet. First, you need to understand 1-2-3's data types.

Data Types

The basic unit of 1-2-3 data storage is the *worksheet cell*. A worksheet cell can hold two basic types of data: values and labels. A *value* is a number, while a *label* is any sequence of characters that is not a value. When you enter data into a worksheet cell, the first character entered tells 1-2-3 whether the entry is a value or a label. A value entry is signalled by the first character being a numeral, a currency symbol (such as $), or one of the following:

(+ − . # @

All other characters signal a label entry. When you begin entering data, the 1-2-3 mode indicator shows VALUE or LABEL, depending on the data type being entered.

 Note: 1-2-3 for Windows recognizes two basic data types: values (numbers) and labels (text).

70

Entering Values

Values are entered from the keyboard. To enter a value in a worksheet cell:

1. Move the cell pointer to the desired cell.
2. Type the desired value.
3. Confirm the entry by pressing Enter, by using the keyboard to move the cell pointer to another cell, or by clicking the check box next to the entry.

When you start typing an entry, it appears in the contents box of the control line. The parts of the control line are illustrated in Figure 5.1, which shows how the worksheet would appear after you move the cell pointer to cell B3 and type 123.

The parts of the control line are listed here:

The *contents box* displays the current entry as it is being typed, or the contents of the current cell if no entry is being made.

The *address box* gives the address of the current cell.

The *confirm box* and *cancel box* are used to confirm or cancel an entry with the mouse. They appear on the control line only during data entry.

The *indicate box* tells what kind of data is being entered.

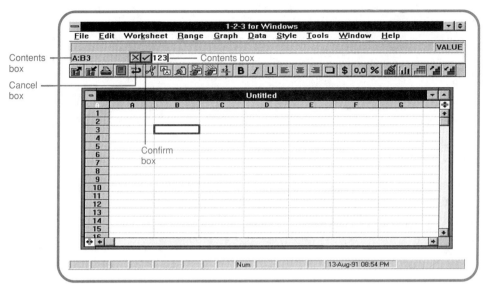

Figure 5.1 As you type in data, it appears in the contents box on the control line.

71

When you're finished typing in data, you confirm it and then 1-2-3 enters it in the worksheet. If other data existed in the current cell, it is replaced by the new entry. To confirm a data entry with the mouse, click the confirm box on the control line. To confirm an entry with the keyboard, press Enter or use any navigation key to move the cell pointer. Figure 5.2 shows the worksheet from Figure 5.1 after you confirm the data by pressing Enter or clicking the confirm box.

If you make a mistake or change your mind while making a data entry (but before confirming it) you can edit or cancel the entry. To cancel a data entry, click the cancel box on the control line or press Esc. To edit a data entry, press Backspace to erase the mistake, and then type replacement characters. You can also edit data by pressing F2 to put 1-2-3 into EDIT mode. You can then edit the entry as described in the "Editing Data" section later in this chapter.

 Note: If a value is too wide to display, 1-2-3 may display a row of asterisks in the cell.

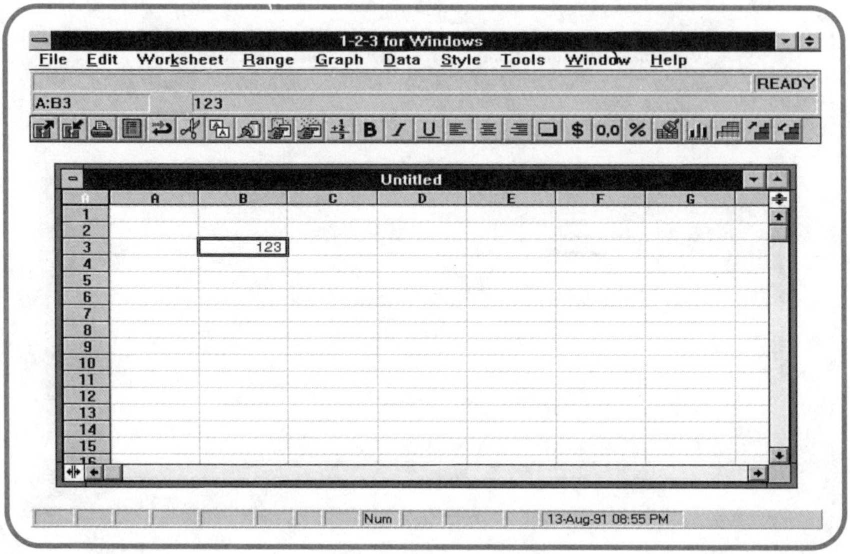

Figure 5.2 *The data entry has been confirmed, and the value is now entered in the worksheet.*

Entering Labels

1-2-3 for Windows stores labels with a label prefix character at the beginning. The label prefix character identifies the entry as a label, and also controls how it is displayed in the cell. The label prefix character is not displayed in the worksheet, but is shown in the contents box when the cell pointer is on a label cell. This is shown in Figure 5.3.

There are four label prefix characters that determine how the label is displayed in the cell:

'	Left aligned in the cell.
"	Right aligned in the cell
^	Centered in the cell.
\	Repeated across the cell.

The effects of these alignments are shown in Figure 5.4.

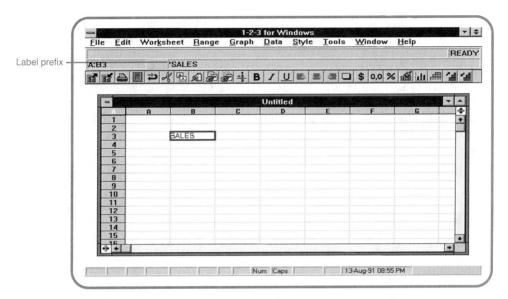

Figure 5.3   The label prefix character ' is not displayed in the worksheet, but is shown in the contents box.

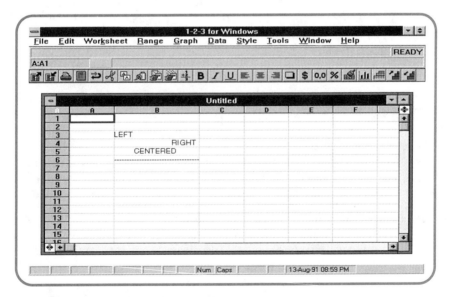

Figure 5.4   Illustration of left aligned, right aligned, centered, and repeated labels. The entry in cell B6 is \- so the hyphen character repeats across the width of the cell.

1-2-3 automatically inserts the default label prefix character when you start typing a label entry. The default label prefix is normally left aligned ('), but you can change this with the Worksheet Global Settings command, which is covered in Chapter 15. To enter a label that begins with a numeral, such as an address, you must type in the label prefix character yourself followed by the entry. Otherwise, 1-2-3 will think it's a value entry and will get confused since the entry has letters. When you confirm the entry, 1-2-3 beeps and enters EDIT mode, so you can correct the entry.

A label can be up to 512 characters long. This means that you can enter a label that is much wider than the cell width. If the cell or cells to the immediate right are empty, 1-2-3 will display across the empty cells and the entire label is seen. If the cells to the right are occupied, 1-2-3 will display only part of the label. The entire label, however, is stored in one cell. You can widen the column the cell is in to the required width to display the label.

74

> ▶ **Tip:** When entering a ZIP code, enter it as a label; that way ZIP codes that begin with 0 appear correctly in the cell. If you simply type 02345 and press Enter, 2345 appears in the cell. But if you type '02345, the correct ZIP code is entered because the number is read as a label.

Entering Dates and Times

Dates and times can be used simply as identifying labels, in which case they are entered and treated like any other 1-2-3 label. Remember to start the entry with a label prefix character (' " or ^) if the date or time label starts with a number, such as 5/28/91.

Dates and times can also be entered as values, which allows 1-2-3 to use them in calculations (for example, determining the number of days between two dates). Date and time values are maintained as special serial numbers, as follows:

Date	A value between 1 and 73050 representing the number of days since December 31, 1899.
Time	A decimal fraction between 0 and 0.99999 representing the 24 hour day.

Table 5.1 gives some examples of date and time values.

Table 5.1   Example Date and Time Values

Serial number	Date or time
1	January 1, 1900
73050	December 31, 2099
32978	April 15, 1990
0.0	12:00:00 AM
0.5	12:00:00 Noon
0.25	6:00:00 AM
0.99999	11:59:59 PM

> **Caution:** 1-2-3 for Windows stores dates and times as serial numbers. You need to use the Format command to make the serial number appear as a date.

It's not much use to have dates and times displayed as serial numbers, nor is it an easy matter to calculate the serial number corresponding to a certain date. Fortunately, 1-2-3 for Windows can handle these problems for you. To enter a date, enter it directly in a cell in one of the following formats:

Day-month-year	20-Jul-91
Day-month	20-Jul
Long international	7/20/91

1-2-3 will automatically recognize the entry as a date and convert it to a date serial number. You can also use the @DATE function (@functions are covered in Chapter 6). The @DATE( ) function converts a day, month, and year to the corresponding date serial number. For example, to enter July 20, 1991 as a serial number, type `@DATE(91,7,20)`. For the date formats that omit the year, the current year is assumed.

Entering times into a worksheet is similar. You can enter a time directly, and 1-2-3 will convert it into the corresponding serial number. The allowed time formats are:

Long AM/PM	11:30:45 PM
Short AM/PM	11:30 PM
Long 24 hour	23:30:45
Short 24 hour	23:30

You can also use the @TIME( ) function to convert hours, minutes, and seconds into a time serial number. For example, enter `@TIME(12,30,45)` to obtain the serial number for 12:30:45 PM (the serial number is 0.521354166666666667).

Date and time serial numbers are no different from other values and will display as such unless you change the cell's display format. Use the Range Format Date command, covered in Chapter 7, to display date and time serial numbers in standard date and time formats.

76 Copying Data

A worksheet cell can contain value or label data. A cell can also have cell properties attached to it. You'll learn the details of cell properties in Chapter 7. For now, all you need to know is that cell properties are settings that affect the appearance of the cell: font type and size, underlining, color, and so on.

When you copy data, the data is duplicated, and it is present in both the original and new locations.

Copying with Edit Quick Copy

1-2-3's Edit Quick Copy command lets you copy data and/or cell properties from one worksheet cell or range to another cell or range in the same or another worksheet file. After executing an Edit Quick Copy command, the data exists in both the old and the new locations. When you copy data, relative cell addresses in formulas are adjusted. (You'll learn about this topic in Chapter 6.) Copying involves three steps:

1. Specify the source of the data, called the FROM range.
2. Specify copy options, if desired. Two options are available:

   The *Styles Only* option copies only cell properties without copying cell data. The TO range receives the FROM range's cell properties while retaining its original data.

   The *Convert to Values* option is relevant only if the FROM range contains formulas. This option causes the result of the formulas to be copied rather than the formulas themselves.
3. Specify the destination for the data, called the TO range. If the TO range is multicell, you need specify only the upper left corner of the range.

   The Edit Quick Copy command does not use the Windows clipboard. The following Quick Steps lead you through the Edit Quick Copy procedure.

 Copying Data with Edit Quick Copy

1. Select the FROM range.	The FROM range is high-lighted (Figure 5.5).
2. Select Edit Quick Copy.	The Edit Quick Copy dialog box is displayed (Figure 5.6).
3. Select the To text box, then specify the address of the cell in the upper left corner of the TO range.	
4. Select the Styles Only and/or Convert to Values options, if desired.	
5. Select OK.	The data and/or cell properties is copied to the TO range (Figure 5.7). ☐

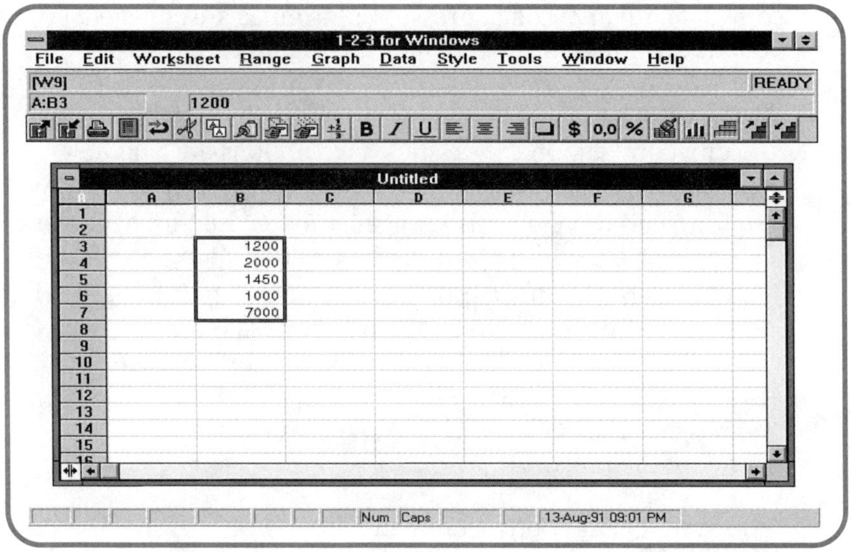

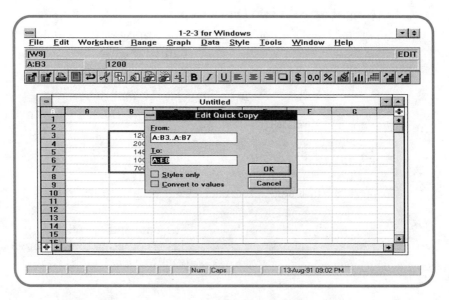

Figure 5.5   The first step in copying data is to specify the FROM range.

Figure 5.6   Next, display the Edit Quick Copy dialog box.

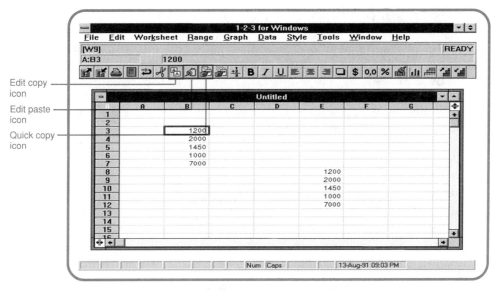

Figure 5.7   After the copy is complete, the data exists in both the TO and FROM ranges.

Mouse users also can perform a quick copy with the Quick Copy icon (see Figure 5.7). Select the FRONT range, click the icon, then specify the TO range with the mouse. The Edit Quick Copy procedure will overwrite any existing data and cell properties in the FROM range. Remember, you can specify a single cell TO range no matter how large the FROM range, and the entire FROM range will be copied with its upper left corner in the specified TO cell. Thus, if the FROM range is A1..C5 and you specify E1 as the TO range, the effective TO range will be E1..G5. Under certain circumstances, you can use Edit Quick Copy to make multiple copies of data:

▶   If the FROM range is a single cell and the TO range is a multiple cell range, the data in the FROM cell is duplicated in each cell in the TO range.

▶   If the FROM range consists of several cells in one column, and the TO range spans more than one column, the FROM cells are duplicated in each column in the TO range.

Copying Data with Edit Copy

The Edit Copy command provides another method of copying data. Edit Copy uses the Windows clipboard, a temporary data storage location shared by all Windows applications. Edit Copy can be used to copy data within an application (for example, from one worksheet location to another) or between applications (for example, from 1-2-3 for Windows to your Windows word processor). When using Edit copy:

▶ You must specify the FROM range before selecting the command.

▶ You have no copy options available, such as Styles Only.

The following Quick Steps describe how to use the Edit Copy command.

 Copying Data in a Worksheet Using Edit Copy

1. Select (that is, highlight) the FROM range.

2. Select Edit Copy, press Ctrl-Ins, or click the Edit Copy icon. | The data in the selected range is copied to the clipboard.

3. Move the cell pointer to the first cell in the TO range.

4. Select Edit Paste, click the Edit Paste icon, or press Shift-Ins. | The data is copied from the clipboard to the TO range, overwriting any existing data. □

The data that has been put on the clipboard remains there until replaced by another Edit Copy operation. You can paste the data multiple times if desired. For additional information on using the clipboard to copy data within and between applications, please see your Microsoft Windows documentation.

Moving Data

Moving data moves data and/or cell properties from one location to another.

Moving Data with Edit Move Cells

1-2-3's Edit Move Cells command lets you move data and/or cell properties from one worksheet range to another range in the same worksheet file. After executing an Edit Move Cells command, the data and cell properties exist in the new location and have been erased from the old location. When you move data, relative cell addresses in formulas elsewhere in the worksheet that refer to the moved range are adjusted. (You'll learn about this topic in Chapter 6.) Moving data involves three steps:

1. Specify the source of the data, called the FROM range.
2. Specify copy options, if desired. One option is available:

   The *Styles Only* option moves only cell properties without moving cell data. The TO range receives the FROM range's cell properties while retaining its original data; the FROM range reverts to the default cell properties while retaining its original data.
3. Specify the destination for the data, called the TO range. You need specify only the upper left corner of the TO range.

Edit Move Cells does not use the Windows clipboard and cannot be used to move data between worksheet files. The following Quick Steps review the procedure.

81

 Moving Data with Edit Move Cells

1. Select the FROM range.	The range is highlighted (Figure 5.8).
2. Select Edit Move Cells.	The Edit Move cells dialog box is displayed (Figure 5.9).
3. Select the Styles Only option, if desired (see Figure 5.8).	
4. Select the To: text box, and then specify the address of the cell in the upper left corner of the TO range.	
5. Select OK.	The data and/or cell properties are moved to the TO range (Figure 5.10). □

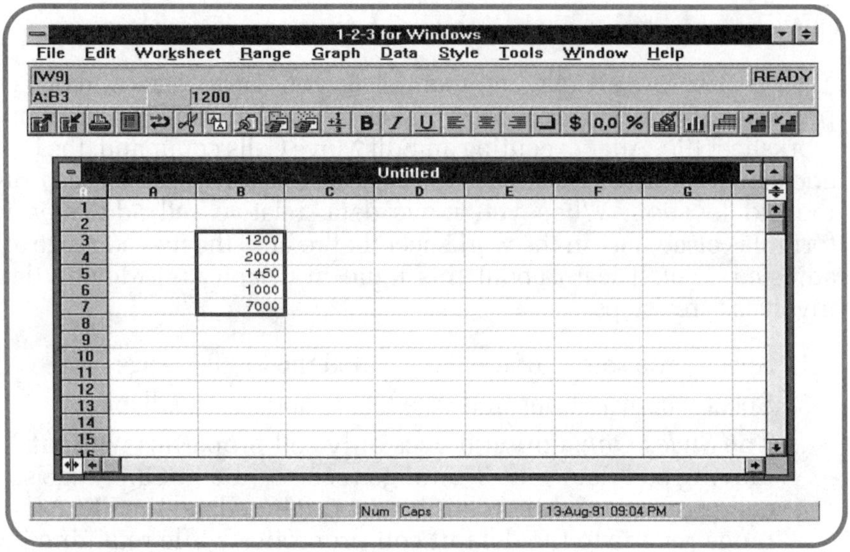

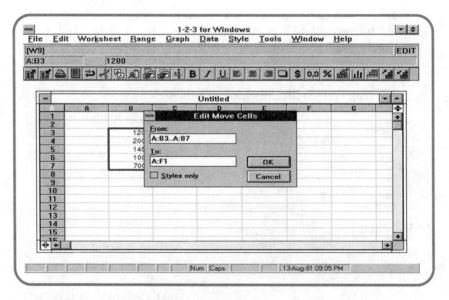

Figure 5.8   The first step in moving data is to specify the FROM range.

Figure 5.9   Next, display the Edit Move Cells dialog box.

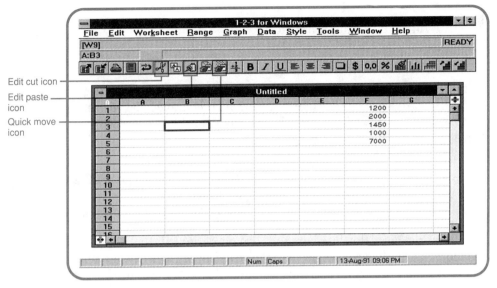

Edit cut icon

Edit paste icon

Quick move icon

Figure 5.10   After the move is complete, the data has been moved to the TO range and erased from the FROM range.

83

Moving Data with Edit Cut

The Edit Cut command provides another method of moving data. Like the Edit Copy command discussed previously, Edit Cut uses the Windows clipboard. Edit Cut can be used to move data within an application or between applications. Unlike Edit Move Cells, Edit Cut can be used to move data between worksheet files. When using Edit Cut:

► Relative cell addresses adjust to the address they are pasted into after a cut.

► You must specify the FROM range before selecting the command.

► You have no copy options available, such as Styles Only.

The next Quick Steps describe how to use Edit Cut.

Q **Moving Data Using Edit Cut**

1. Select (that is, highlight) the FROM range.

2. Select Edit Cut, click the Edit Cut icon (Figure 5.10), or press Shift-Del.

    The data in the selected range is moved to the clipboard.

3. Move the cell pointer to the first cell in the TO range.

4. Select Edit Paste, click the Edit Paste icon, or press Shift-Ins.

    The data is copied from the clipboard to the TO range, overwriting any existing data. □

You can paste the data from the clipboard multiple times if desired. For additional information on using the clipboard to move data within and between applications, please see your Microsoft Windows documentation.

Mouse users can perform a quick move with the Quick Move icon (see Figure 5.10). Select the range to move, click the icon, then specify the TO range with the mouse.

Erasing Data

You can erase data and/or cell properties from ranges of cells. You can also erase entire rows, columns, and worksheets.

Erasing a Range of Cells

You have two options when you want to erase a range of cells. Edit Clear erases all information—data, cell properties, graphs, etc.—from the range. Edit Clear Special lets you specify which information is to be erased. With Edit Clear Special, your options are:

Cell Contents deletes the data in the cells but does not erase cell properties.

Number Format resets all numeric formats in the range to the default format. Formats are set with the Range Format command (covered in Chapter 7). Cell data and other cell properties are not affected.

Style deletes all cell properties set with the Style command (covered in Chapter 6), such as font, borders, and shading. Cell data and other cell properties are not affected.

Graph deletes a graphic from the range. The graphic is not deleted from memory, and the data on which the graphic is based is not affected.

To erase data, graphics, and/or cell properties from a worksheet range, use the following Quick Steps.

 Clearing Cell Information

85

1. Select the range to delete.	The range is highlighted (Figure 5.11).
2a. *To delete all data, properties, and graphics in the range,* select Edit Clear, press Del.	All information in the selected range is deleted.
2b. *To delete selected information,* select Edit Clear Special.	The Edit Clear Special dialog box is displayed (Figure 5.12).
3. Select options in the dialog box depending on the specific information you want deleted from the range.	
4. Select OK.	The specified types of information are deleted from the range (Figure 5.13). □

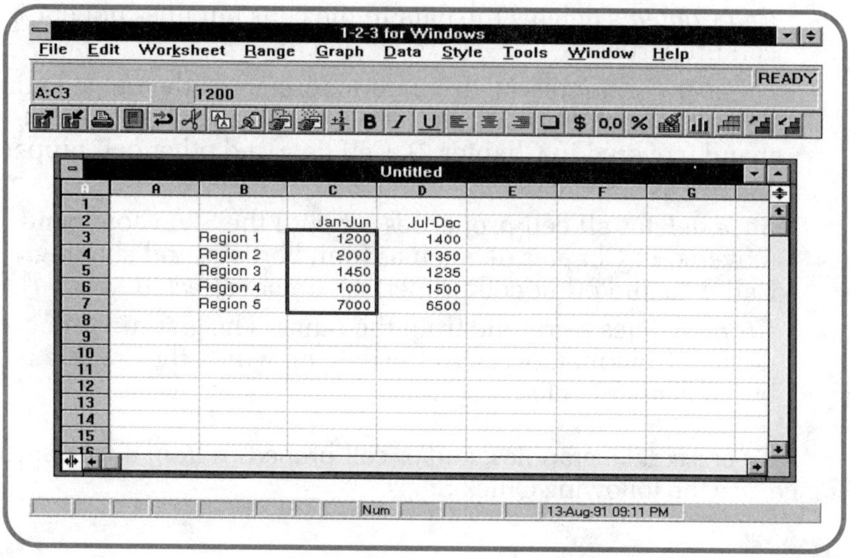

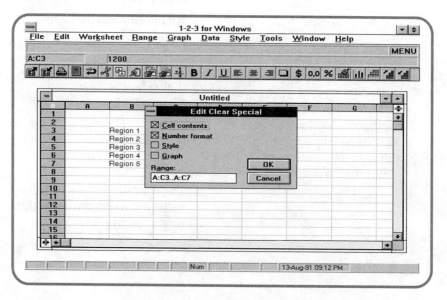

Figure 5.11   To delete data from a worksheet, first select the range.

Figure 5.12   Next, display the Edit Clear Special dialog box.

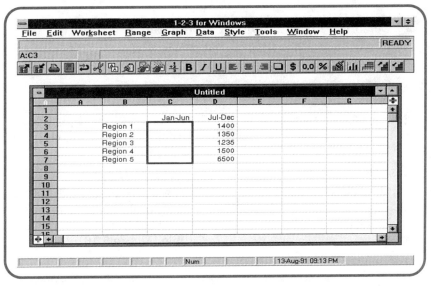

Figure 5.13   After selecting options in the dialog box and selecting OK, data is erased from the specified range.

87

 Note: To quickly delete all data from a single cell, move the cell pointer to that cell and press Del.

Deleting Rows, Columns, and Worksheets

You can delete entire rows, columns, or worksheets from the current worksheet file. When you delete a row, column, or worksheet, you are not simply erasing the data it contains. You are actually removing the row, column, or worksheet from the worksheet file. For example, if you delete row 2 from a worksheet, the lower rows move up to fill in the deleted row: the data in row 3 will now be in row 2, and so on. Likewise, if you delete worksheet C:, the data in worksheet D: will move to the left. This will be made clearer by the examples contained in the following Quick Steps.

Deleting a Row, Column, or Worksheet

1. Select a range that includes at least one cell in each row, column, or worksheet to be deleted.

   The range is highlighted (Figure 5.14).

2. Select Worksheet Delete.

   The Worksheet Delete dialog box is displayed (Figure 5.15).

3. Select Row, Column, or Sheet.
4. Select OK.

   The selected row(s), column(s), or sheet(s) are deleted from the worksheet file (Figure 5.16). □

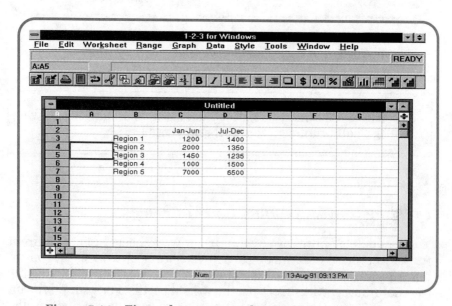

Figure 5.14   First select a range that includes at least one cell in each row, column, or worksheet to be deleted.

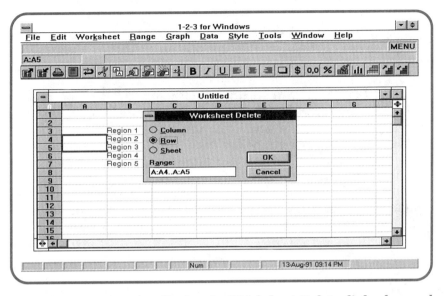

Figure 5.15 *Next, display the Worksheet Delete dialog box and select the type of item to be deleted. In this case, Row is selected.*

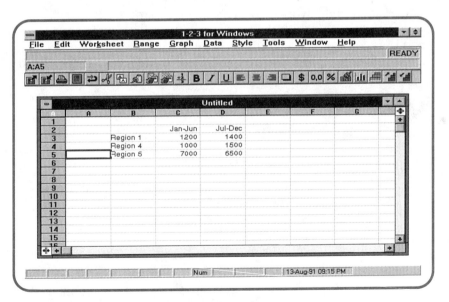

Figure 5.16 *Select OK, and the selected items are deleted. In this case, rows 4 and 5 were deleted. The space left by the deletion is closed up.*

> ⊘ **Caution:** Worksheet Delete deletes entire rows, columns, or worksheets—not just the portion visible on the screen.

In GROUP mode (explained in Chapter 3), deleting rows or columns in one worksheet deletes the same rows or columns in all worksheets in the file. If you delete an entire range whose address is used in a formula, the formula evaluates as ERR. If you delete an entire named range whose name is used in a formula, the name remains in the formula and is treated as an undefined range name (as explained in Chapter 4). When worksheet data moves to fill in a deleted area, 1-2-3 automatically redefines named ranges and adjusts cell addresses and range addresses in formulas.

Editing Data

90

You will sometimes need to modify data or formulas that have already been entered in the worksheet. This is done using 1-2-3's EDIT mode. Do not confuse this with the Edit command on the main menu. EDIT mode lets you modify the contents of a cell without completely retyping it. The following Quick Steps explain how to edit an existing cell entry.

 Editing an Existing Cell Entry

1. Move the cell pointer to the cell whose contents you want to edit.

2. Press F2 or click the contents box to enter EDIT mode.   The mode indicator reads EDIT.

3. Use the editing keys and mouse actions in Table 5.2 to make the necessary changes.

4. To confirm the changes you have made, press Enter, use the navigation keys to move the cell pointer, or click the Confirm box.   You are returned to READY mode, and the modified data is entered in the cell.

5. To cancel the changes, press Esc or click the Cancel box.

You are returned to READY mode with the original cell contents unchanged. □

Table 5.2 *Editing the Cell Entry While in EDIT mode*

Desired Result	Key or Mouse Action
Move the cursor one character at a time	Right and left arrow keys
Move the cursor to the beginning or end of the text	Home or End key
Highlight one character to the right or left of the cursor	Shift-left arrow or Shift-right arrow key
Highlight all characters between the cursor and the beginning or end of the text	Shift-Home or Shift-End key
Highlight characters with the mouse	Move mouse pointer to the first character, hold down the left mouse button, and drag the highlight over the desired characters. Alternatively, click on the first character, hold down the shift key, and click on the last character.
Highlight one word with the mouse	Double-click on the word
Delete all highlighted characters or one character to the right of the cursor	Del key
Delete one character to the left of the cursor	Backspace key

91

Finding and Replacing Entries

You can search for and optionally replace entries in a worksheet. You can search in labels, formulas, or both. You cannot search value cells. The following sets of Quick Steps describe how to find, then find and replace, cell entries.

Q Finding Cell Entries

1. Specify the range in which you want to search.

   The range is highlighted (Figure 5.17).

2. Select Edit Find.

   The Edit Find dialog box is displayed (Figure 5.18).

3. Under Action, select Find. Then, in the Search For text box, enter the target text, that is, the characters to be found. You may enter up to 512 characters.

4. Under Search Through, specify the type of cell entries to be searched: Labels, Formulas, or Both.

5. Select Find Next.

   The first occurrence of the search characters is highlighted

6. To continue the search, select Find Next again.

   The next occurrence of the search characters is highlighted

7. To terminate the search, select Cancel.

   1-2-3 for Windows returns to READY mode.   ☐

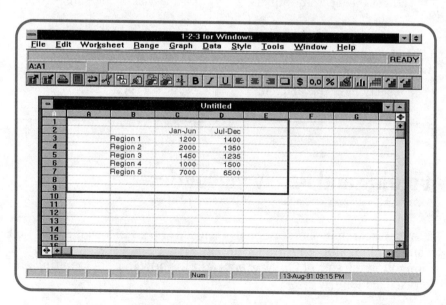

Figure 5.17 *To search for and optionally replace text, first specify the range to be searched.*

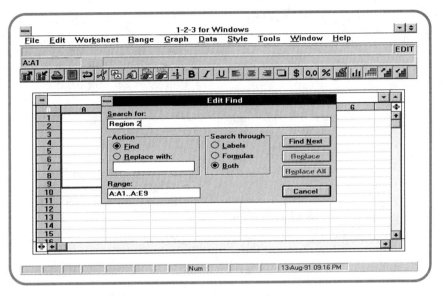

Figure 5.18 In the Edit Find dialog box, enter the target text in the Search For text box.

93

 Finding and Replacing Entries

1. Select the worksheet range to be searched.	The range is highlighted.
2. Select Edit Find.	The Edit Find dialog box is displayed (Figure 5.18).
3. Under Action, select Replace With.	
4. In the Search For text box, enter the characters you want to replace.	
5. In the Replace With text box, enter the replacement text (Figure 5.19).	
6. Select Find Next.	1-2-3 for Windows highlights the first occurrence of the search characters (but does not replace them).

7. To replace the characters, select Replace.

The highlighted characters are replaced with the replacement characters, and the next occurrence of the search characters is highlighted.

8. Repeat step 7 as needed. Or, select Replace All to replace all remaining occurrences of the search characters.

9. To terminate the search, select Cancel.

1-2-3 returns to READY mode.   □

If the search reaches the end of the search range without finding a match, 1-2-3 for Windows displays a message to that effect.

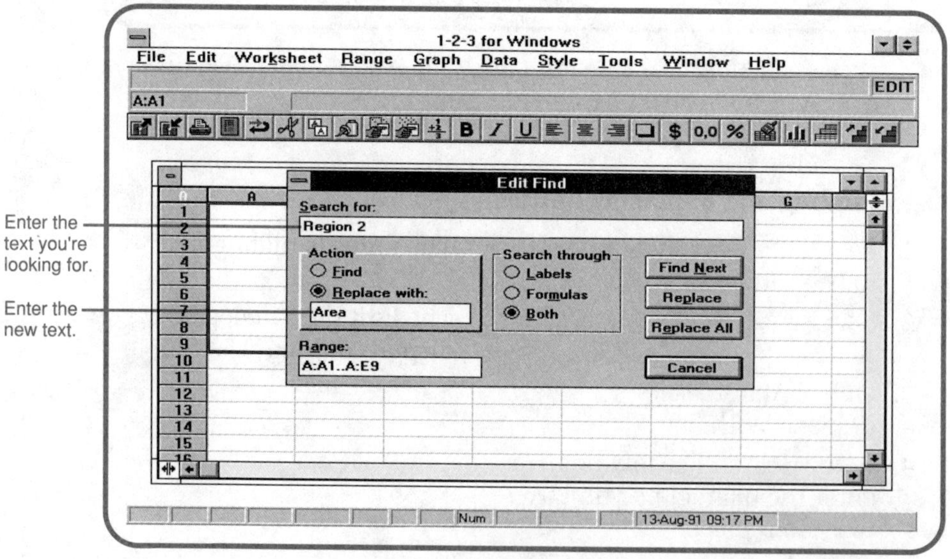

Figure 5.19   If you select Replace With, enter the replacement text in the Replace With text box.

The Undo Command

What if you mistakenly erase some valuable data or make another error? The Edit Undo command can usually save you. Many (but not all) 1-2-3 for Windows commands or actions can be undone, or reversed, with this command. Generally speaking, you can undo any action or command that changes worksheet data or settings. Here are some examples:

►   Deleting data.

►   Changing a cell entry.

►   Moving or copying data.

►   Changes in numeric format, font, and other cell properties.

And here are some things that *cannot* be undone:

►   Changes to disk files.

►   A previous use of Undo.

►   Formula recalculation.

►   Printer activity.

►   Cell pointer movement caused by F5 (Goto), F6 (pane), or the navigation keys.

95

   To undo your latest action, press Alt-Backspace or select Edit Undo. The Undo feature can be turned on or off. 1-2-3's default is for Undo to be on. The Undo feature uses some memory, so you may at times want to turn it off. This is done with the Tools User Setup command, which will be covered in Chapter 15.

What You Have Learned

►   1-2-3 for Windows works with two basic data types: values and labels.

►   Data is entered into worksheet cells from the keyboard.

▶ A worksheet stores dates and times as special serial numbers. 1-2-3 for Windows has functions to convert dates and times between standard formats and serial numbers.

▶ Use the Edit Quick Copy command to copy data and/or cell properties to another worksheet location. Use the Edit Copy command to copy data using the Windows clipboard.

▶ Use the Edit Move Cells command to move data and/or cell properties to another worksheet location. Use the Edit Cut command to move data using the Windows clipboard.

▶ You can erase any worksheet data from a single cell to an entire worksheet.

▶ Use the Edit Find command to search for and optionally replace worksheet data.

▶ The Edit Undo command can undo many worksheet actions, allowing you to recover from errors.

96

Formulas and Functions

In This Chapter

▶ *Writing your own worksheet formulas*
▶ *Using relative and absolute cell addresses*
▶ *Using 1-2-3 for Windows' built-in formulas, called functions*

Writing Formulas

You learned in Chapter 5 that a worksheet cell can contain either a value or a label. A cell can also contain a formula that performs a calculation based on data in a worksheet. This is one of 1-2-3 for Windows' most powerful features. A formula can contain numbers and labels, and can also use values and labels in other worksheet cells. Whenever data in the worksheet changes, formulas are automatically recalculated, keeping the worksheet up to date. There are three types of formulas:

Numeric formulas evaluate to a value.

Logical formulas perform tests on numeric or string values and evaluate as either TRUE or FALSE. 1-2-3 uses the value 1 to represent TRUE and 0 to represent FALSE.

String formulas evaluate to a string.

The term *string* refers to any sequence of characters. A string can be a worksheet label or a sequence of characters enclosed in quotation marks. Table 6.1 gives some examples of simple formulas.

Table 6.1   Example Formulas

If you enter	The cell displays
`20/4`	5 (20 divided by 4)
`+B3`	The contents of cell B3—0 if B3 is blank.
`+B1+B2+B3`	The sum of the values in cells B1, B2, and B3.
`+Total`	The contents of the cell that has been assigned the range name "Total".
`"1-2-3 for"&" Windows"`	The string `1-2-3 for Windows`.
`@SUM(A1..A5)`	The sum of all values in the range A1..A5 (this is an @function, one of 1-2-3 for Windows' built-in functions).
`+B2=B3`	1 (TRUE) if the values in cells B2 and B3 are the same; `0` (FALSE) otherwise. (This is a logical formula.)

You enter a formula into a cell like any other entry. A formula must begin with a number, a left parenthesis, a cell reference preceded by a plus or minus sign, or the name of an @function. (These are 1-2-3 for Windows' built-in formulas, discussed later in this chapter.) When a cell contains a formula, the result (rather than the formula itself) is displayed in the worksheet. The formula is displayed in the contents box when the cell pointer is on the cell. See Figure 6.1.

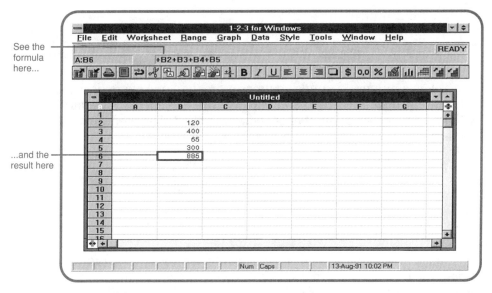

See the formula here...

...and the result here

Figure 6.1 *The worksheet displays the result of a formula, but the contents box displays the formula itself.*

99

Formula Operators and Operator Precedence

An *operator* is a symbol that instructs 1-2-3 to perform a certain operation in a formula. 1-2-3's operators have a precedence that determines the order in which they are performed. There are three types of operators: *mathematical, logical,* and *string*.

Mathematical Operators

1-2-3 for Windows can use the five standard *mathematical* operators to perform numeric calculations in formulas:

+   (addition)

−   (subtraction)

* (multiplication)
/ (division)
^ (exponentiation)

When a numeric formula contains more than one operator, 1-2-3 performs the operations in a particular order, or precedence. Operators with lower precedence number are performed first. The precedence of operators is:

Precedence	Operator(s)
1	^
2	* /
3	+ −

Operators with the same precedence are performed in left-to-right order. You can use parentheses to modify the order in which calculations are performed, as operations enclosed within parentheses are always performed first. Table 6.2 shows some examples. Values are used here for clarity, but the same rules apply for calculations using cell addresses or range names.

100

Table 6.2   Order of Precedence Examples

Formula	Result	Explanation
+5+2*3	11	The * is performed first, giving 6, then the 5 is added.
(5+2)*3	21	The parentheses force the + to be performed first, giving 7. The 7 is then multiplied by 3.
+6^2+2	38	The ^ is performed first, giving 36, then the 2 is added.
+6^(2+2)	1296	The + is performed first giving 4, then the ^ is performed.
+2^2+2*2	8	The ^ is performed first, giving 4. The * is performed next, also giving 4. Finally the + is performed.
+2^((2+2)*2)	256	The + is performed first, giving 4. The 4 is then multiplied by 2, giving 8. Finally the ^ is performed.

The Logical Operators

The *logical* operators evaluate conditions and return TRUE/FALSE answers. Remember, 1-2-3 uses the numerical values 1 and 0 to represent TRUE and FALSE, respectively. The logical operators and their precedence levels are listed in Table 6.3.

Table 6.3 **Logical Operators**

Precedence level	Operator	Meaning
5	=	Equal to
5	<>	Not equal to
5	<	Less than
5	>	Greater than
5	>=	Greater than or equal to
5	<=	Less than or equal to
6	#NOT#	Not *condition*
7	#AND#	Both *condition 1* and *condition 2*
7	#OR#	Either *condition 1* or *condition 2*

101

Note that the logical operators all have precedence lower than that of the mathematical operators. This means that if a formula contains a combination of mathematical and logical operators, the mathematical operations will be performed first (unless parentheses are used to modify the order, of course).

The first 6 logical operators in Table 6.3 above are used to perform comparisons between values. In effect, they ask questions and return either 1 or 0 depending on whether the answer to the question is TRUE of FALSE. Here are some examples:

Formula	Meaning
+A5>5	Is the value in cell A5 greater than 5?
(B1+B2)=A10	Is the sum of the values in cells B1 and B2 equal to the value in cell A10?
@SUM(A1..A5)>=TOTAL	Is the sum of the values in the range A1..A5 greater than or equal to the value in the cell assigned the range name TOTAL?

The #NOT# operator simply reverses a TRUE/FALSE value. Here are two examples:

Formula	Meaning
`#NOT#A1`	TRUE if the formula in cell A1 evaluates as FALSE; FALSE if the formula in A1 evaluates as TRUE.
`#NOT#(A1<A2)`	TRUE if A1 is greater than or equal to A2; FALSE if A1 is less than A2. (Could also be written as +A1>=A2.)

The #AND# and #OR# operators are used to combine two logical results, or *conditions*. The #AND# operator evaluates as TRUE only if both conditions are true. The #OR# operator evaluates as TRUE if either condition is true. Here are some examples:

Formula	Meaning
`+A1#AND#A2`	TRUE if both A1 and A2 are TRUE; FALSE otherwise.
`(B2=<10)#AND#(B2>=5)`	TRUE if B2 is between the values of 5 and 10; FALSE otherwise.
`(A2=10)#OR#(B2=10)`	TRUE if either A2 or B2 (or both) equals 10; FALSE otherwise.
`(A2+A3>B3)#OR#(B3=0)`	TRUE if the sum of A2 and A3 is greater than B3, or if B3 equals 0; FALSE otherwise.

The String Operator

There is one *string* operator: & (ampersand sign). It stands for *concatenation*, or the joining of two strings or labels together. The concatenation operator has precedence level 7. For these examples, assume that cell A1 contains the label `Ajax Industries` and Cell C3 contains the label `1991 Sales`.

Formula	Displays
`+A1&" "&C3`	`Ajax Industries 1991 Sales`
`+"Annual report for "&A1`	`Annual report for Ajax Industries`

> ⊘ **Caution:** If you try to concatenate a cell that contains a value, you will get an error. You can, however, use the @STRING function to make the value compatible with concatenation. For example, if cell A1 contained 1965 and cell A2 contained Mustang, the formula @STRING(A1,0)&A2 would produce 1965 Mustang.

Using Built-in Formulas

1-2-3 for Windows has an array of built-in formulas, called @functions ("at" functions), that you can use in your worksheets. Some @functions provide a quick way of performing commonly needed calculations, such as summing a group of numbers. Other @functions let you do complex calculations, such as calculating loan payments, without you having to write the formulas yourself. 1-2-3 @functions fall into 8 categories:

103

- ▶ Mathematical
- ▶ Database
- ▶ Financial
- ▶ Statistical
- ▶ Logical
- ▶ Date and Time
- ▶ String
- ▶ Special

1-2-3 for Windows has over 100 @functions, and space limitations preclude covering them all in detail. This section shows you the basics of how they are used, and you can refer to the 1-2-3 for Windows documentation for details on specific functions.

Each @function consists of the function name (which always begins with the @ symbol) followed by a list of one or more arguments enclosed in parentheses. The arguments are the values or cell addresses that the function is to use in its calculations. A function's arguments can be values, cell addresses, range names, or even another @function. Here are some examples:

@function	Result
@SUM(SALES)	The sum of all values in the range named SALES.
@PMT(2000, 0.10/12,24)	The monthly payment on a $2000, 24 month loan at 10% annual interest.
@MIN(A:A1..A:C20)	The minimum value in the range A:A1..A:C20.
@AVG(B2..B10)	The average of the values in the range B2..B10.
@SQRT(@SIN(B1))	The square root of the sine of the value in cell B1.
@YEAR(A1)	The year corresponding to the date serial number in cell A1.

104

You should spend some time becoming familiar with 1-2-3 for Windows' @functions. They can be great time savers. And, you would not want to spend a lot of time writing a formula that duplicates an @function!

Point Mode

Most formulas you use will reference other worksheet data. You can reference a named range (as covered in Chapter 4) by entering the range name in a formula, and you can reference any cell or range by entering its address in a formula. You can type in the address directly, but it is often easier to use POINT mode to enter cell addresses into formulas. In POINT mode, you actually point to the cell or cells of interest, and 1-2-3 automatically enters the corresponding address into the formula. You may find that using POINT mode is quicker and more accurate than typing the address. The following Quick Steps summarize how to enter a cell or range address into a formula in point mode.

 Pointing to a Range

Using the Mouse:

1. Move the cell pointer to the cell that will contain the formula.

2. Enter the formula up to the point where a cell or range address is needed. For example, type @SUM(into the cell.

3a. *For a single cell address,* click the desired cell.

   1-2-3 displays the POINT mode indicator and enters the cell address in the formula, as shown in the contents box (Figure 6.2).

3b. *For a range address,* point at a corner of the range and drag the highlight over the range, then release the mouse button.

   1-2-3 enters the range address in the formula, as shown in the contents box (Figure 6.3).

4. Continue typing the formula, usually by entering a close parenthesis. If another address is needed, return to step 3a or 3b.

5. When the formula is complete click the confirm box.

   1-2-3 enters the formula in the cell, evaluates it, and displays the result (Figure 6.4).

105

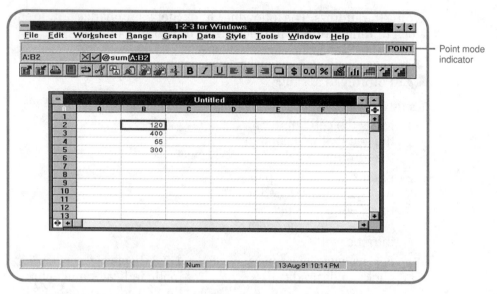

Point mode indicator

Figure 6.2   To enter an address in a formula using POINT
mode, type in the formula up to where an address is needed,
then move the cell pointer to the first cell.

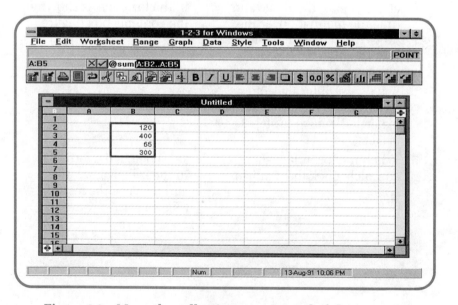

Figure 6.3   Move the cell pointer to one end of the range, press
. (period), and then expand the highlight over the desired range.

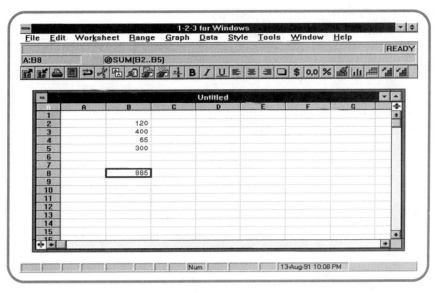

Figure 6.4   When the formula is complete, press Enter.

 Pointing to a Range *(continued)*

Using the Keyboard:

1. Move the cell pointer to the cell that will contain the formula.

2. Enter the formula up to the point where a cell or range address is needed. For example, type `@SUM(` into the cell.

3. Use the navigation keys to move the cell pointer to the first cell in the range.

   1-2-3 displays the POINT mode indicator and enters the cell address in the formula, as shown in the contents box (Figure 6.2).

4a. *For a single range address,* proceed to step 5.

   1-2-3 enters the range address in the formula in the contents box (Figure 6.3).

4b. *For a multicell range address,* press . (period) to anchor the range, then use the navigation keys to adjust the highlighted rectangle so it covers the desired range. If you make a mistake, press Esc to unanchor the range, and return to step 3.

5. If the address is correct, continue entering the formula (usually by entering a close parenthesis). If another address is needed, return to step 3.

6. When the formula is complete, press Enter.

1-2-3 enters the formula in the cell, evaluates it, and displays the result (Figure 6.4).

□

Relative and Absolute Cell Addresses

108

To use formulas effectively, you must understand the distinction between *relative* and *absolute* cell references. When used in a formula, a cell reference is, by default, relative. This means that it does not refer to a fixed worksheet location, but to a location that is relative to the cell containing the formula.

An example will make this clearer. In cell A:A3, enter the formula @SUM(A:A1..A:A2). Because A:A1..A:A2 is a relative cell reference, the formula's meaning is "sum the two cells immediately above this cell." If you use the Copy command to copy the formula to another cell in the same worksheet, it retains its relative meaning. If, for example, you copy it to cell A:D8, the formula is changed to @SUM(A:D6..A:D7), retaining its original meaning: sum the two cells immediately above this cell. Note that the sheet letter is automatically removed by 1-2-3 since the addresses refer to the same sheet.

Relative worksheet references are adjusted as well. For example, if you copy the above formula from A:A3 to B:A3 it will change to read @SUM(B:A1..B:A2. If you copy it to B:D8, it will be adjusted to read @SUM(B:D6..B:D7). In both cases the meaning remains "sum the two cells immediately above this cell in this worksheet."

Relative cell references are appropriate for most 1-2-3 formulas. For example, you might have several dozen columns of numbers to sum. You can write the summing formula in the cell below one column, then copy it across to the cells below each of the other columns. The relative cell addresses will be adjusted so that each formula sums the column above it. This is shown in Figures 6.5 and 6.6.

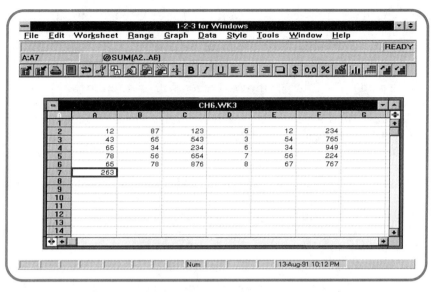

Figure 6.5   The formula @SUM(A:A2..A:A6) *is entered in Cell A:A7.*

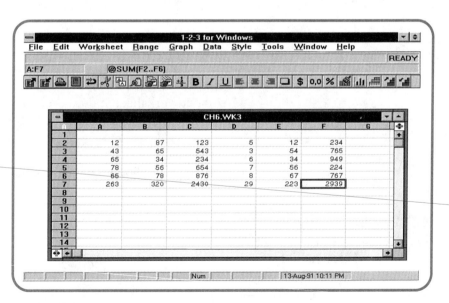

Figure 6.6   When that formula is copied to cells A:B7..A:F7, the relative cell references are adjusted so that each formula sums the column of numbers above it.

At times, however, you want a cell reference in a formula to refer to a specific cell or range no matter where the formula is copied to. In this case you use an absolute reference.

An absolute range name is denoted by a $ (dollar sign) before the range name. The $ can be inserted when you first define the range with Range Name Create, or can be added when you type the range name into a formula. If the range A1..A4 has been named Data, the formula @SUM($Data) will return the sum of cells A1..A4 no matter where in the worksheet it is copied, while the formula @SUM(Data) will sum A1..A4 only where first entered. When it is copied, the range name will be converted to the cell address of a range that has the same relative position to the new location as the range Data had to the original location. For example, assume that the range name Data refers to cells A1..A4, and that the formula @SUM(Data) is entered in cell A5. If you copy the formula to cell C5, it will change to read @SUM(C1..C4).

An absolute address is denoted by a dollar sign before the worksheet letter, the column letter, and/or the row number (for example, $A:$A$1). In a mixed cell address, one or two of the three address components (worksheet, column, row) is absolute, and the remaining part is relative. Here are some examples of absolute and mixed addresses in formulas:

@SUM($A:$B$1..$A:$B$4)	Absolute address. When the formula is copied, no adjustments are made.
@SUM(A:B$1..A:B$4)	Mixed, with row absolute. When copied, worksheet and column are adjusted but row is not.
@SUM($A:$B1..$A:$B4)	Mixed, with worksheet and column absolute. When copied, row is adjusted but worksheet and column are not.

> ⊘ **Caution:** Use care in entering absolute addresses. If you are inconsistent—for example, @SUM(B5..$B10)—you may get inaccurate results when you copy the formula.

You can enter absolute references by simply including the $ in the appropriate places as you type or edit the formula. You can also use the F4 (Abs) key to have 1-2-3 automatically cycle through the possible relative, absolute, and mixed entries, as the following Quick Steps demonstrate.

 Cycling through Absolute, Relative, and Mixed Cell References

1a. *If entering a formula,* type in the cell or range address, then stop.

1b. *If editing a formula,* move the editing cursor onto the cell address or range name.

2. Press F4 (Abs) one or more times until the address or range name is at the desired state.

Each time you press F4, the address or range name changes.

3. Continue entering or editing the formula.

□

111

Worksheet Recalculation

Most formulas you write will reference data in other worksheet cells. When worksheet data changes, the formulas must be recalculated for their results to be accurate. 1-2-3 for Windows' default is to automatically recalculate formulas whenever the values they depend on change. You can modify when and how formulas are recalculated with the Tools User Setup Recalculation command. This command is covered in detail in Chapter 15.

The ERR Indicator

1-2-3 will display ERR in a formula cell when there is a problem evaluating the formula. This can occur when you first enter a formula.

It can also happen that a formula that was working correctly suddenly displays ERR after some worksheet manipulation. Some common causes of ERR are:

▶ A @function that requires a single cell argument is passed a multicell range as an argument—for example, `@cos(A1..A4)`.

▶ A portion of the worksheet referenced by the formulas has been deleted.

▶ A cell referenced by a string formula is blank or contains a number.

▶ The formula attempts to perform a mathematically meaningless operation, such as `@sqrt(-4)`.

What You Have Learned

▶ You can write formulas in 1-2-3 for Windows cells that perform calculations based on worksheet data.

▶ There are three basic types of formulas: numeric, string, and logical.

▶ Formula operators have a precedence that determines the order in which they are performed.

▶ Cell references in formulas can be absolute, relative, or mixed.

▶ 1-2-3 for Windows includes many built in formulas, called @functions, that perform commonly needed calculations.

Chapter 7

Worksheet Format and Style

In This Chapter

▶ *Displaying numbers, dates, and times in different formats*
▶ *Changing column width and row height*
▶ *Using borders, colors, shading, and drop shadows*
▶ *Using different fonts in your worksheets*

Format and Style—What are They?

The format and style of a worksheet affect only the appearance of the worksheet (and of printouts), and have no effect on the worksheet's data. Format and style can have a major influence on the readability and impact of your worksheets and printed reports. *Format* refers to the way in which numeric values are displayed in cells. *Style* involves worksheet enhancements such as colors, fonts, and borders.

Formatting Numbers

1-2-3 for Windows offers many different numeric display formats, with one suitable for every imaginable need. Remember that changing the numeric format of worksheet cells affects only the way numbers are displayed. Numbers are always stored with full 15-digit accuracy.

Numeric formats are applied to individual worksheet cells. You can change the format of a single cell, a range of cells, or an entire worksheet. When you start a new worksheet, it has a default numeric format that will be used for all cells whose format is not explicitly changed. 1-2-3 for Windows' normal default format is General; you can change the default format with the Worksheet Global Settings Format command (covered in Chapter 15).

You modify numeric display formats with the Range Format command. Before seeing how to use this command, you should be familiar with the various formats that are available. As you'll see, the way formats display on the screen depends in some cases on column width.

General format displays numbers with as many decimal places as needed, and displays negative numbers with a minus sign. Thousands separators are not used. If there are too many digits to the right of the decimal point to fit in the column width, the number is rounded as needed. If there are too many digits to the left of the decimal point to fit in the column width, the number is displayed in scientific format. Following are some examples of values displayed in General format.

Value	Displayed as
106.99	106.99
−0.015	−0.015
125000000000	1.250E+11 (default column width)

Fixed format is essentially the same as General format, but the number of decimal places displayed (0-15) is specified by the user. If the number of specified decimal places is too few, the number is displayed rounded off (but remains stored with full precision). If the number is too wide for the column width, a row of asterisks is displayed. Simply widen the column, and the number will correctly display. Here are some examples:

Value	Displayed as
106.99	`107.0` (1 decimal place)
106.99	`106.9900` (4 decimal places)
125000000000	`************` (default column width)

Currency format displays numbers with a currency symbol, thousands separators, and 0-15 user specified decimal places. Negative numbers are displayed with a minus sign or in parentheses (the default). The symbols used for currency and thousands separator, and the negative number format, depend on the International settings (set with the Tools User Setup International command, covered in Chapter 15). These examples are formatted as currency:

Value	Displayed as
1000	`$1,000.00` (2 decimal places)
−50.95	`-$50.9500` (4 decimal places, sign for negative values)
−50.95	`($50.95)` (2 decimal places, parentheses for negative values)

Comma format is identical to currency format except that no currency symbol is displayed. The thousands separator symbol and the negative number format depend on the International settings.

Percent format displays numbers multiplied by 100, with a percent sign and 0-15 user-specified decimal places, as the following examples illustrate:

Value	Displayed as
0.15	`15%` (0 decimal places)
1.15	`115.00%` (2 decimal places)

Scientific format displays numbers as a value between 1 and 10 (the *mantissa*) multiplied by a power of 10 (the *exponent*). Scientific notation is sometimes called *exponential notation*. The number of decimal places in the mantissa can be specified between 0 and 15. Use scientific notation for very large and very small numbers, such as those included among the following examples:

Value	Displayed as
1.25	`1.25E+00` (2 decimal places)
−0.0000055	`5.500E-06` (3 decimal places)
5656500000000	`5.66E+12` (2 decimal places)

Hidden format hides the data in the cell. The cell appears blank, but when the cell pointer is on the cell, its data appears in the contents box.

> ⊘ **Caution:** Be careful when applying Hidden format. Because the cell appears empty, you may inadvertently type in new data, overwriting the old.

Automatic format displays existing values in General format. If a new entry is made, the entry is analyzed, and the cell is formatted accordingly:

▶ If a new entry is typed in Currency, Comma, Fixed, Percent, or Scientific format, the cell is given the corresponding format.

▶ If an entry is typed in a date or time format, the cell is given the corresponding Date or Time format, and the entry is converted to, and stored as, a date or time serial number.

▶ If the entry starts with a number followed by any nonnumeric character, or if the entry is an invalid formula, it is stored as a label.

> ▶ **Tip:** If you need to type in many addresses, format the column as Automatic. That way you won't have to precede each address with an apostrophe—simply type the address and press Enter.

Text format displays the text of formulas rather than the formula's results. Numbers are displayed in General format. Use text format to display formulas during worksheet debugging.

Label format displays existing numbers in General format, and treats all new entries, whether numeric or text, as labels.

Parentheses format offers the option of displaying numbers enclosed in parentheses. This format operates in conjunction with, not instead of, other formats. Thus, if you select Parentheses format for a cell already formatted as Percent, it will display as (50%).

+/– format displays positive and negative numbers as a row of + or – signs. The number of + or – signs displayed equals the entry's integer value. Numbers between –1 and 1 display as a period. This format can be used to create simple bar charts within the worksheet.

Following are examples of entries formatted as +/–.

Value	Displayed as
7	+++++++
–5.4	-----
0	.
4.8	++++

The date and time formats display date and time serial numbers in one of the available date or time formats. Here are examples of the five date formats, which also appear on the Range Format menu:

Menu Choice	Format
31-Dec-90	Day-Month-Year
31-Dec	Day-Month
Dec-90	Month-Year
Long Intl. Date	Month/Day/Year (for example, 12/31/90)
Short Intl. Date	Month/Day (for example, 12/31)

117

Following are the four time formats that appear on the Range Format menu:

Menu Choice	Format
11:59:59 AM	HH:MM:SS AM/PM
11:59 AM	HH:MM AM/PM
Long Intl. Time	HH:MM:SS (for example, 11:59:59)
Short Intl. Time	HH:MM (for example, 11:59)

You can use the Tools User Setup International command (covered in Chapter 15) to modify the Long and Short International Date and Time formats. The preceding examples show the initial default international formats.

> ▶ **Tip:** When the cell pointer is on a cell that has been assigned a format by the user, the cell's format abbreviation is displayed at the left end of the indicator line. For example, a cell with a format for Currency, 2 decimal places will show a (C2) at the left end of the indicator line.

Changing the Numeric Display Format

Each worksheet cell has its own numeric display format, which can be changed independently of all other worksheet cells. Initially, every cell is set to the default format, which is General unless you have changed it with the Worksheet Global Settings Format command (see Chapter 15). To change the format of a range of cells, use the Range Format command, as described in the following Quick Steps.

Q **Changing the Numeric Display Format**

1. Select the range whose format you want to change.

   The range is highlighted.

2. Select Range Format.

   The Range Format dialog box is displayed (Figure 7.1).

3. Select the desired format from the list box.

4. If necessary, enter the desired number of decimal places in the Decimal Places text box.

5. To add parentheses to the selected format, select the Parentheses option box.

   Select OK.

   □

The highlighted range is displayed in the selected format.

If you click on Parentheses, and the negative value is set to Parentheses rather than Sign (under Tools User Setup International Negative Values), a negative number appears with 2 sets of parentheses—for example, ((12)).

> ► **Tip:** The default icon palette (see Figure 7.1) has buttons for comma, currency, and percent format (all with 0 decimal places). To set these formats, you can highlight the range and click the appropriate icon.

118

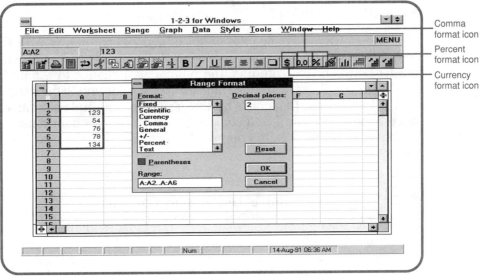

Figure 7.1   The Range Format dialog box.

If you want to reset formatted cells to the default display format, use the following Quick Steps.

Resetting a Cell Range to the Default Display Format

1. Select the range whose format you want to reset.

   The range is highlighted.

2. Select Range Format.

   The Range Format dialog box is displayed (Figure 7.1).

3. Click the Reset box.

   The range is reset to the default format.   □

Changing Row and Column Size

Every worksheet cell has a width and a height. Its width is determined by the width of the column it is in, and its height is determined by the height of the row it is in. You can adjust the width and height of each column and row in a worksheet.

Changing Column Width

The easiest way to change the width of a single column is with the mouse. Move the mouse pointer to the worksheet frame and point at the border between two columns; the pointer will change to a double-headed arrow. Press the mouse button, drag the column to the desired width, then release the mouse button. To change multiple columns at once, for greater control, or if you don't have a mouse, you must use the Worksheet Column Width command, as explained in the next Quick Steps.

 Changing the Width of One or More Columns

1. Select the range of columns to change. The range must include at least one cell in each column. For example, to change the width of columns A through C you could select the range B2..C2.

   The range is highlighted (Figure 7.2).

2. Select Worksheet Column Width.

   The Worksheet Column Width dialog box is displayed (Figure 7.3).

3. Select Set Width To (if not already selected), and enter the desired width, in characters, in the text box. Select Reset to Global to reset the columns to the global column width.

   You can select from 1 to 240.

4. Select OK.

   The selected columns change to the new width (Figure 7.4). □

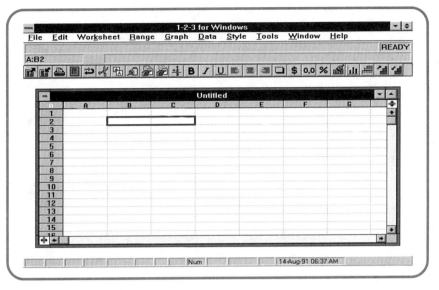

Figure 7.2 *To change column widths, first select a range containing at least one cell in each column.*

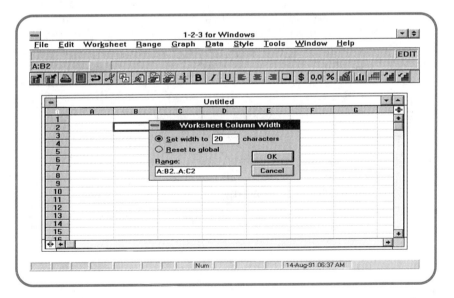

Figure 7.3 *Next, display the Worksheet Column Width dialog box and enter the desired column width.*

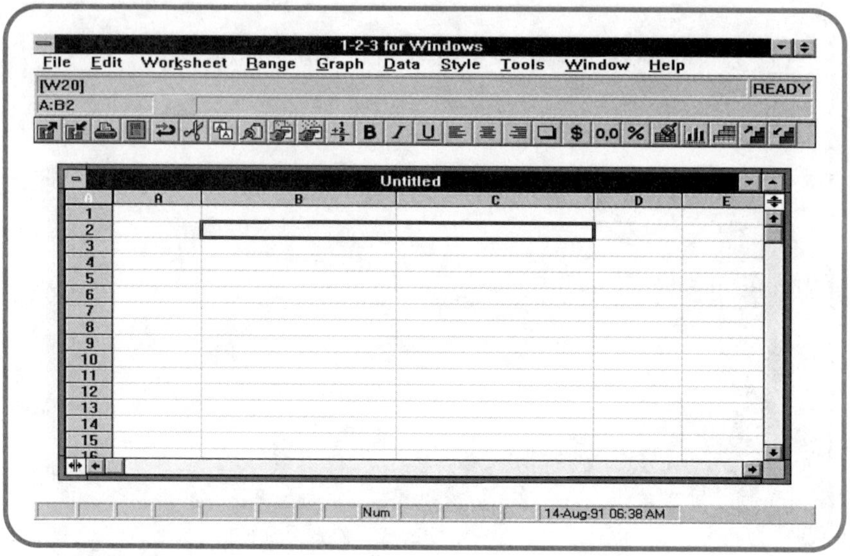

Figure 7.4   Select OK, and the selected columns change to the
new width.

The initial global column width is 9 characters. You can change
this setting with the Worksheet Global Settings command, discussed in
Chapter 15. Column width is specified in terms of characters in the
default font, which is Swiss 12 point. If you change a cell's font (as
described later in this chapter), the actual number of characters that will
display may be greater or less than the set column width, depending on
the new font size.

▶ **Tip:** When the cell pointer is in a column whose width has
been changed from the global setting, the width setting is
displayed in the indicator line.

Changing Row Height

1-2-3 for Windows automatically sets the height of each row to accommodate the largest font in that row. You can manually adjust row height

as well. To change the height of a single row with the mouse, move the mouse pointer into the worksheet frame that contains the row numbers. Grab a row border, below the row being changed; the pointer will change to a double-headed arrow. Press the mouse button, drag the row to the desired height, and then release the mouse button.

To change multiple rows at once, for greater control, or if you don't have a mouse, you must use the Worksheet Row Height command, as follows.

Q Changing the Height of One or More Rows

1. Select the range of rows to change. The range must include at least one cell in each row. For example, to change the width of rows 3 through 5 you could select the range B3..B5.

   The range is highlighted (Figure 7.5).

2. Select Worksheet Row Height.

   The Worksheet Row Height dialog box is displayed (Figure 7.6).

3. Select Set Height To if it is not already selected, and enter the desired height in the text box. Select Reset Height to reset the rows to automatic height.

4. Select OK.

   The select rows change to the new height (Figure 7.7).   □

123

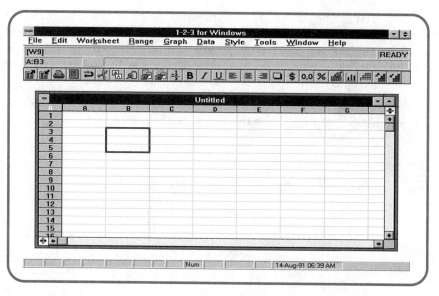

Figure 7.5 *To change row height, first select a range that includes at least one cell in each row.*

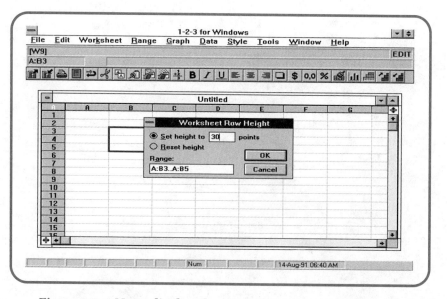

Figure 7.6 *Next, display the Worksheet Row Height dialog box and enter the desired row height.*

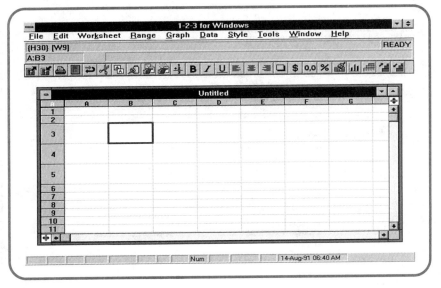

Figure 7.7   Select OK, and the selected rows change to the new height.

125

Changing Styles

The style commands are used to change worksheet appearance, enhance printouts, and use colors. These commands are found on the Style menu.

Changing Fonts

A *font* is a style and size of type used to display data on the screen and in printed reports. By using different fonts for different regions of the worksheet, you can increase the clarity and impact of your worksheets and printouts. Some of the fonts and sizes available in 1-2-3 for Windows are shown in Figure 7.8. The exact fonts you have available will depend on your Windows installation and your printer. A 1-2-3 for Windows worksheet can display as many as eight different fonts at one time.

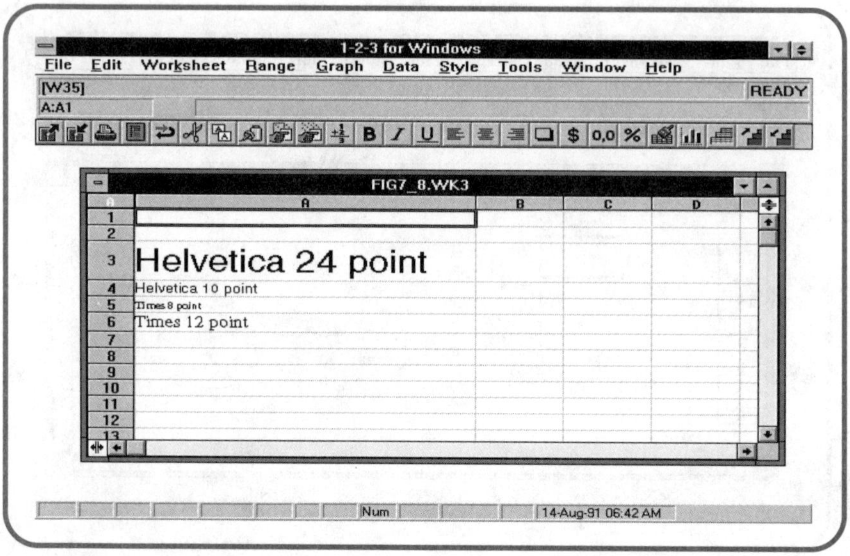

Figure 7.8   Some of 1-2-3 for Windows' available fonts.

Each font has a name that identifies the type style, such as Helvetica or Times. Each type style is usually available in several different sizes. Font sizes are measured in *points*. One point equals 1/72 inch. Thus, the Times 18 point font would be approximately 1/4 inch high. 1-2-3 lets you add special attributes, such as boldface, italics, and underlining, to any font. The following Quick Steps summarize how to change the font (both the display font and the print font) for a cell range.

Q Changing the Font for a Cell Range

1. Select the range whose font you want to change.

   The range is highlighted (Figure 7.9).

2. Select Style Font.

   The Style Font dialog box is displayed (Figure 7.10).

3. In the list box, select the desired font.

4. If desired, select the Bold, Italics, and/or Underline options. If you select Underline, choose the desired underline style from the drop-down box.

5. Select OK.

The range is displayed in the selected font (Figure 7.11). Row heights are adjusted, if necessary, to accommodate larger fonts.   □

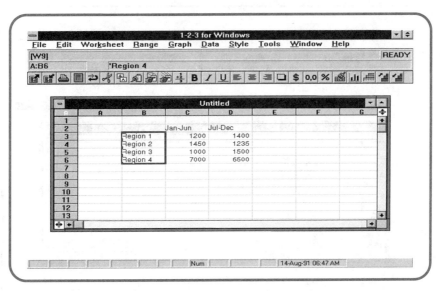

Figure 7.9   To change font, first select the range.

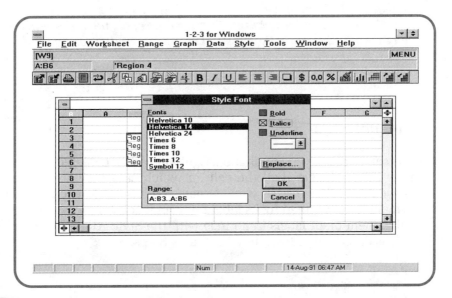

Figure 7.10   Next, select the font and font attributes you want from the Style Font dialog box.

127

> ▶ **Note:** The Adobe Type Manager is a separate program, included in your 1-2-3 package, that provides additional control over fonts. Please refer to the program documentation for information.

128

Indicator line —

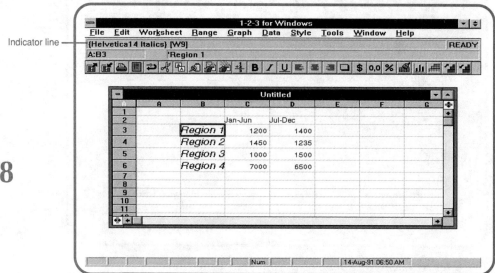

Figure 7.11 Select OK, and the range is displayed in the selected font and attributes. For this figure, we have Helvetica 14 with italics. Note that the left side of the indicator line tells us this information.

Changing Label Alignment

Labels can be displayed left-aligned, right-aligned, or centered in a cell (unless they're longer than the cell, in which case they are always displayed left-aligned). As you learned in Chapter 5, each label's alignment is determined by its label prefix character. You can change the alignment of all labels in a range with the Style Alignment command, as described in the following Quick Steps.

Q Changing Label Alignment in a Range

1. Select the range.   The range is highlighted.
2. Select Style Alignment.   The Style Alignment dialog box is displayed (Figure 7.12).

3. Select the desired alignment: Left, Right, or Center.
4. Select OK.   Labels in the range are aligned as specified. Value cells are not affected.   □

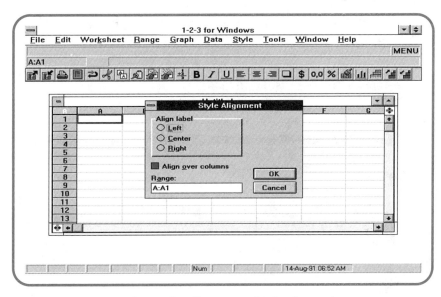

129

Figure 7.12   The Style Alignment dialog box.

When you change label alignment with Style Alignment, the label prefix character in the cells is changed.

The Style Alignment dialog box has an option button labeled Align Over Columns (see Figure 7.12). This option is used to align a column of labels over a range of two or more adjacent columns. When you select

Align Over Columns, a fourth option, Even, appears in the dialog box along with the Left, Right, and Center options in the Align Label group. When Align Over Columns is selected, these options have the following effects:

Left aligns labels with the left edge of the range.

Center centers labels in the range.

Right aligns labels with the right edge of the range.

Even expands space between letters and words in the label to stretch the label over the range width. Even has no effect on labels that end with a period, exclamation point, question mark, or colon.

The effect of Align over Column is illustrated in Figure 7.13. For this worksheet the labels were entered in cells B2..B6. The 2-column range B2..C6 was selected, and Align over Columns command with the Center option was given. The result is that the labels are centered in the range—between columns B and C.

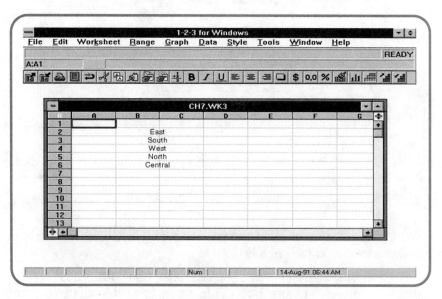

Figure 7.13 Centering labels over two columns with the Align over Columns option.

Adding Borders and Drop Shadows

1-2-3 for Windows lets you add borders and drop shadows to your worksheets. Borders can be used to set different data areas off from one another, and drop shadows can be effective for adding emphasis to a worksheet or printed report. The following Quick Steps show how to add a border or drop shadow to a worksheet range.

Adding Borders or Drop Shadows to a Worksheet Range

1. Select the range of cells.

   The range is highlighted.

2. Select Style Border.

   The Style Border dialog box is displayed (Figure 7.14).

3. Select the locations to place borders in the range (see below). Use the drop-down boxes to select the line style for each border.

131

4. Select Drop Shadow to place a drop shadow to the lower right of the range.

5. Select OK.

   The range is displayed with the selected borders and/or drop shadow.   □

The options for border placement are:

All edges places a line around each cell in the range.

Top places a line at the top edge of each cell in the range.

Bottom places a line at the bottom edge of each cell in the range.

Left places a line at the left edge of each cell in the range.

Right places a line at the right edge of each cell in the range.

Outline places a border around the outer edge of the entire range.

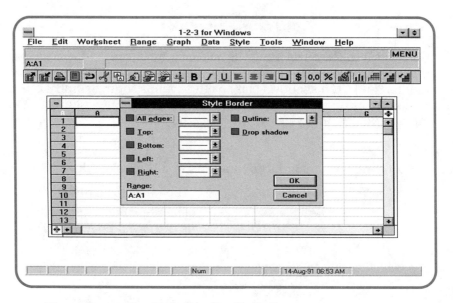

Figure 7.14   *The Style Border dialog box.*

For each of the border placement options, you can select a thin single line, a thick single line, or a double line. Figure 7.15 shows a worksheet with some Style Border enhancements.

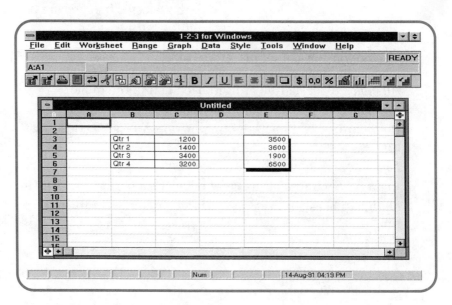

Figure 7.15   *The range B3..C6 has a heavy single line applied to all edges; the range E3..E6 has a light single line applied as an outline, plus a drop shadow.*

Changing Color

You can change the colors that 1-2-3 for Windows uses to display the worksheet on the screen (color monitors only, of course!). If you have a color printer, these colors will appear in printouts as well. You can also have 1-2-3 display negative values in red. The following Quick Steps tell how to select colors for worksheet display.

 Changing Worksheet Display Colors

1. Select the range to change.   The range is highlighted.
2. Select Style Color.   The Style Color dialog box is
                                           displayed (Figure 7.16).

3. To change the color
   used to display data,
   select a color from the
   Cell Contents drop-
   down box.

4. To change the color
   used for cell background,
   select a color from the
   Background drop-down
   box.

5. To display negative
   values in red, select the
   Negative Values in Red
   option.

6. Select OK.   The range is displayed in the
                                           selected colors.   □

▶ **Tip:** You can hide values by setting the same contents and background colors.

133

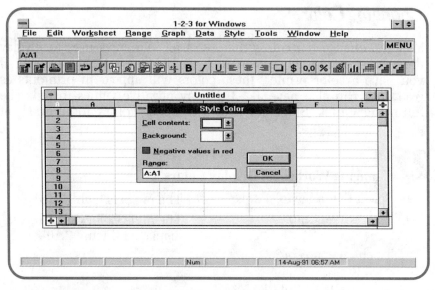

Figure 7.16   *The Style Color dialog box.*

Adding Background Shading

To add background shading to a range, use the Style Shading command. There are four shading options:

Light adds light gray shading.

Dark adds dark gray shading.

Solid adds black shading.

Clear removes shading.

The following Quick Steps make changing the shading for a range a breeze.

Adding Background Shading to a Range

1. Select the range.   The range is highlighted.
2. Select Style Shading.   The Style Shading dialog box
                                              is displayed (Figure 7.17).

3. Select the desired shading
   for the range, or select Clear
   to remove shading.

4. Select OK.   The range is displayed
                                              with the selected shading
                                              (Figure 7.18).   □

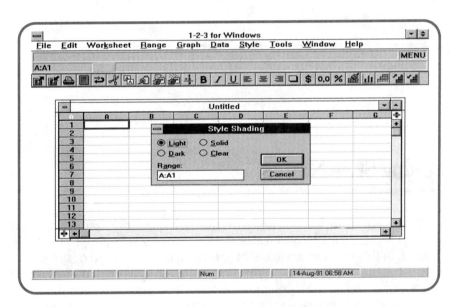

Figure 7.17   The Style Shading dialog box.

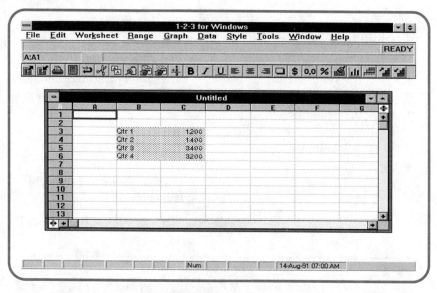

Figure 7.18   This worksheet has dark shading applied to the range B3..C6.

136

Using Style Names

1-2-3 for Windows lets you assign a name to commonly used styles, then assign those styles to new worksheet ranges by referring to the style name. In this context, style refers to those aspects of a cell or range that are set with the Style menu. You can have as many as eight named styles in a worksheet. Before you can name a style, you must use the Style commands to assign that style to at least one worksheet cell. The Quick Steps that follow explain how to assign a style name.

 Creating a Named Style

1. Move the cell pointer to a cell that has the desired style.

2. Select Style Name.   The Style Name dialog box is displayed (Figure 7.19).

3. In the dialog box, select the style (1-8) to define.

4. In the corresponding Name text box, type a name for the style. The name can be up to 6 characters long.

5. Optionally, type a description of the style, up to 25 characters long, in the Description text box.

6. Select OK.

The style of the current cell becomes associated with the name you assigned. ☐

137

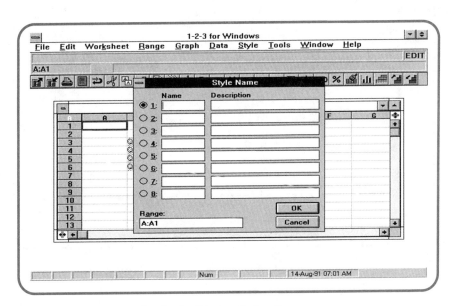

Figure 7.19 The Style Name dialog box.

When you have assigned styles to one or more of the eight style slots, their names appear on the Style menu and can be quickly assigned to other worksheet ranges, as the following Quick Steps demonstrate.

Q Applying a Named Style to a Worksheet Range

1. Select the range.   The range is highlighted.

2. Select Style.   The Style pulldown menu is displayed, and lists named styles (Figure 7.20).

3. Select the desired style.   A dialog box is displayed giving the style number and the selected range (Figure 7.21).

4. Select OK.   The selected style is applied to the range.   □

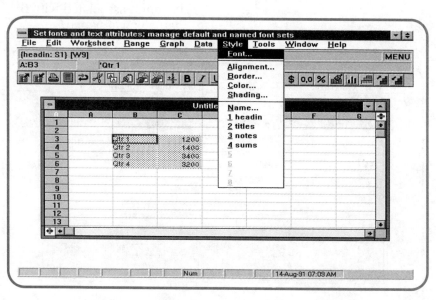

Figure 7.20   The Style pulldown menu lists named styles.

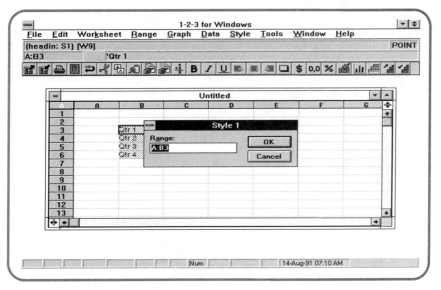

Figure 7.21   After you select a named style, a dialog box appears giving the style number and the address of the selected range. Select OK to apply the style to the range.

Group Mode

When you assign styles and formats to a range in one worksheet in a multiple worksheet file, those styles and formats normally apply only to the one worksheet. By using Group mode, you can assign styles and formats to one worksheet and have them automatically applied to all worksheets in the file. For example, in Group mode, assigning Currency numeric format to cells A1..C10 in worksheet A: would assign that format to cells A1..C10 in all worksheets in the file.

Group mode can be useful if your file contains multiple worksheets that require the same format, such as a 12 sheet annual sales report that has one identically formatted sheet for each month's data. To activate Group Mode, select the Group Mode option in the Worksheet Global settings dialog box. In Group Mode, the word Group appears on the status line at the bottom of the screen.

The following Quick Steps illustrate Group Mode.

Q Using Group Mode

1. Start with a worksheet file that contains at least two worksheets.

2. Select Worksheet Global Settings.

   The Worksheet Global Settings dialog box appears.

3. Select the Group Mode option.

   An X appears in the Group Mode check box.

4. Select OK.

   The dialog box closes and the GROUP indicator appears in the status line.

5. Perform the desired format or style changes in one worksheet.

   The format and style changes are applied to the same range in all worksheets. □

The Indicator Line

As you learned in Chapter 2, the line in the main 1-2-3 window just below the title bar is called the indicator line. The right end of this line displays the 1-2-3 mode indicator. The left portion displays formatting and style information about the current cell and the width of the current column. If the cell pointer is on a cell that has had no special formatting or styles applied (that is, the cell still has the default numeric format and style), the indicator line will display nothing. If the column width has not been changed, the indicator line will display nothing. If a nondefault format or style has been applied, the line will display abbreviations of the format and style. For example, for a cell that has been assigned currency format with 2 decimal places, green data color, and a border on all sides, the line will display `{Green LRTB} {C2}`.

Removing Styles from a Range

To remove all styles and/or numeric formatting from a range, use the Edit Clear Special command, as the following Quick Steps describe.

 Removing Styles and/or Numeric Formatting from a Range

1. Select the range.

   The range is highlighted.

2. Select Edit Clear Special.

   The Edit Clear Special dialog box is displayed (Figure 7.22).

3. To clear styles, select the Style option box. To clear numeric formatting, select the Number Format option box. Be sure the Cell Contents box is not selected unless you also want to erase the range's data.

4. Select OK.

   The numeric formatting and/or styles are cleared from the range. All cells in the range return to the worksheet's default format and style. □

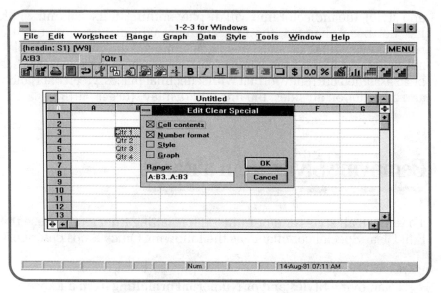

Figure 7.22   The Edit Clear Special dialog box.

142

⊘ **Caution:** Edit Clear Special will not affect protected cells.

▶ **Tip:** To clear only data, but not format or style, from a range, select only the Cell Contents option in the Edit Clear Special dialog box.

Screen Display, Printed Output , and Draft Mode

In its normal display mode, 1-2-3 for Windows' screen appears almost identical to the way a printed report of the worksheet will appear. At times, you may want to switch to draft display mode. In draft mode, all data is displayed in a monospace font, and borders and other style settings are not shown. Cell style is indicated in the indicator line, however. Draft mode has the advantage of faster screen display, particularly when complex styles are in use. You can also display more data on the screen when you have selected large fonts. Draft display mode does not affect printed output.

Using the Worksheet Titles Command

Many worksheets use labels at the top of columns and/or the left of rows as titles to identify the data in the columns or rows. If your worksheet is large, however, scrolling through your data may cause the titles to move off the screen, making it difficult to identify the data you are working with. The Worksheet Titles command lets you "freeze" one or more rows and columns on the screen so that the titles remain visible no matter where in the worksheet you scroll to.

143

 Freezing Titles on the Screen

1. Position the cell pointer one row below the row(s) you want to freeze, and one column to the right of the column(s) you want to freeze.

2. Select Worksheet Titles.

   The Worksheet Titles dialog box is displayed (Figure 7.23).

3. Select Horizontal to freeze the rows above the cell pointer. Select Vertical to freeze the rows to the left of the cell pointer. Select Both to freeze both rows and columns.

4. Select Clear to unfreeze all rows and/or columns.

5. Select OK.

The specified rows and/or columns are frozen in place and will not scroll out of the window. □

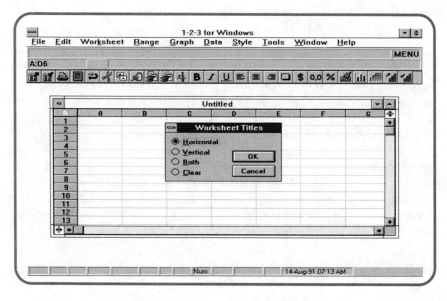

Figure 7.23   The Worksheet Titles dialog box.

144

What You Have Learned

▶ Format and style affect only worksheet appearance, not worksheet data.

▶ Number format controls the way that values are displayed in worksheet cells.

▶ You can change the size of single columns and rows with the mouse.

► 1-2-3 for Windows normally adjusts row height to fit the largest font in the row.

► A 1-2-3 for Windows worksheet can use as many as 8 different fonts.

► Use the Style menu to change fonts, borders, shading, and colors.

► Combinations of styles can be named for future use.

145

Writing Macros to Automate Worksheet Tasks

In This Chapter

147

- ▶ *Writing and naming macros*
- ▶ *Playing back macros*
- ▶ *Recording keystrokes*
- ▶ *Finding macro errors*

Macro Basics

A macro is a series of 1-2-3 instructions that is stored in a worksheet and can be "played back," or executed, to perform worksheet tasks. Macros are very useful for automating complex and repetitive worksheet tasks. Using a macro, you can perform a task with a couple of keystrokes that would require hundreds of keystrokes to perform otherwise. Not only do macros speed up your work, but they also reduce the possibility of errors when performing complex operations.

Most macros contain keystrokes that duplicate the effect of keyboard input. When you run a macro, the effect is the same as if you had entered those keystrokes from the keyboard. Keystroke macros can be used for data entry, formatting, printing, and so on. A macro can also contain macro commands. The 1-2-3 for Windows macro commands are similar in concept to the commands found in programming languages. Macro commands let you manipulate the Windows clipboard, control the flow of macro execution, control the screen, transfer data between 1-2-3 for Windows and other Window applications, etc.

Let's look at a simple example. In Figure 8.1, cells D3 and D4 contain a macro that formats the column of values starting in cell A1 as Currency with 2 decimal places.

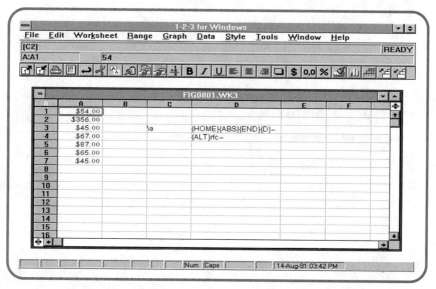

Figure 8.1   Cells D3 and D4 contain a simple macro.

Now we'll look at the components of the macro. The first line reads {HOME}{ABS}{END}{D}~:

{HOME} is the macro command that represents pressing the HOME key. This moves the cell pointer to cell A1.

{ABS} is the macro command for the F4 (ABS) key, which anchors a range.

{END}{D} are two commands that stand for pressing the END key followed by pressing the down arrow key. The result is to expand the range to the end of the column of cells.

~ (tilde) stands for pressing Enter.

The effect of the first line of the macro is, therefore, to select the entire column of cells starting in A1 all the way to its end. Now let's look at the second line of the macro, which reads {ALT}rfc~:

{ALT} is the macro command for pressing the ALT key, which activates the menu.

The next three entries, rfc, are keystrokes that stand for themselves (the "r" key, the "f" key, etc.).:

▶ The r after ALT displays the Range pulldown menu.
▶ The f displays the Range Format dialog box.
▶ The c selects Currency format.

The macro terminates with another ~ representing Enter.

The \a in cell C3 is the macro's name, which is used to run the macro. This macro requires only 2 keystrokes to run, but does the work of 10 keystrokes. Many macros are much longer, and save a greater number of keystrokes. I hope this brief introduction gives you an idea of how useful macros can be! Now let's look at the details of writing and using macros.

149

Storing Macros

Macros are stored as labels in a worksheet. A short macro may occupy only a single cell. Longer macros are stored in two or more successive cells in a single worksheet column. More than one macro can share a worksheet column, as long as you leave at least one blank row between the last cell of one macro and the first cell of the next macro (It's a blank cell that signals the end of a macro). Since a cell can hold a label up to 512 characters long, that's also the length limit for macro entries. It's best to use shorter entries, however, to facilitate editing, reading, and documenting macros.

It's a good idea to set aside a separate worksheet for macro storage, one that does not contain data. If you must store macros in a worksheet that contains data, place the macros in a location where they will not be affected by data operations such as deleting or inserting rows or columns.

Naming Macros

You must name a macro in order to execute it. A macro name is nothing more than a range name that you assign to the first cell of the macro. For documentation purposes it is good practice to put the macro name, as a label, in the cell immediately to the left of the first macro cell. This also enables you to use the Range Name Label Create command to assign the macro name to the first macro cell. There are two types of macro names:

> *Backslash names* consist of a single letter preceded by a backslash, \P for example. You are limited to 26 such names, of course. Assign backslash names to your most frequently used macros because they can be executed by pressing Ctrl-*letter*.

> *Multiple-character names* are ordinary range names and follow the same rules as names for data ranges. Multiple-character names let you assign each macro a name that describes its function.

Executing Macros

When you execute a macro, 1-2-3 starts with the commands in the first macro cell and works down, executing commands in each subsequent cell in the column. Macro execution halts when an empty cell is reached, or when the user presses Ctrl-Break. You can run a macro in READY mode.

 Tip: To stop macro execution before normal termination, press Ctrl-Break.

The procedure for executing a macro depends on the type of name assigned to it. To execute a macro with a backslash name, press Ctrl-*letter*, where *letter* is the single-letter name assigned to the macro. To execute a macro with a multiple-character name, select Tools Macro Run or press RUN (Alt-F3). 1-2-3 displays a dialog box containing a list of all named ranges (Figure 8.2). Select the name of the macro to run, and press Enter. Note that 1-2-3 displays all ranges, not just macro ranges, so you'll need some way to tell macro names from data range names.

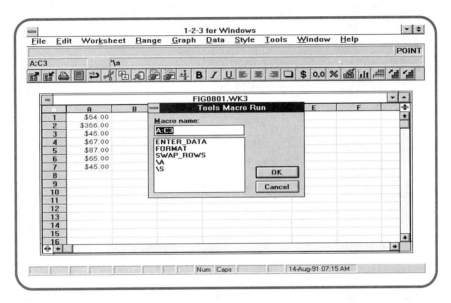

Figure 8.2   The Tools Macro Run dialog box.

151

Keystroke Macros

Some macros contain only a sequence of keystrokes. Most keys, such as letters and numerals, are entered in macros as themselves. Other keys, such as Enter, are entered as a special symbol or as a keyword enclosed in curly braces. The 1-2-3 for Windows Help system contains a complete list of these keywords and symbols. The most commonly used ones are presented in Table 8.1.

Table 8.1   Special Macro Keywords

Function keys

Key	Macro command
F1 (HELP)	{HELP}
F2 (EDIT)	{EDIT}
F3 (NAME)	{NAME}
F4 (ABS)	{ABS}
F5 (GOTO)	{GOTO}
F6 (PANE)	{PANE}
F7 (QUERY)	{QUERY}
F8 (TABLE)	{TABLE}
F9 (CALC)	{CALC}
F10 (MENU)	{MENU} or {ALT}

Navigation keys

Key	Macro command
Down arrow	{DOWN} or {D}
Up arrow	{UP} or {U}
Right arrow	{RIGHT} or {R}
Left arrow	{LEFT} or {L}
End	{END}
Home	{HOME}
PgUp	{PgUp}
PgDn	{PgDn}
Ctrl-Left arrow	{BACKTAB} or {BIGLEFT}
Ctrl-Right arrow	{BIGRIGHT}

Other keys

Key	Macro command
Ins	{INS} or {INSERT}
Esc	{ESC} or {ESCAPE}
Del	{DEL}
{ (left brace)	{{}
} (right brace)	{}}
Backspace	{BS} or {BACKSPACE}
Ctrl	{CTRL}

Macro commands are not available for the following keystrokes, so they cannot be used in macros:

Alt-Backspace (Undo)
Alt-F1 (Compose)
Alt-F2 (Step)
Alt-F3 (Run)
CAPS LOCK
NUM LOCK
PRINT SCREEN
SCROLL LOCK
SHIFT

Entering a Keystroke Macro

A keystroke macro may consist of only a few keystrokes performing a simple task. It may also contain hundreds of keystrokes that perform a sequence of complicated worksheet operations. Keystrokes in a macro can execute worksheet commands, enter data, or a combination of the two. When writing a complicated macro, it's wise to proceed in steps, getting each section of the macro to work properly before starting on the next. Techniques for finding macro errors (*debugging*) are described later in the chapter. Steps for recording a keystroke macro in a worksheet are listed here.

153

1. Test the keystroke sequence to be sure it performs the desired actions (this is optional, but certainly a good idea!).

2. Move the cell pointer to the cell where the macro is to begin.

3. Enter the macro key sequence, using macro commands for special keys. If the macro begins with a numeric character, start the entry with a label prefix character.

4. For long macros, continue in the cell directly below the current one. Each macro command must be contained in a single cell, although a single cell can contain more than one macro command. Do not leave blank cells within the macro.

5. When the macro is complete, return the cell pointer to the first macro cell, then move it left one cell.

6. Enter the macro name in the cell as a label, using either a backslash name or a multicharacter range name. In the latter case, use a name that describes the macro's function.

7. Use the Range Name Labels Create Right command to assign the macro name to the first macro cell.

The Macro Commands

1-2-3's macro commands provide a great deal of flexibility and power. In essence, these commands provide a programming language built into your worksheets. Here are some examples of things that you can do with macros that use the macro commands:

▶ Create a menu structure, allowing inexperienced users to work with complex worksheet models.
▶ Control the size and position of screen windows.
▶ Automatically print sophisticated reports and graphs.
▶ Accept and manipulate data input from the keyboard.
▶ Execute different tasks depending on data in the worksheet.
▶ Move data between 1-2-3 for Windows and other programs.
▶ Use macro subroutines, and pass macro execution along different branches based on user input.

The macro commands consist of over 50 separate commands, each of which consists of the command name enclosed in curly braces. Macro commands can be used alone in macros, and can also be used in conjunction with keystroke commands. Macro commands are available only in macros—they cannot be directly accessed from the keyboard.

Even a brief treatment of all of 1-2-3 for Windows' macro commands is beyond the scope of this book. The 1-2-3 for Windows documentation and Help system includes complete descriptions of all the commands. To give you a taste of their power, I've listed a few command descriptions in Table 8.2. You'll also see a few examples in the Sample Macros section later in this chapter.

Table 8.2   Examples of Macro Commands

Command	Function
{GRAPHON}	Displays a graph.
{GETNUMBER}	Displays a prompt, accepts data from the keyboard, and stores the data in a worksheet cell.
{BRANCH}	Transfers macro execution to another worksheet location.
{READLN}	Reads a line of data from a disk file into a worksheet cell.
{LINK-CREATE}	Opens a data link between 1-2-3 for Windows and another Windows application.
{BLANK}	Erases a cell or range.
{MENUCALL}	Displays a custom menu, then branches based on the user's selection.

155

Autoexecute Macros

The *autoexecute macro* is a macro that is executed automatically when you open the worksheet file it is in. An autoexecute macro is created simply by assigning it the name \0 (backslash zero). Each worksheet file can contain only one autoexecute macro.

Execution of autoexecute macros can be turned on (the default) or off by selecting the Tools User Setup command. When you enter this command, the dialog box shown in Figure 8.3 is displayed. Turn the Run Autoexecute Macros option on or off to control macro execution, then select OK. To have the changed setting remain in effect for future 1-2-3 for Windows sessions, select Update before selecting OK.

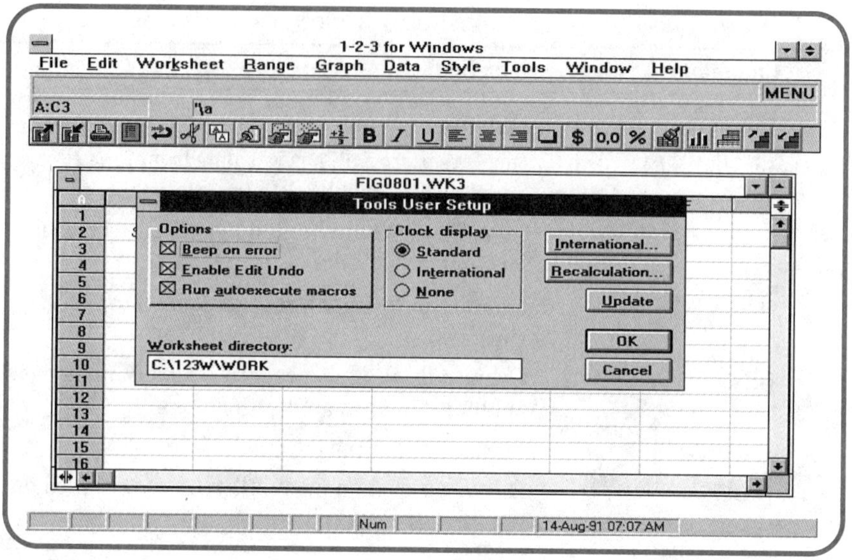

Figure 8.3   Use the Tools User Setup dialog box to control autoexecute macro execution.

Recording Keystrokes with the Transcript Window

When developing macros, it is often easier to create a macro by recording keystrokes and commands as you actually perform the action. The Transcript window records keystrokes and commands as you enter them. You can edit the recorded commands and transfer them to the worksheet for inclusion in a macro. Keys that you press are recorded as themselves, as special characters, or as macro commands, whichever is appropriate for inclusion in a macro. Thus, letter keys are recorded as themselves, the F4 key is recorded as {ABS}, and Enter is recorded as ~. Mouse actions are recorded as the keystroke equivalents.

The Transcript window can hold up to 512 characters. When the Window fills up, keystrokes are discarded from the beginning of the window to make room for new ones added at the end. If you're recording a long sequence, avoid losing keystrokes by cutting them from the window and pasting them in the worksheet.

The Transcript window records your keystrokes whenever you are using 1-2-3; there is no need to turn it on. When you're ready to record a macro, you must display the Transcript window and clear it of existing keystrokes. The following Quick Steps explain how to use the Transcript window to record a macro.

Q Recording a Macro with the Transcript Window

1. Get your worksheet to the point where you're ready to begin macro recording.

2. Select Tools Macro Show Transcript.

   The Transcript window is displayed (Figure 8.4). It contains any previously recorded keystrokes.

3. Make the Transcript window active by clicking it or pressing Ctrl-F6 one or more times.

   The Transcript window becomes active, and the Transcript menu appears in the menu bar (Figure 8.5).

4. Select Edit Clear All to clear the Transcript window.

   The contents of the Transcript window are erased (Figure 8.6).

5. If desired, move the Transcript window to a location in the work area where it will be visible.

6. Make the worksheet window active, and start entering the keystrokes for the macro.

   The keystrokes are recorded in the Transcript window (Figure 8.7).

7. When the action is complete, make the Transcript window active.

8. Select the keystrokes you want to copy to the worksheet. With the mouse, drag the highlight over the characters. With the keyboard, move the cursor to the first character, press and hold Shift, then use the navigation keys to expand the highlight.

   The selected characters are highlighted (Figure 8.8).

157

9. Select Edit Copy from the Transcript window.

The selected characters are copied to the Windows clipboard.

10. Make the worksheet window active, and move the cell pointer to the cell where you want the macro inserted.

11. Select Edit Paste.

The keystrokes are pasted into the cell (Figure 8.9).

12. Name the macro, as described earlier in this chapter.

□

▶ **Tip:** You can press the End key to highlight to the end of the line. You can click in one spot, holding down the Shift key, and click to the end of where you want to highlight.

158

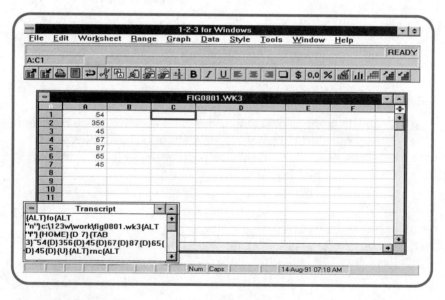

Figure 8.4 When you first display the Transcript window, it contains any previously recorded keystrokes.

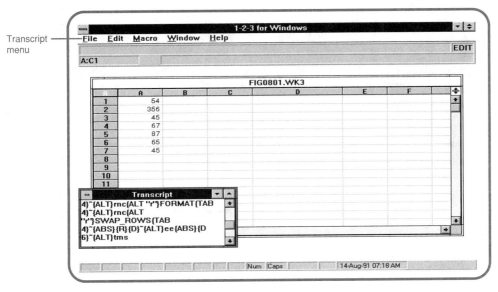

Figure 8.5   When you make the Transcript window active, the Transcript menu appears in the menu bar.

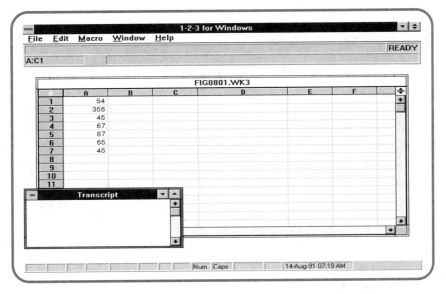

Figure 8.6   Select Edit Clear, and the Transcript window is cleared.

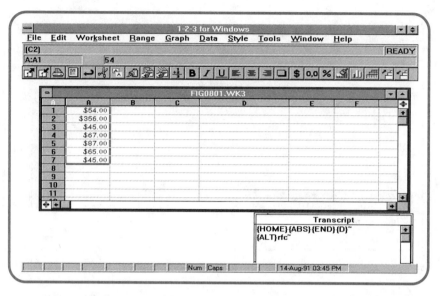

Figure 8.7   Make the worksheet window active, and enter keystrokes. They are recorded in the Transcript window.

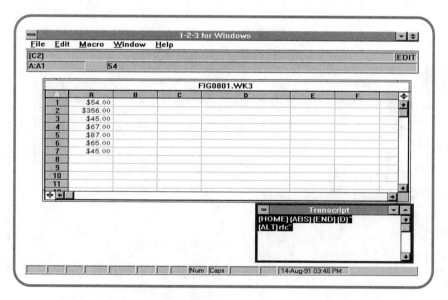

Figure 8.8   When done, select the keystrokes in the Transcript window, Copy them to the clipboard....

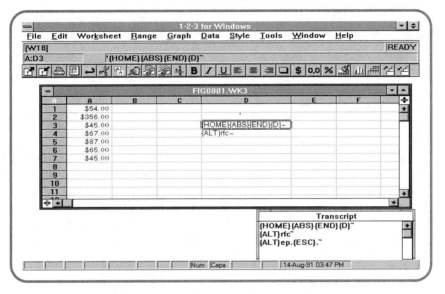

Figure 8.9   Then paste them into the worksheet.

If the keystrokes being pasted are wider than the column width, they will be pasted into two or more cells starting at the current cell and working downward. For example, in Figure 8.9 the keystrokes have been pasted into cells D3 and D4.

When the Transcript window is active, you can edit its contents just like you would edit data in a cell. You can also play back keystrokes from the Transcript window before pasting them in a worksheet. This can be useful for testing a recorded macro before moving it to your worksheet. The next Quick Steps describe how to play back the keystrokes in the Transcript window.

Q **Playing Back Keystrokes from the Transcript Window**

1. In the worksheet, move the cell pointer to the desired current cell.

2. Make the Transcript window active.

3. Select (highlight) the keystrokes you want to play back. To play back the entire contents of the Transcript window, select nothing.

4. Select Macro Run from the Transcript menu.

The selected keystrokes are played back. □

Macro Errors

One kind of macro error occurs when the macro runs, but does not do what you expect it to. This is usually due to one or more incorrect instructions in the macro, or to a simple typing or formatting error. You can correct macro instructions by moving the cell pointer to the offending cell and using EDIT mode to make corrections.

The other kind of macro error is when 1-2-3 cannot run the macro because the instructions in the macro are incorrect or incomplete. The macro will run to the location of the error, then 1-2-3 will halt with an error message indicating the address of the macro cell where the error occurred. Examine that cell closely. Here are some common causes of macro errors:

▶ A missing ~ (Enter) at the end of a macro instruction.
▶ Misplaced spaces, either placed where they shouldn't be or omitted where they should be.
▶ Missing braces around macro key words.
▶ Errors in spelling keywords or range names.
▶ Incorrect logic in macro flow control statements.

If the cause of a macro error is not immediately found, you may need to use 1-2-3's macro debugging capabilities to find it.

Debugging Macros

1-2-3 for Windows offers two features that can assist you in tracking down macro errors:

162

STEP mode executes a macro one command at a time, so you can view the effect of each command as it executes.

TRACE mode displays a window that shows the macro command about to be executed.

It is probably most effective to use STEP and TRACE modes together. This lets you step through a macro one command at a time, viewing each command and its effects as the macro executes. It will be clear when the error occurs and which command caused it. The next Quick Steps walk you through the procedure for using STEP and TRACE modes.

 Debugging a Macro Using STEP and TRACE Modes

1. Select Tools Macro Debug.

   The Tools Macro Debug dialog box is displayed (Figure 8.10).

2. Select the Single Step and Trace options, then select OK.

   The STEP indicator and the Macro Trace window are displayed.

3. Start the macro. Press any key to execute each macro instruction.

   The Macro Trace window shows the location and contents of the instruction being executed (Figure 8.11).

4. When you locate the error, terminate macro execution by pressing Ctrl-Break, then Esc. Then, edit the macro to correct the error.

5. Return to step 3 to retest the macro. When it is running correctly, turn TRACE and STEP modes off. ☐

163

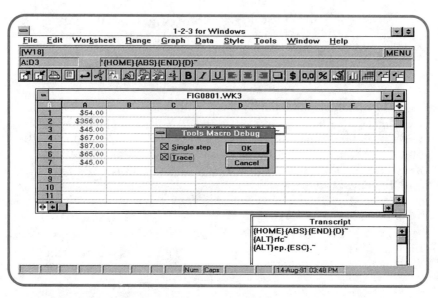

Figure 8.10   The Tools Macro Debug dialog box.

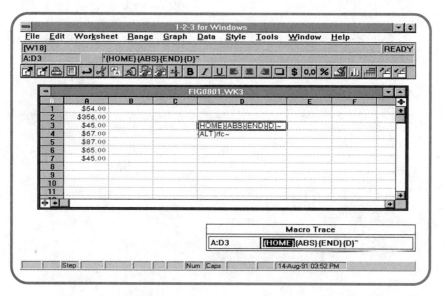

Figure 8.11   In TRACE mode, the Macro Trace window displays
the current macro instruction.

Some Example Macros

The next two sections contain sample macros you can create in your worksheet files to make your operations more efficient.

Saving the Current Worksheet File

When you are using a worksheet file, its contents are stored in your computer's random access memory. It's wise to save the file to disk regularly during a work session to guard against data loss caused by a power outage, computer crash, or other problem. For a file that has already been saved to disk at least once, you can save it by clicking the File Save icon on the icon palette. If you prefer the keyboard, the commands are File Save. This requires only a few keystrokes, but you might find a macro more convenient. The following macro does the trick:

165

```
{ALT}fs
```

Name this macro \s, and you can save your file at any time simply by pressing Ctrl-S.

Entering a Column of Numbers

Worksheet data entry often requires keyboard entry of long columns of numbers. Experienced typists may want to enter numbers using the number and Enter keys on the numeric keypad (in NUMLOCK mode, of course). To do this, you need a macro that accepts a number followed by Enter, puts the number in the current cell, then moves the cell pointer down one cell. Here's one way to do it:

```
{?}
{D}
{BRANCH \n}
```

Name this macro \N. To use the macro, move the cell pointer to the first cell in the column, press NUMLOCK, then press Ctrl-N. The first line of the macro accepts keyboard entry terminated by Enter, and places it in the current cell. The second line moves the cell pointer down one cell. The third line restarts the macro. When data entry is finished, press Ctrl-Break to terminate the macro.

> ▶ **Note:** 1-2-3 for Windows can run macros created for earlier versions of 1-2-3, as well as the Microsoft Excel spreadsheet macros.

What You Have Learned

- ▶ Macros save time and reduce errors by automating repetitive worksheet tasks.
- ▶ A macro can contain any keystrokes you would enter from the keyboard, as well as special macro commands.
- ▶ You can record keystrokes for use in a macro with the Transcript window.
- ▶ To find macro errors, use STEP and TRACE modes.

Chapter 9

Printing Reports

In This Chapter

167

- ▶ *Printing worksheet data*
- ▶ *Printing a graph*
- ▶ *Previewing your printout*
- ▶ *Selecting print options*

Printing a Report

A *report* is a printout containing worksheet data and/or graphs. It can be as simple as a single column of numbers for your own reference, or as complicated as a multipage, formatted document for distribution in your company. Creating a printout of your worksheet using the default print settings is very easy.

To print, you must have installed a printer during the Windows installation procedure. The printer must be connected to your system, turned on, and on-line. The following Quick Steps give the basic printing procedure.

Printing All or Part of a Worksheet

1. Select the range to print, or select the entire worksheet.

   The range is highlighted.

2. Select File Print, or click the File Print SmartIcon on the Icon Palette (Figure 9.1).

   The File Print dialog box is displayed (see Figure 9.1).

3. Select OK.

   The range is printed.   □

168

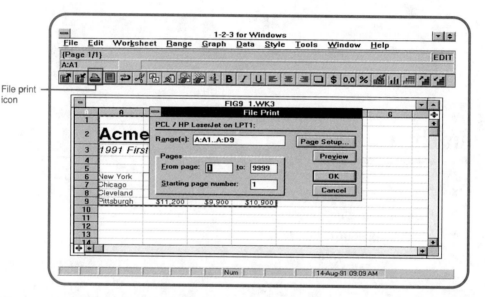

File print icon

Figure 9.1   The File Print dialog box.

 Tip: To select the entire worksheet, press Home, F4, End, and then Home.

Previewing a Print Job

The normal 1-2-3 for Windows screen shows you a close approximation of what your printout will look like. Fonts, outlines, shading, and so on are similar in the printout to what you see in your worksheet. For an exact preview of the way the printout will look, you can use 1-2-3 for Windows' *print preview* feature, as described in the following Quick Steps.

 Previewing a Print Job

1. Select the range to print.

   The range is highlighted.

2. Select File Preview, or click the File Preview SmartIcon (Figure 9.2).

   The File Preview dialog box is displayed (Figure 9.2).

3. To preview only a subset of the report's pages, enter the start and stop pages in the dialog box.

4. Select OK.

   The first page of the range is displayed in the Print Preview window (Figure 9.3).

5. Press Enter to display the next page of the report. Press Esc to return to the worksheet.

169

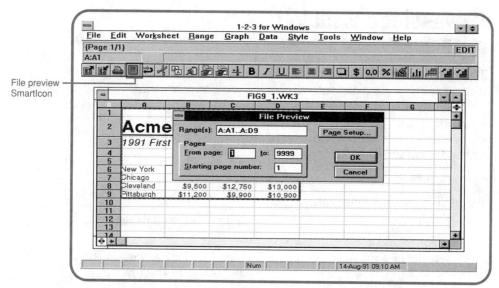

File preview
SmartIcon

Figure 9.2   The File Preview dialog box.

Figure 9.3   The Print Preview window with a page displayed.

On the Print Preview screen, 1-2-3 displays a solid line to indicate the positions of the page margins. Layout enhancements such as footers and page numbers are displayed as well. After you return to the worksheet, the print range is surrounded by a dotted line.

Changing Page Setup

The *page setup* is the way certain aspects of the printed page appear: margins, headers and footers, etc. Page setup is controlled from the Page Setup dialog box (Figure 9.4). You can display this dialog box by selecting File Page Setup, or by clicking the Page Setup button in either the File Print or File Preview dialog box.

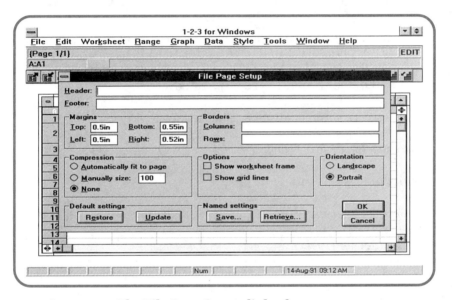

Figure 9.4   The File Page Setup dialog box.

171

Headers and Footers

A *header* is text that is printed at the top of every page, and a *footer* is text that is printed at the bottom of every page. In the Page Setup dialog box, enter the desired text in the header and/or footer text boxes. A header or footer can be up to 512 characters long, but 1-2-3 will not print any portion that would extend past the page's right margin. The header and footer will be separated from the other text on the page by two blank lines.

There are several special characters you can include in header or footer text:

▶ To include the current date (as set on your computer's clock), use the symbol @. The date is printed in the format specified for Date—International with the Tools User Setup command.

▶ To include a page number, use the symbol #.

▶ To include text contained in a worksheet cell, use a backslash \ followed by the cell address or range name where the text is located. If you refer to a multicell range, the contents of the upper left cell in the range is used.

▶ To justify header or footer text, include one or two ¦ (vertical bar) symbols. Text to the left of the first ¦ is left-justified; text after the first ¦ but before the second ¦ is centered; text to the right of the second ¦ is right-justified.

Here are some examples. The header text:

```
Acme Manufacturing¦page #¦@
```

results in this header:

```
Acme Manufacturing              page 1          22-Jul-91
```

The header text:

```
\A:A5¦¦\NAMES
```

results in the header:

```
XYZ Consulting                                  John Smith
```

if cell A5 contains the label XYZ Consulting and the named range NAMES has the label John Smith in its upper left cell.

Margins

A *margin* is the width of blank paper left between the printed area and the edge of the page. The default margins are 0.50 inch top, left, and right, 0.55 inch bottom. To change the margin, enter a new value in the corresponding text box. To specify the margin in inches, follow the value with `in`. For centimeters or millimeters, follow the value with `mm` or `cm`.

Compression

Settings made here let you compress or expand a printout. When you compress a printout, printed data is made smaller so more data fits per page. When you expand a printout, printed data is made larger so less data fits per page. There are three compression options:

None disables compression. Data is printed at its normal full size (this is the default).

Automatically Fit to Page compresses the print range, attempting to fit the entire print range on one page, if possible. This setting will compress by a factor of up to 7.

Manual lets you specify an exact compression/expansion factor. To compress the print range, enter a percentage factor between 15 and 99. To expand the print range, enter a percentage factor between 101 and 1000. For example, 50 compresses to half normal size, while 200 expands to double normal size.

173

Orientation

There are two orientation options:

Portrait (the default) prints the data with worksheet rows parallel to the short edge of the paper.

Landscape prints the data with worksheet rows parallel to the long edge of the paper. This mode is not available on all printers.

> ▶ **Tip:** Use landscape orientation and a compression factor of less than 100 to fit wide worksheet ranges on single pages.

Options

You can select all, some, or none of these options:

Show formulas prints worksheet formulas, rather than their results. Use this option for debugging and documenting worksheets.

Grid prints the worksheet grid (the vertical and horizontal lines between cells).

Frame prints the worksheet frame (row numbers and column letters) on each page.

Borders

174

Borders specifies worksheet rows and columns to include on every printed page. Under Rows, specify the worksheet row(s) to be printed at the top of each page. Under Columns, specify the worksheet columns to be printed at the left edge of every page. The range you specify must include at least one cell in each row or column. You can press the period key to jump back to the spreadsheet and highlight the cells.

Use the Borders option with multipage reports to include identifying labels on every report page. Do not include the row(s) and/or column(s) of the border in the print range, or they will be printed twice on some pages.

Saving and Restoring Page Setups

Each worksheet file has a default page setup associated with it. It consists of the page setup settings that will be used if you do not make any changes in the Page Setup dialog box. If you do make changes, they will be in effect only for the current print job. You can change and retrieve a file's defaults from the Page Setup dialog box:

Select *Update* to make the current page settings the new defaults for the worksheet file.

Select *Restore* to set all Page Setup options to the defaults.

You can also save page setups on disk, in a *page layout library file*. Page layout library files let you keep frequently used page layouts for future use, and also easily share page layouts between worksheet files. The following Quick Steps tell you how to save a page layout library file.

Saving the Current Page Setup in a Page Layout Library File

1. Display the Page Setup dialog box.

2. Make any desired changes to the page setup options.

3. Under Named Settings, select Save.

   The File Page Setup Named Save dialog box is displayed (Figure 9.5).

175

4. The list box displays the names of any existing page layout library files. Use the Directories list box and the Drives drop-down box to change drive and/or directory, if needed. Select a file to change, or enter a new filename in the text box.

5. Select OK.

   The current page setup is saved in the specified file. □

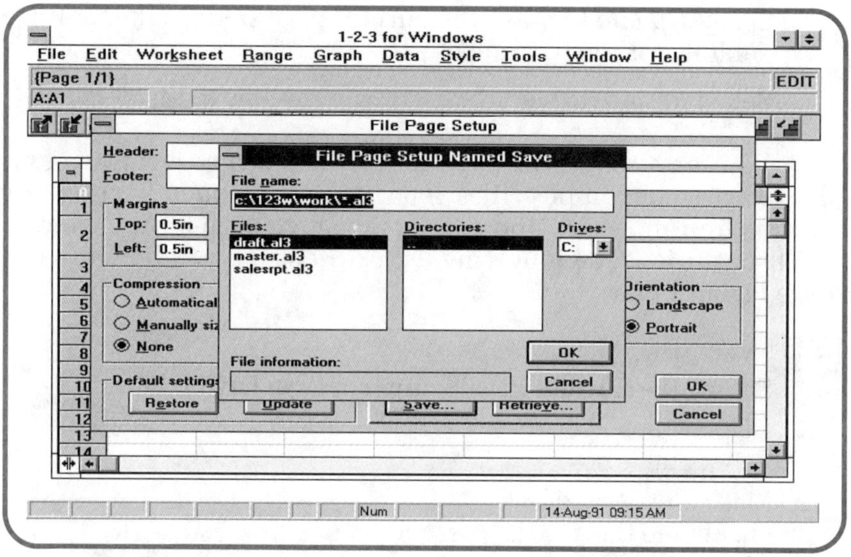

Figure 9.5   File Page Setup Named Save dialog box.

Printing a Graph

1-2-3 can print a graph and worksheet data together on the same page. This allows you to create professional-looking reports. Printing a graph requires only two steps:

1. Insert the graph in the worksheet at the desired location.
2. Print a worksheet range that includes the graph.

You'll learn how to insert a graph in the worksheet in Chapter 10.

Controlling Page Breaks

A *page break* is where 1-2-3 starts printing on a new page. Normally, 1-2-3 automatically places page breaks where needed. You can manually place page breaks if your report requires it. For example, you may need to add a page break to prevent a table from being split between two pages. The following Quick Steps provide instructions for inserting manual page breaks.

Inserting a Vertical and/or Horizontal Page Break

1. Move the cell pointer to the location of the page break. For a horizontal page break, this is the first row to print at the top of the new page. For a vertical page break, this is the first column to print at the left edge of the new page.

2. Select Worksheet Page Break.

   The Worksheet Page Break dialog box is displayed (Figure 9.6).

3. Select Vertical or Horizontal (or select Both) to place vertical and/or horizontal breaks at the cell pointer.

4. Select OK.

   The page break(s) are placed in the column and/or row. □

177

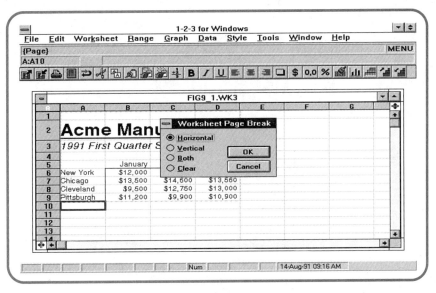

Figure 9.6   The Worksheet Page Break dialog box.

In the worksheet window, 1-2-3 displays vertical or horizontal lines to indicate the location of page breaks (if Window Display Options Page Break is selected). To remove page breaks, move the cell pointer to a cell in the row or column and then select Worksheet Page Break Clear.

> **Note:** When the cell pointer is in a row or column that contains a page break, the indicator line displays {MPage}.

What You Have Learned

178

▶ 1-2-3 for Windows can create printed copies of your worksheet data and graphs.

▶ You can display a screen preview of your printouts with the File Preview command.

▶ You can print with the default page setup, or change it from the Page Setup dialog box.

▶ Headers and footers in a printout can contain a page number or the current date.

▶ Use the Worksheet Page Break command to manually place page breaks in your report.

Graphs — the Basics

In This Chapter

▶ *Graph components*
▶ *Types of graphs*
▶ *Selecting data to graph*
▶ *Saving a graph*
▶ *Adding a graph to a worksheet*

Graph Basics

1-2-3 for Windows can display and print graphs of your worksheet data. A *graph* is a visual representation of numerical data and can be a very effective tool for summarizing and communicating information. 1-2-3 for Windows' graphing features are extensive and powerful, and will be covered in three chapters. This chapter covers the basics, and more advanced graph topics are covered in Chapters 11 and 12.

If you've ever used a spreadsheet program, you are probably familiar with the components of a graph. Figure 10.1 shows a 1-2-3 for Windows graph with its components labelled. Every 1-2-3 graph contains some or all of these components.

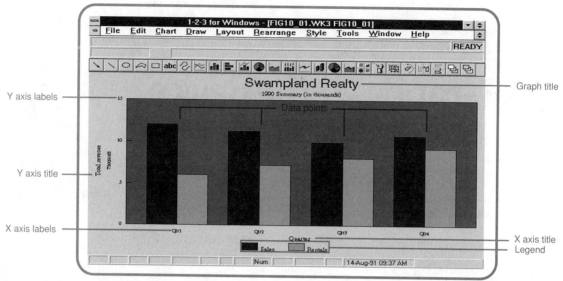

Figure 10.1   *The components of a graph.*

180

In this and the following chapters, you'll see that there are three steps involved in creating a graph:

1. Specify the data to be graphed.
2. Specify the type of graph.
3. Enhance the graph with titles, legends, and other additions.

These steps need not be carried out in this order.

Selecting the worksheet data to be graphed means selecting a data range, which contains one or more data series. A data series is a single row or column of worksheet data that appears as a plot in the graph. The data series for a graph are usually grouped together in a rectangular worksheet range, but they can also be located in different regions of the worksheet or in different worksheets.

Each graph contains at least one Y-series, which consists of data values that are plotted against the graph's Y axis (or, in pie graphs, as wedges). A graph can contain as many as six Y-series. Y-series are identified by the letters A through F. A graph usually contains a single X-series, which consists of labels, values, or dates that are plotted on the graph's X axis. The details of selecting data series are covered later in this chapter.

Selecting a graph type means choosing one of 1-2-3 for Windows' eleven different graph types, which are suitable for just about every imaginable need. The different types of graphs are described later in this chapter, as are methods of selecting graph type.

Enhancing the graph means to add explanatory text and labels, change colors, move and resize graph objects, and so on. By enhancing a graph, you clarify its message and enhance its impact.

To help clarify the concept of data range and data series, let's look at an example. Figure 10.2 shows the worksheet data that is graphed in Figure 10.1. The X data range is B5..B8, and the two Y data ranges are C5..C8 and D5..D8.

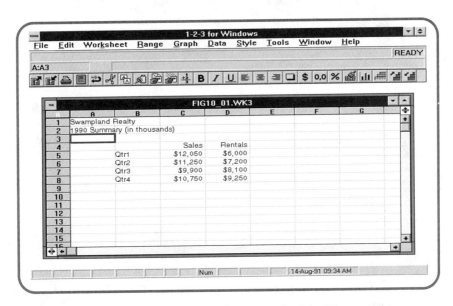

Figure 10.2   The worksheet data graphed in Figure 10.1.

When you create a graph, it is displayed in a window. A graph window is similar to other windows in that it can be moved, resized, reduced to an icon, etc. The title bar of a graph window displays the graph's title. In Figure 10.1, the graph window has been maximized. When a graph window is active, the 1-2-3 menu bar displays the graph menu, and the icon palette changes to show icons for commonly needed graph commands (refer to Figure 10.1). Before getting to the details, however, let's see how to create a basic graph.

Creating a Basic Graph

For this demonstration I'll use the worksheet shown in Figure 10.3. We want a graph that illustrates each month's sales by city. The following Quick Steps demonstrate how to create a basic graph.

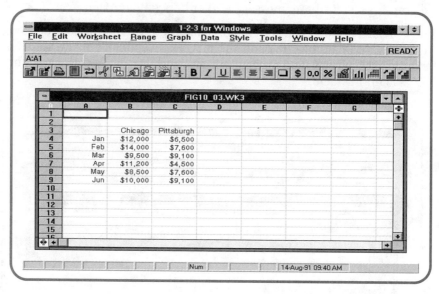

Figure 10.3   Data for the sample graph.

Q Creating a Basic Graph

1. Select the data to be graphed (in this example, A4..C9). — The data range is highlighted.

2. Select Graph New, or click the Graph New icon. — The Graph New dialog box is displayed (Figure 10.4).

3. In the Graph Name text box, 1-2-3 displays a default worksheet and graph name (i.e. *worksheet* GRAPH*n*, where *worksheet* is the worksheet name and *n* is a sequential number whose value depends on the number of graphs you have created). You can accept this name or (preferably) enter your own descriptive graph name.

4. Select OK.

1-2-3 opens a window and displays a line graph of the selected data (Figure 10.5). The name assigned to the graph is displayed in the window title bar.

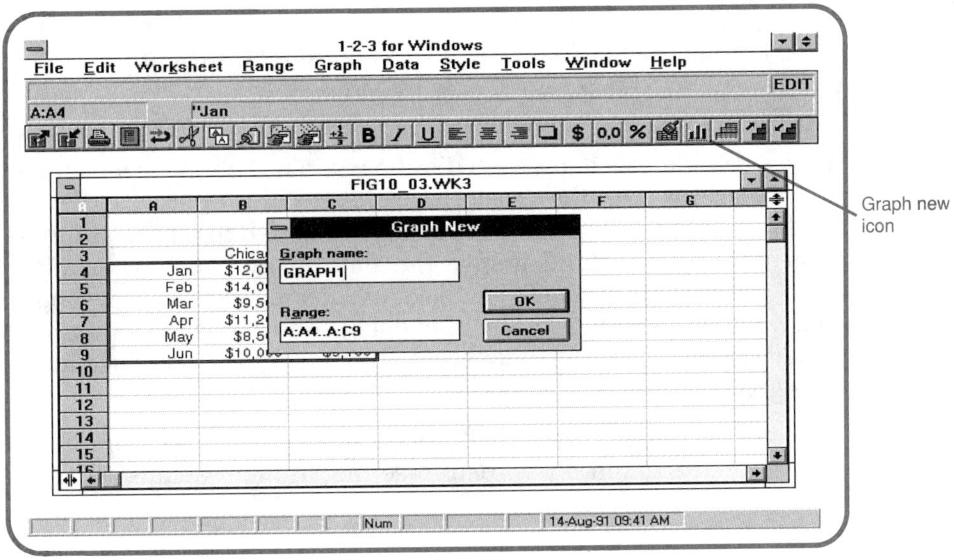

Figure 10.4   The Graph New dialog box.

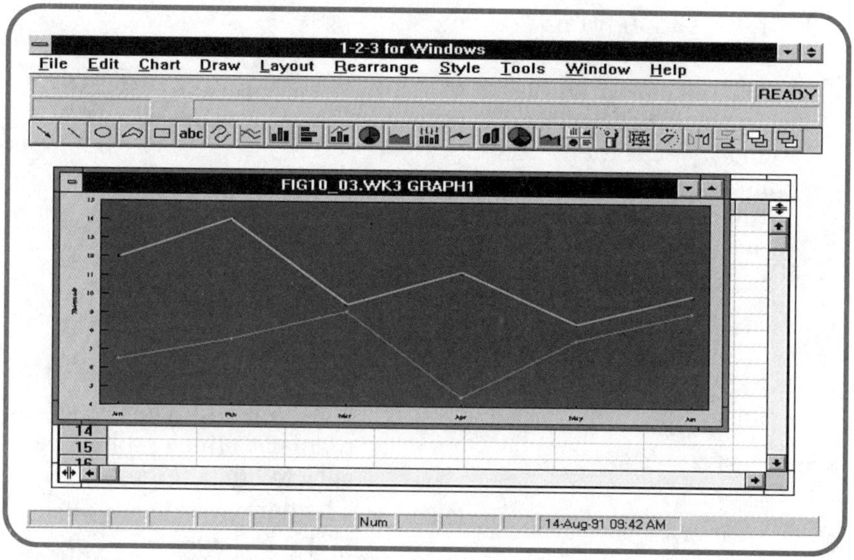

Figure 10.5   *A graph created with the Graph New command.*

That was pretty easy! You now have a graph that can be printed, saved, or modified. You'll see how to do these things in this and the next two chapters. For now, note two things.

First, to create this graph all we did was specify a rectangular range of worksheet data; 1-2-3 did the rest. The Graph New command automatically uses the labels in the first column as X axis labels and plots each column of values as a separate line on the graph. For this type of automatic graph, the data range must be organized in a specific way, which you'll learn later in the chapter. You are not limited to creating graphs from data in one worksheet range. Later, you'll see how to plot data from different worksheet locations in one graph.

Second, I mentioned that this graph is called a *line graph*. Line is one of 1-2-3's graph types. Before getting to more details of creating graphs, you need to become familiar with 1-2-3 for Windows' various types of graphs.

Graph Types

1-2-3 for Windows offers 11 different graph types. When creating a graph, you select the type depending on your data and the point you are trying to make.

Line Graph

A *line graph* plots each data value as a point or symbol, and connects the data points in each data series with a line. Line graphs are well suited for illustrating changes that occur over time. The table below gives yearly sales totals for imported and domestic typewriters. Figure 10.6 shows this data plotted as a line graph. The graph makes it clear that the domestic manufacturers are gaining market shares.

185

Year	Domestic	Imported
1984	115	85
1985	124	72
1986	132	64
1987	140	62
1988	156	50
1989	166	49
1990	172	44

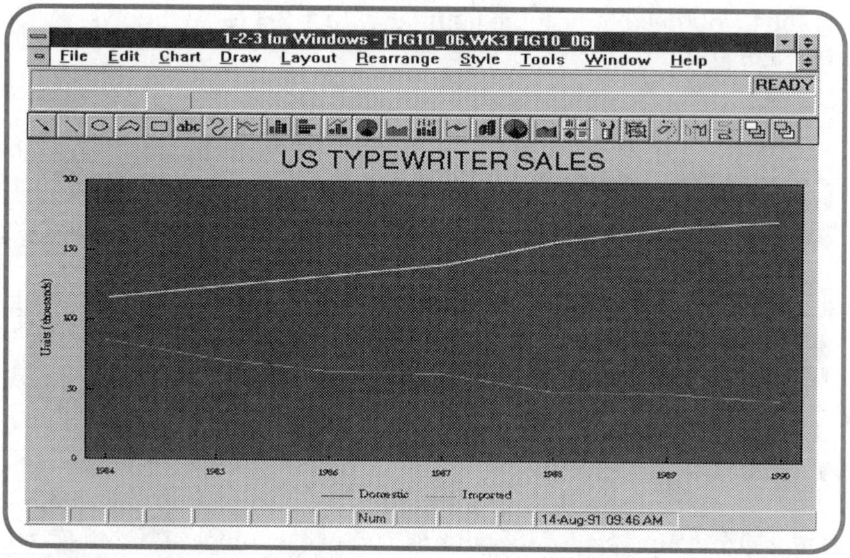

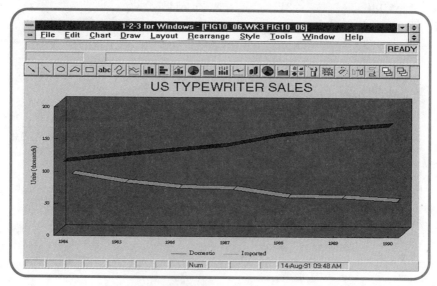

Figure 10.6   Sales data plotted as a line graph.

3-D Line Graph

A *3-D line graph* has the same basic structure as a line graph, but displays data in a three-dimensional perspective. Figure 10.7 shows the same data as Figure 10.6 plotted as a 3-D line graph.

Figure 10.7   A 3-D line graph.

Area Graph

An *area graph* is a line graph in which data series are plotted "stacked" on each other, and the regions between plots are filled with a color or pattern. Use an area graph to illustrate trends over time when you want to show overall totals as well as the contribution of each series to the totals. The table below gives sales by flavor for the Fizzy Soda Pop Company. Figure 10.8 shows this data as an area graph. It's clear from the graph that overall sales are not changing significantly, but the proportion of sales for different flavors is changing.

Year	Orange	Root Beer	Cola
1986	74	64	100
1987	65	62	115
1988	45	50	156
1989	21	49	188
1990	20	44	195

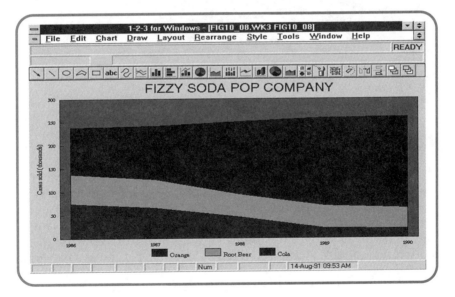

Figure 10.8   The soda sales-by-flavor data plotted as an area graph.

3-D Area Graph

A *3-D area graph* is an area graph displayed with a three-dimensional perspective. The same data in Figure 10.8 is shown in Figure 10.9 as a 3-D area graph.

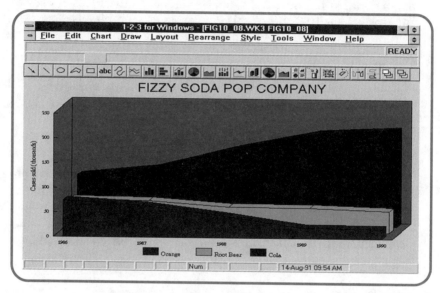

Figure 10.9 A 3-D area graph.

Bar Graph

A *bar graph* displays numerical values as a set of vertical rectangular bars along the X axis. Each number is plotted as a single bar, and the height of each bar is proportional to the corresponding value. Bar graphs are appropriate for comparing totals for several categories. For example, the following data gives total sales for four flavors of ice cream sold at two store locations. Figure 10.10 shows this data plotted as a bar graph.

	Downtown	**Mall**
Vanilla	27	32
Chocolate	14	20
Strawberry	16	22
Rocky Road	11	15

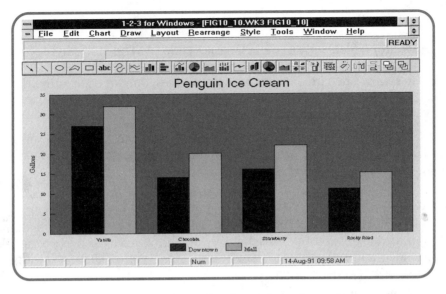

Figure 10.10   Ice cream sales data plotted as a bar graph.

3-D Bar Graph

A *3-D bar graph* is identical to a bar graph except that each individual bar is given three-dimensional perspective and appears solid. Figure 10.11 shows the same graph as Figure 10.10 plotted as a 3-D bar graph.

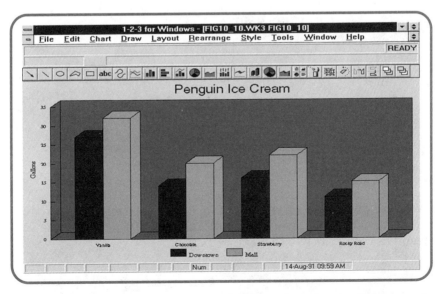

Figure 10.11   The ice cream sales data plotted as a 3-D bar graph.

Pie Graph

A *pie graph* plots only a single Y-series, series A. The plot is in the form of a circle, with the entire circle representing the total of all values in the data series. The circle is divided into wedges, one for each value. The size of each wedge represents the percentage that the corresponding value contributes toward the total.

A pie graph data range can include a second and third data series. These series are not plotted, but rather control how the first data series is plotted.

The values in data series B control the color used to display the corresponding wedge. The numbers 1-14 correspond to the 14 available screen display colors. The values in data series B also control whether a wedge is *exploded*, or offset slightly from the other wedges. To explode a wedge, add 100 to the corresponding series B value. To hide a wedge, use a negative B-series value.

The values in data series C determine whether a percent value is displayed next to each wedge. A series C value of 0 hides the percent value for the corresponding pie wedge. An empty cell in the C-series displays the percent value for the corresponding pie wedge. If you do not include a B- and C-series, pie graphs are displayed with default colors with a percent label.

The following list shows sales totals by salesperson for the Clunker Used Car Company. This data as a pie graph is shown in Figure 10.12. The second column of numbers was specified as series B.

	Units Sold	
Smith	10	1
Wilson	8	2
Jones	19	103
Baker	4	4
Adams	9	5

3-D Pie Graph

A *3-D pie graph* is identical to a regular pie graph, but with added three-dimensional perspective. The graph in Figure 10.13 shows the same graph as Figure 10.12 as a 3-D pie graph.

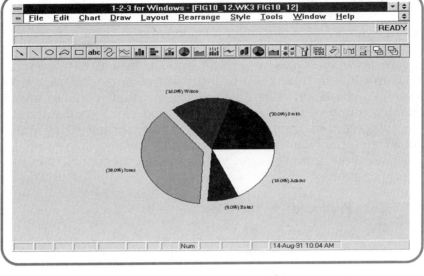

Figure 10.12   Auto sales data plotted as a pie graph.

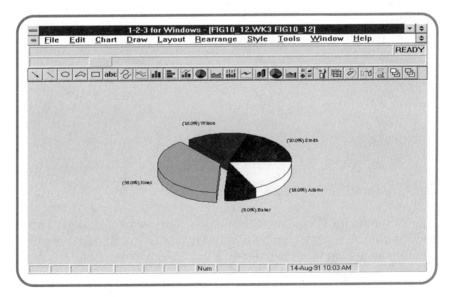

Figure 10.13   A 3-D pie graph.

XY Graph

The *XY graph*, sometimes called a *scattergram*, is the only 1-2-3 graph type that plots **values** on the X axis (the other graph types all plot **categories** on the X axis). Use an XY graph to display the relationship, or correlation, between two or more sets of numerical values. For example, you could determine the cost per unit produced at your manufacturing plant on a weekly basis, and plot it against the total number produced. Sample data shown in the following list is plotted as an XY graph in Figure 10.14. The graph clearly shows that the plant operates at maximum efficiency when producing approximately 250 units per week.

Units Produced	Unit Cost
330	90
333	92
340	82
345	72
349	73
350	74
354	75
365	76
369	88
370	80
375	86
380	88

HLCO Graph

HLCO stands for High-Low-Close-Open. This is a specialized kind of graph used for stock market data. An HLCO graph plots a stock's performance over time, usually on a day-by-day basis. For each day or other time period, four values are plotted:

High: the stock's highest value during the time period.

Low: the stock's lowest value during the time period.

Open: the stock's value at the start of the time period.

Close: the stock's value at the end of the time period.

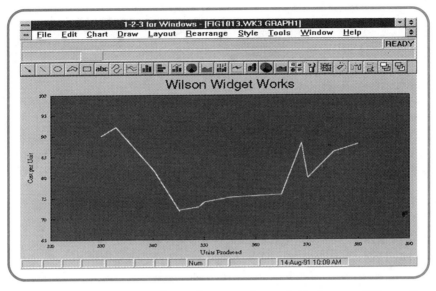

Figure 10.14   Manufacturing cost data plotted as an XY graph.

193

For each time period, the High and Low values are represented by a vertical line on the graph. The top end of the line represents the High, and the bottom end represents the Low. The Close and Open values are represented by small "flags" or tick marks extending horizontally from the line. The Open value is represented by a flag to the left, and the Close value by a flag to the right. Figure 10.15 illustrates an HLCO graph (with added bars as described in the next section).

HLCO graphs can display additional elements. One additional data series can be plotted as bars, using a second Y axis that is displayed on the right edge of the graph. Bars are often used to show daily trading volume for the stock. A second additional data series can be plotted as lines on the graph. You must assign data ranges properly when defining an HLCO graph:

Data series	Graph element
A	High values
B	Low values
C	Close values
D	Open values
E	Bars (optional)
F	Line (optional

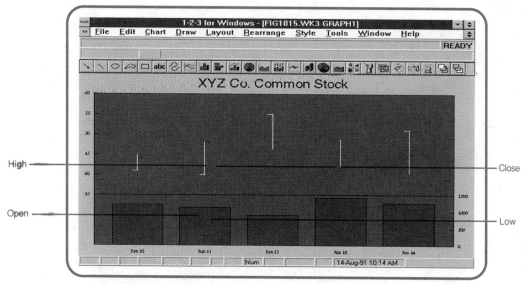

Figure 10.15   Stock market prices plotted on an HLCO graph.

194

While specialized for stock market information, HLCO graphs can be used for any data that fluctuates within discrete time periods, such as daily temperatures.

Mixed Graph

A *mixed graph* combines bar and line types in one graph. Data series A-C are plotted as bars, while series D-F are plotted as lines. Figure 10.16 shows a mixed graph.

Selecting Graph Type

To select a graph type, a graph window must be active so that the main graph menu is displayed in the menu bar. To make a window active, click it with the mouse or press Ctrl-F6 one or more times.

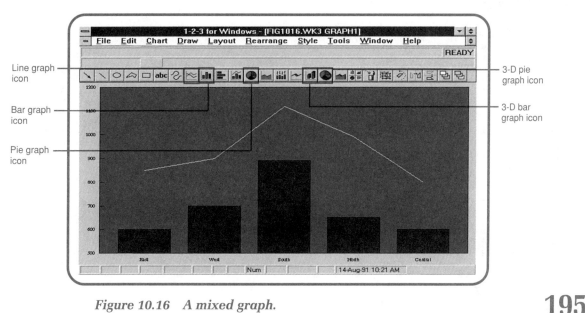

Figure 10.16   A mixed graph.

195

When you select a graph type, you can also select from several other options:

Style refers to how a specific graph type is displayed. For example, an XY graph can be displayed with symbols only, lines only, or symbols connected by lines. Each graph type offers one or more different style options, which are displayed as miniature sample graphs in the Graph Gallery section of the Chart Type dialog box (Figure 10.17).

Orientation can be either vertical (the default) or horizontal. Vertical orientation displays the Y axis vertically and the X axis horizontally. Horizontal orientation reverses this. The orientation option is not applicable to all graph types.

The *Table of Values* option includes in the graph a text table of the actual values displayed in the graph. The Table of Values option is available only for some graph types.

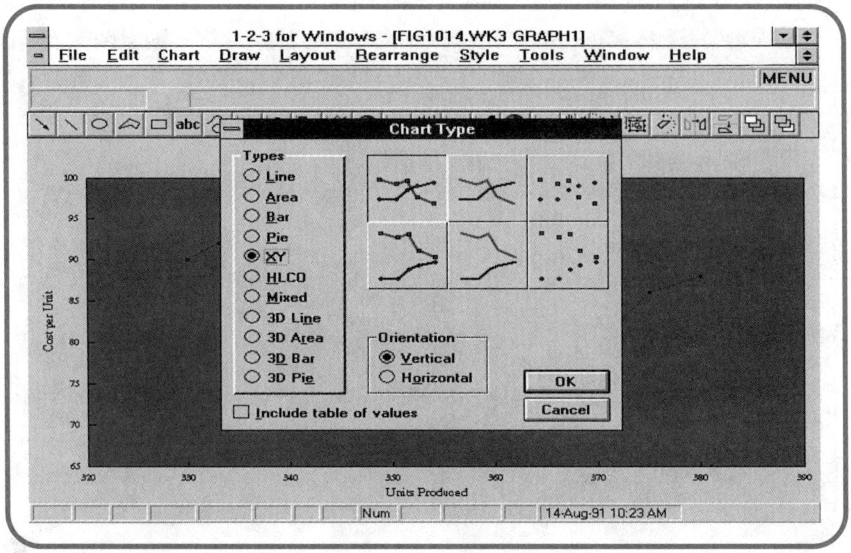

Figure 10.17 The Chart Type dialog box. Note that the icon palette provides icons for changing the graph type.

The following Quick Steps summarize how to change graph types.

Selecting or Changing Graph Type

1. Make the graph window active.

2. From the main graph menu, select Chart Type.

   The Chart Type dialog box is displayed (Figure 10.17).

3. Select the desired chart type.

   The style options for that type are displayed in the dialog box to the right of the type options.

4. Select a chart style from the Graph Gallery, or accept the default style.

5. Select Orientation and Table of Values options if desired.

6. Select OK.

   The graph in the window changes to the selected type.

> ▶ **Note:** The default icon palette for the charting function
> contains icons for changing type to bar, 3-D bar, pie, 3-D
> pie, or line (see Figure 10.16).

Dual Y Axes

Normally, graph types that use a Y axis have a single Y axis, located at
the left side of the chart. All data series are plotted relative to the single
Y axis. You can create a chart with dual Y axes that have different scales.
One axis is located in the normal position at the left of the chart, and the
second one is located at the right of the chart. Use dual Y axes to plot data
series with widely differing values on the same graph. A dual Y axis
graph is shown in Figure 10.18. You select dual Y axes from the Chart
Ranges dialog box, which is covered later in this chapter.

197

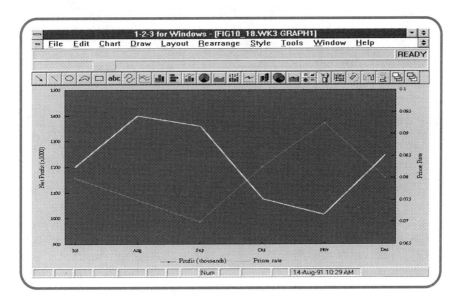

Figure 10.18   A graph with dual Y axes.

Selecting Data Ranges

A *data range* consists of one or more columns or rows of values (data series) and, in most cases, some labels that identify the values. The task of creating graphs is much easier if your worksheet data is organized appropriately. Fortunately, the type of data organization that is best for graphs is also the organization most commonly used for worksheet data: related numerical values in adjacent columns or rows, with identifying labels as row or column headings. An example of this organization is shown in Figure 10.19.

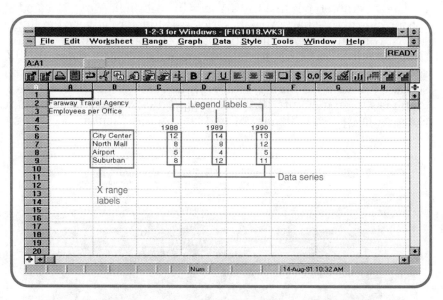

Figure 10.19   The proper worksheet data organization makes graphing operations easier.

Sometimes you may need a single graph that combines data series from different worksheets or from nonadjacent ranges in the same worksheet. 1-2-3 can do this, but it's better to combine separated data series into a single, contiguous data range that will be used for graphing. You can use formulas or the Edit Quick Copy command to create a data range for graphing while leaving the original data in its original location. Using formulas has the advantage that the graph data range will be automatically updated if the original data ranges are modified.

Automatic Graphs

If you specify a data range before selecting the Graph New command, 1-2-3 will attempt to assign data series properly. It can do this only if the data in the range is organized in a certain way.

▶ Data values must be organized in adjacent columns, one column per series. You may have a maximum of six series.

▶ If the first column of the range contains labels, they are used as X axis labels in the graph.

▶ If the first row of the range contains labels, they are used as the graph legend.

1-2-3 will attempt to create a graph from any data range, even if it is not organized correctly. In this case, you will get unpredictable results! You can manually assign rages to data series, giving you complete control over the graph contents. To do this, select Graph New *without* first selecting a data range. 1-2-3 opens an empty graph window. You can then use the Graph menu commands to specify data ranges, as explained in the next section.

199

Manual Range Selection

To manually select data ranges, first open an empty graph window as described above. Then, use the Chart Ranges command to specify the ranges for each data series. The following Quick Steps describe this process.

 Manually Specifying Data Series

1. From the worksheet window, select Graph New without a data range selected.

   The Graph New dialog box is displayed.

2. Enter a name for the new graph in the text box, then select OK.

   An empty graph window is opened.

3. Select Chart Ranges.

   The Chart Ranges dialog box is displayed (Figure 10.20).

4. In the X Data Range text box, enter the worksheet range to be used as the X-series. Remember, you can enter cell addresses, enter a range name, or use POINT mode.

5. In the A: through F: text boxes, enter the worksheet ranges to be used for the A through F data ranges.

6. Select the second Y check box for any ranges you want plotted against the second Y axis.

7. Select OK.

The graph is displayed. If you did not specify a type, Line type (the default) is used. □

200

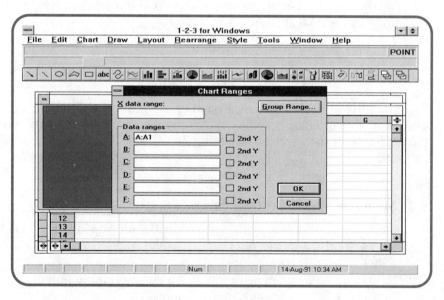

Figure 10.20   The Chart Ranges dialog box.

Using Group Range

If your data is contained in a single, rectangular worksheet range, but not exactly as the Graph New command requires, you can use the Group Range command to tell 1-2-3 how to assign the data ranges. For example, you can have rows of numbers, rather than columns, assigned as data series. You have two options:

Columnwise uses the first column of the range as the X data series and each succeeding column as the A-F data series.

Rowwise uses the first row of the range as the X data series and each succeeding row as the A-F data series.

Use these Quick Steps to assign group ranges.

 Assigning Group Ranges

201

1. Open an empty graph window and select Chart Ranges.	The Chart Ranges dialog box is displayed (Figure 10.20).
2. In the dialog box, select Group Range.	The Chart Ranges Group Range dialog box is displayed (Figure 10.21).
3. In the Range text box, enter the range of rows or columns containing the data to be graphed.	
4. Select Columnwise or Rowwise.	
5. Select OK.	The Chart Ranges dialog box is redisplayed.
6. Select 2nd Y for one or more data series if desired.	
7. Select OK.	The graph is displayed. ☐

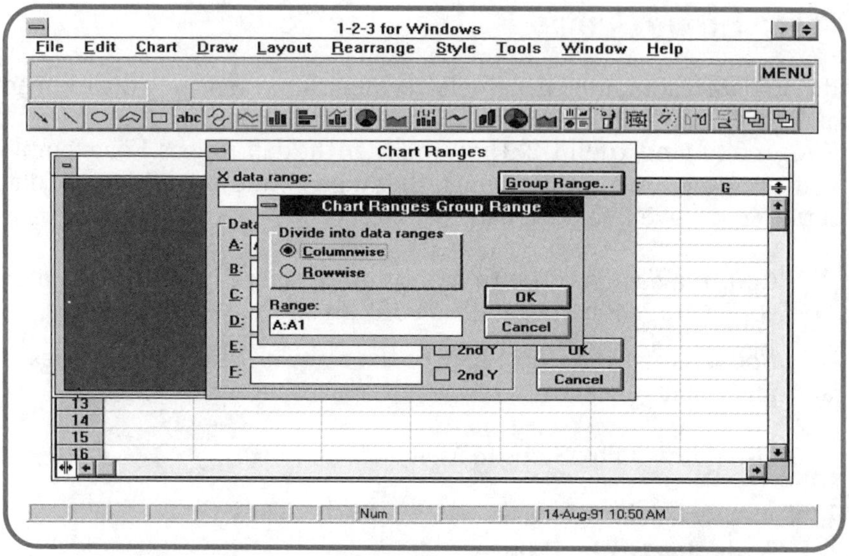

Figure 10.21   The Chart Ranges Group Range dialog box.

Viewing and Saving Graphs

A worksheet file can have multiple graphs defined. Remember, each
graph is assigned a name when it is first created. To open a graph
window and display an existing graph, use the Graph View command,
as the following Quick Steps explain.

Viewing an Existing Graph

1. Select Graph View.

The Graph View dialog box is
displayed (Figure 10.22).

2. In the list box, select the
   name of the graph to view.

3. Select OK.

A graph window opens
and displays the selected
graph.

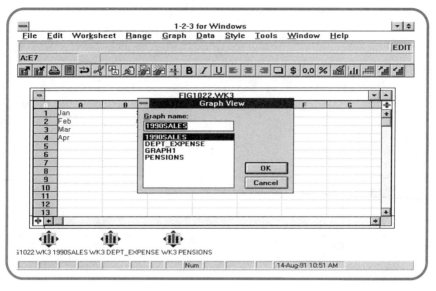

Figure 10.22   The Graph View dialog box.

Graphs are associated with the worksheet file that contains their data. When you save the worksheet file, all of its graphs are saved with it.

Inserting a Graph in the Worksheet

Once you have created a graph in a graph window, you can insert it in a worksheet range. The graph will be displayed in the worksheet window and will be printed if you print the worksheet range that contains the graph. By inserting graphs in worksheets, you can create sophisticated reports that include both data and graphs together. Use the following Quick Steps to insert graphs.

 Inserting a Graph in the Worksheet

1. In the worksheet window, select the range to contain the graph.

   The range is highlighted (Figure 10.23).

2. Select Graph Add to Sheet.

> The Graph Add to Sheet dialog box is displayed (Figure 10.24).

3. In the list box, select the graph to be added.

4. Select OK.

> The worksheet is displayed with the graph in the selected range (Figure 10.25). □

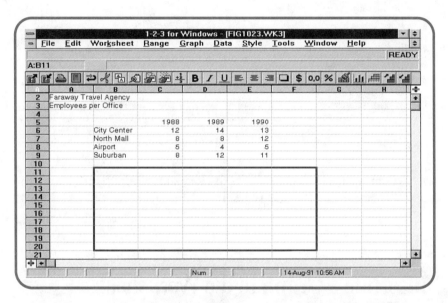

Figure 10.23   To add a graph to a worksheet, first select the graph range.

When a graph is added to a worksheet, it is automatically scaled to fit in the specified range. Worksheet data in that range is not affected, but is not visible because it is hidden by the graph. If you return to the graph window and modify the graph (for example, by changing its type), the changes will automatically be reflected in the worksheet graph when you next make the worksheet window active. If you change the data that the graph is based on, you must update the graph by selecting Graph Refresh from the worksheet window. This command updates all graphs in the current file.

To move to an inserted graph, select Graph GoTo. A dialog box is displayed listing the names of all inserted graphs. Select the desired graph, and the cell pointer is moved to the upper left cell in that graph's insert range.

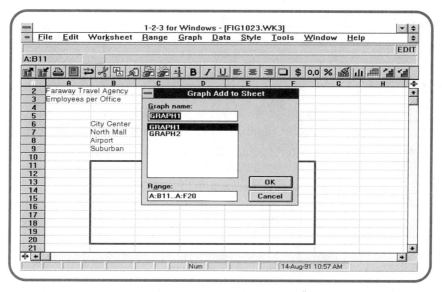

Figure 10.24   Next, display the Graph Add to Sheet dialog box and select the graph name.

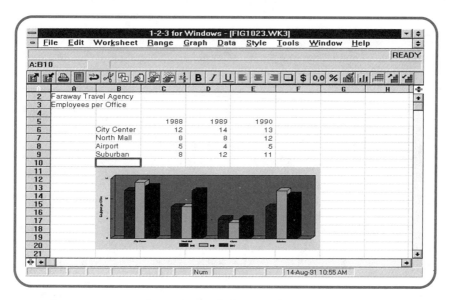

Figure 10.25   Select OK, and the graph is displayed in the worksheet.

To delete an inserted graph, simply click on a cell within the graph and press Del or choose Edit Clear.

What You Have Learned

▶ 1-2-3 for Windows can display graphs based on data in a worksheet.

▶ There are 11 types of graphs that you can use.

▶ A graph can contain one X-series and as many as six Y-series.

▶ You can specify data ranges manually or have 1-2-3 for Windows select them automatically.

▶ Graphs are saved when you save the associated worksheet file.

▶ When you add a graph to a worksheet, it is displayed and printed along with the worksheet data.

Chapter 11

Graph Enhancements

In This Chapter

- ▶ *Adding titles and footnotes to a graph*
- ▶ *Including a legend and data labels*
- ▶ *Modifying the graph axes*
- ▶ *Controlling graph borders and grids*
- ▶ *Setting color, font, and other options*

Graph Enhancements

In the last chapter you learned how to create a basic graph. In most situations, you will want to go beyond a basic graph and add various *enhancements*. Enhancements consist of additions and modifications to a graph that improve its appearance, clarity, and impact. This chapter and the next show you how to enhance your 1-2-3 for Windows graphs.

Adding Titles and Footnotes

You can add titles and footnotes to a 1-2-3 for Windows graph. Each title or footnote can contain any numbers, letters, or special characters. There are four titles/notes available, as illustrated in Figure 11.1:

The *title* is displayed centered above the graph.

The *subtitle* is displayed centered below the title.

The *footnote* is displayed below the graph in the lower left corner.

The *second footnote* is displayed below the first footnote.

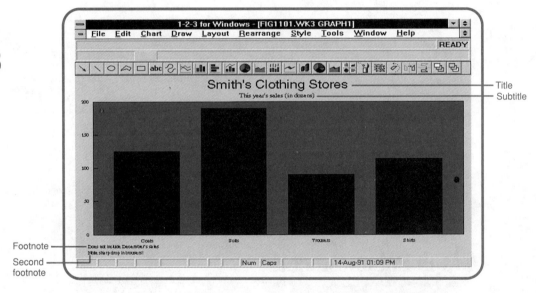

Figure 11.1   A graph with titles and footnotes added.

The following Quick Steps give the procedure for adding graph titles and footnotes.

Adding Titles and Footnotes to a Graph

1. Select Chart Headings.

   The Chart Headings dialog box is displayed (Figure 11.2).

2. In the text box for each title or footnote, enter the desired text. To move to the next text box, press Tab or click the next box using the mouse. To use a worksheet label as a title or footnote, enter the cell address or range name preceded by a backslash. The label can be up to 512 characters, but remember that only a certain number can display on screen.

3. Select OK.

   The titles or footnotes are added to the graph. □

209

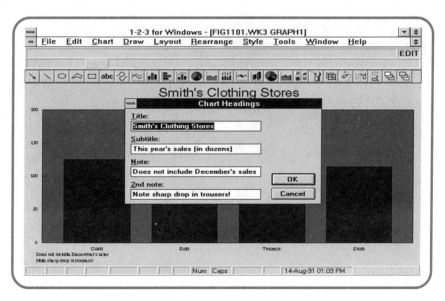

Figure 11.2   The Chart Headings dialog box.

If you specify a cell address for a title or footnote, and later move or delete that cell, 1-2-3 automatically adjusts the cell reference.

Titles and footnotes are displayed using the font and color that you select with the Chart Options command (covered later in this chapter).

Adding a Legend

A *legend* is a key that identifies graph data ranges by the color, hatch pattern, or symbol used to plot them. Graphs that include more than one data range usually need a legend. The default is for a legend to be placed below the graph, as in Figure 11.3. If you have a footnote, the footnote is pushed down below the legend.

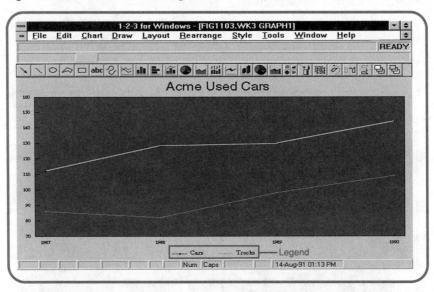

Figure 11.3   A legend is placed below the graph.

Use these Quick Steps to add a graph legend.

 Adding a Legend to a Graph

1. Select Chart Legend.	The Chart Legend dialog box is displayed (Figure 11.4).
2. To enter individual legend labels, enter the desired legend text in the text box for each data range. To use a worksheet label as a legend, enter the cell address or range name preceded by a backslash.	The Chart Legend Group Range dialog box is displayed (Figure 11.5).
3. If the worksheet contains labels in adjacent rows or columns that you want to use for the legend, select Group Range in the Chart Legend dialog box.	
4. In the Range text box, enter the worksheet range that contains the labels, then select OK.	The Chart Legend dialog box is redisplayed.
5. Select OK.	The legend is added to the graph. 1-2-3 automatically puts the appropriate color, symbol, or hatch key adjacent to each legend label. □

211

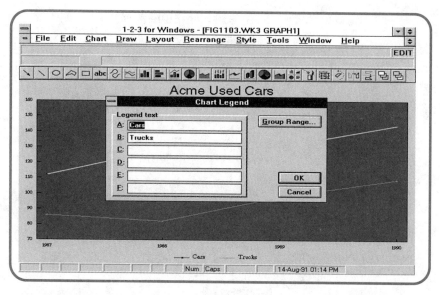

Figure 11.4   You enter legend information in the Chart Legend dialog box.

212

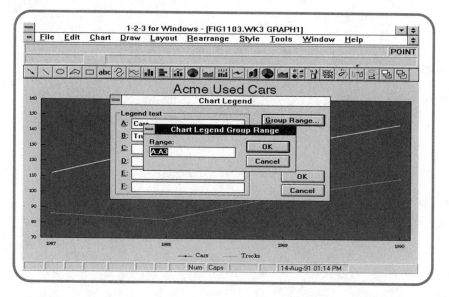

Figure 11.5   To use a range of worksheet labels in the legend, use the Chart Legend Group Range dialog box.

If you specify a cell address for a legend label, and later move or delete that cell, 1-2-3 automatically adjusts the cell reference. Legends are displayed using the font set chosen with Chart Options Font and the color set chosen with Chart Options Colors. (Both of these options are covered later in this chapter.)

Data Labels

A *data label* is a numeric or text label that is displayed adjacent to a data point in the graph. The most common use for data labels is to indicate exact numerical values on a graph. Figure 11.6 shows a graph with data labels displayed.

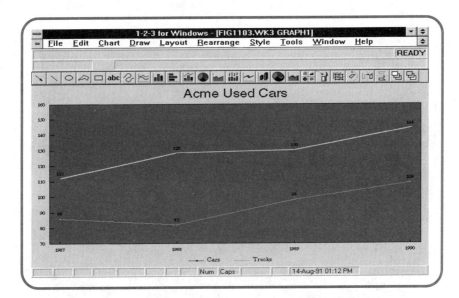

Figure 11.6 A graph with data labels displayed.

Each data point in your graph can only have a single label. You can display a label adjacent to some or all of the data points in each data series. The text to be used for data labels must exist in your worksheet as either labels or values; you cannot type in data labels directly. You add data labels to a data range by specifying the worksheet range that contains the labels. This range must be the same size as the data range. The data in each cell of the data label range is used, in order, as labels for each data point in the data range. To omit the label from one or more data points in the series, include an empty cell or cells at the corresponding locations in the data label range.

An example will make this clearer. In Figure 11.7, the range B1..B12 was specified as data series A and the range C1..C12 was specified as data labels for series A. The resulting graph is shown in Figure 11.8.

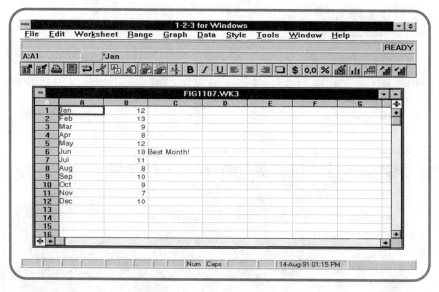

Figure 11.7   The range C1..C12 was specified as data labels for the graph in Figure 11.8.

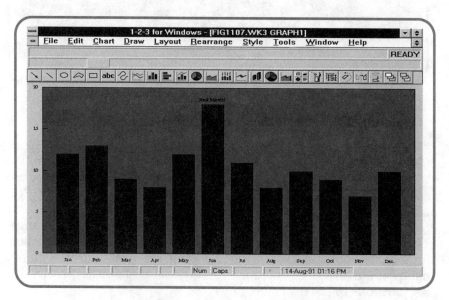

Figure 11.8   Applying data labels to specific data points.

Use the Quick Steps that follow when you want to include data labels on a graph.

Adding Data Labels to a Graph

1. Select Chart Data labels.

   The Chart Data Labels dialog box is displayed (Figure 11.9).

2. In the text box, enter the worksheet range to be used for data labels. Remember, this range must be the same size as the data series range.

3. In the drop-down box, select the position of the data labels with respect to the data point: Center, Above, Below, Left, or Right.

4. Repeat steps 2 and 3 for each data range to have labels.

5. Select OK.

   The data labels are displayed on the graph.

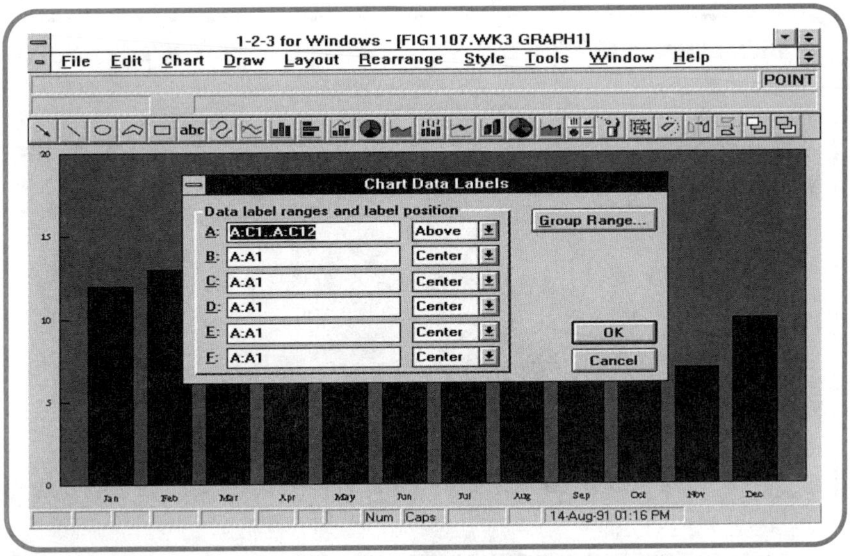

215

Figure 11.9   The Chart Data Labels dialog box.

Graph Axes

With the exception of pie graphs, all 1-2-3 for Windows graphs have at least two axes: the X axis and the Y axis. A graph that includes a 2nd Y axis has a total of three axes. The Y and 2nd Y axes always plot numerical values. In XY graphs, the X axis also plots numerical values; in all other graph types, the X axis plots category data. 1-2-3 for Windows gives you a great deal of control over your graph's axes.

Axis Scale

Axis scale controls the range of values that are displayed on a numerical axis. Axis scale is relevant for the Y and 2nd Y axes in all graphs, and the X axis in XY graphs. 1-2-3 for Windows' default is to scale the axis automatically, setting an axis maximum and minimum based on the data being plotted against the axis. You can also set axis scale manually. This is useful when plotting sets of large data values that differ relatively little from reach other. Figure 11.10 shows a bar graph with automatic Y axis scaling. The differences between the bars are not very obvious. Figure 11.11 shows the same graph with the Y axis scale set manually to 800-1000. Note how the differences are much easier to see.

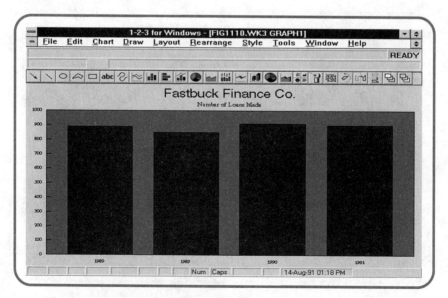

Figure 11.10   With automatic Y axis scaling, small differences between data points can be hard to see.

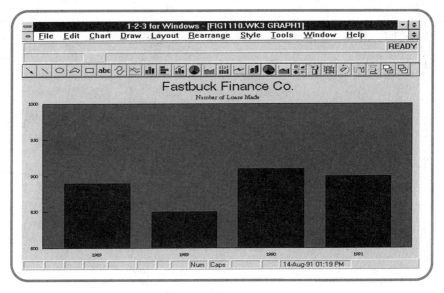

Figure 11.11   With the Y axis scale set manually to 800-1000, the differences are more obvious.

 Changing Axis Scaling

1. Select Chart Axis.

2. From the cascade menu select the axis whose scale you want to change: X, Y, or 2nd Y.

   The Chart Axis X, Chart Axis Y, or Chart Axis 2nd Y dialog box is displayed. These dialog boxes are identical; Figure 11.12 shows the Chart Axis Y dialog box.

3. Under Scale Axis select Manual. In the Show Values Between text boxes enter the desired minimum and maximum axis values.

4. Select OK.

   The graph is displayed with the modified axis scale (as in Figure 11.11).

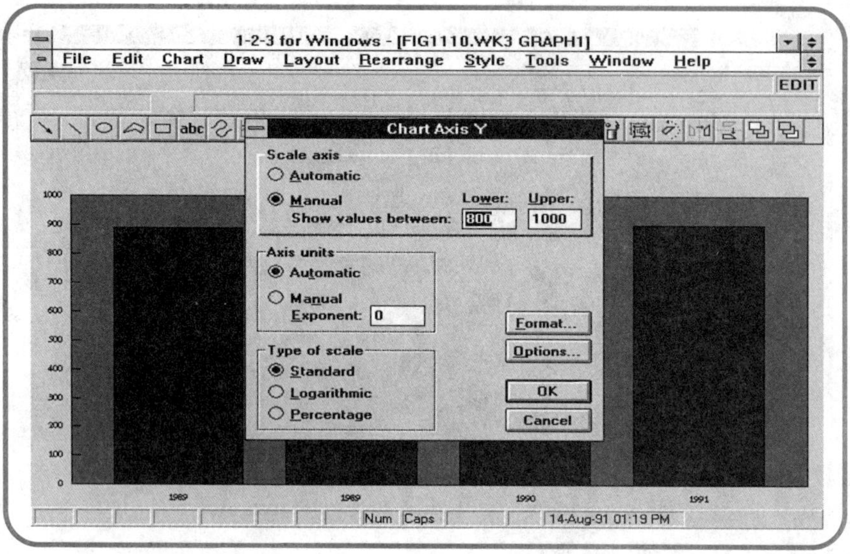

Figure 11.12   The Chart Axis Y dialog box.

218

> ⊘ **Caution:** If you set the axis maximum too low, or the axis minimum too high, some of your data points will not display on the graph. If the axis maximum is lower than the axis minimum, 1-2-3 will display a blank window.

Axis Number Format

For numeric axes, you can specify the format that 1-2-3 uses to display the axis numbers. You have the same format options that are available with the Range Format command, as covered in Chapter 6: Currency, Fixed, Scientific, etc. The default display format is General. The following Quick Steps describe this procedure.

Q   Changing the Display Format for a Numeric Axis

1. Select Chart Axis.

2. From the cascade menu, select the axis whose numeric format you want to change: X, Y, or 2nd Y.

   The Chart Axis dialog box for the selected axis is displayed (for example, Chart Axis Y in Figure 11.12).

3. Select Format.

The Chart Axis Format dialog box is displayed (for example, Chart Axis Format Y in Figure 11.13).

4. From the Format list box, select the desired numeric format. If appropriate, enter the number of decimal places in the Decimal Places text box.

5. Select OK.

The Chart Axis dialog box is redisplayed (for example, Chart Axis Y).

6. Select OK.

The graph is displayed with the select numeric format. □

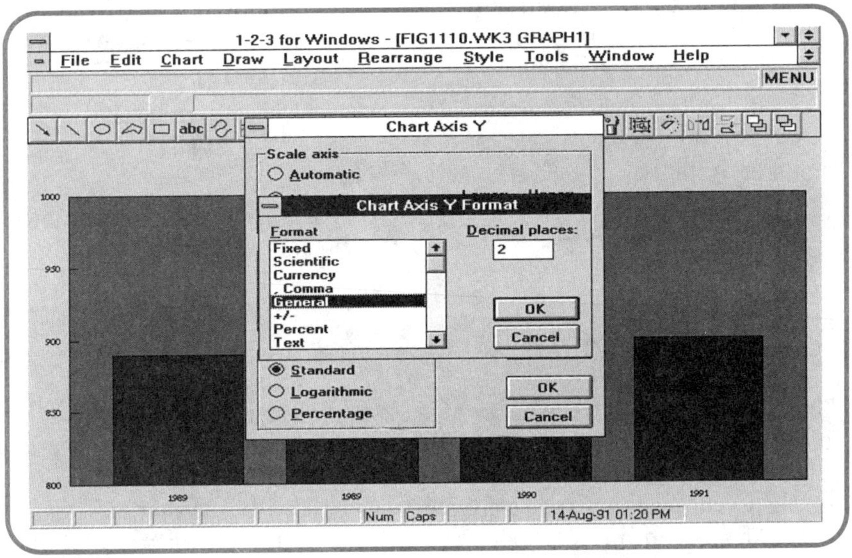

Figure 11.13   The Chart Axis Y Format dialog box.

Setting Axis Scale Type

1-2-3 offers three types of axis scales for numeric axes:

Standard, the default, gives a linear axis, with equal increments between primary tick marks.

Logarithmic gives a logarithmic axis, with exponential increments between primary tick marks.

Percent gives a percent scale, with percentage increments between primary tick marks.

 Note: The Percent type scale is not available for the X axis.

Use these Quick Steps to specify a scale type.

 Selecting a Numeric Axis Scale Type

1. Select Chart Axis.

2. From the cascade menu, select the axis whose scale type you want to change: X, Y, or 2nd Y.

   The corresponding Chart Axis dialog box is displayed (for example, Chart Axis Y in Figure 11.12).

3. Under Type of Scale select Standard, Logarithmic, or Percentage.

4. Select OK.

   The graph is displayed with the selected scale type. □

Selecting Axis Units

The axis units refer to the order of magnitude for a numerical axis scale. In other words, what power of 10 must axis numbers be multiplied by to accurately reflect the data being graphed? For example, if you are graphing values that range between 1 and 10 million, you could use an order of magnitude of 6 (because 10 to the 6th power = 1,000,000). 1-2-3 will automatically set an appropriate order of magnitude based on the data being graphed. You can also set order of magnitude manually, as the following Quick Steps describe.

 Setting an Order of Magnitude for Numerical Axis Units

1. Select Chart Axis.

2. From the cascade menu, select the axis whose units you want to change: X, Y, or 2nd Y.

The corresponding Chart Axis dialog box is displayed (for example, Chart Axis Y in Figure 11.12).

3. Under Axis Units, select Manual, then enter the desired exponenet in the text box. The exponent must be between –95 and 95.

4. Select OK.

The chart is displayed with the selected axis units. ☐

Axis Titles

You can add a title to each axis on the graph to identify the data being illustrated. The X axis title is displayed below the X axis labels and above the legend (if there is a legend). The Y and 2nd Y axis titles are displayed vertically next to the axis.

221

You can enter a title from the keyboard, or use a label in a worksheet cell as a title. Use the Quick Steps that follow to add an axis title.

 Adding a Title to an Axis

1.   Select Chart Axis.

2. From the cascade menu select the axis you want to add a title to: X, Y or 2nd Y.

The corresponding Chart Axis dialog box is displayed. (For example, Chart Axis Y in Figure 11.12.)

3. Select Options.

The Chart Axis Options dialog box for the selected axis is displayed (for example, Chart Axis Options Y in Figure 11.14).

4. In the Axis Title text box, enter the desired axis label text. To use a worksheet label as an axis title, enter the call address or range name preceded by a backslash.

5. Select OK.	The Chart Axis dialog box is redisplayed.
6. Select OK.	The graph is displayed with the axis title. □

If you specify a cell address for an axis title, and later move or delete that cell, 1-2-3 automatically adjusts the cell reference. Axis titles are displayed using the font selected with Chart Options Font and the color selected with Chart Options Colors (covered later in this chapter).

Controlling Borders and Grids

Graph borders are the lines displayed at the four edges of the data area (the lower and left borders are the X and Y axes). Grid lines are lines within the data area corresponding to axis tick marks. 1-2-3's default is to display graphs with all four borders and no grid lines. You can control borders and grid lines with the Chart Borders/Grids command, as the next Quick Steps describe.

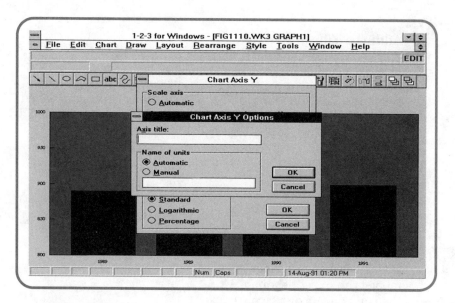

Figure 11.14   The Chart Axis Y Options dialog box.

Modifying Graph Borders and Grid Lines

1. Select Chart Borders/Grids.

   The Chart Borders/Grids dialog box is displayed (Figure 11.15).

2. Under Borders, turn the check boxes on or off for Left, Right, Top, and Bottom borders.

3. Under Grid Lines, select one or more axes to have grid lines.

4. Select OK.

   The graph is displayed with the selected borders and grid lines. □

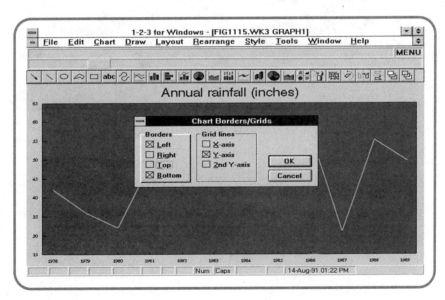

Figure 11.15   The Chart Borders/Grids dialog box.

Grid lines can be placed on any of a graph's axes: X, Y, and 2nd Y (if present). Grid lines are displayed perpendicular to their axis, and have the same spacing as the axis's major tick marks. Figure 11.16 shows a graph displayed with only left and bottom borders, and with grid lines on the Y axis.

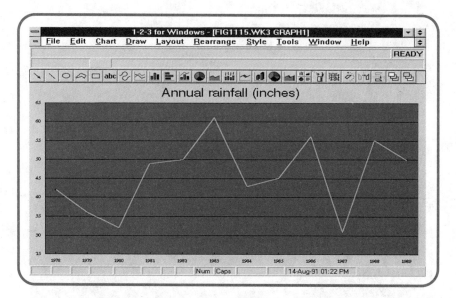

Figure 11.16   A graph with Y axis grid lines, and left and bottom borders.

Setting Chart Options

You use *chart options* to control the colors, hatch patterns, lines, and fonts that are used to display text and data in a graph. You need to modify these settings only if you are not satisfied with 1-2-3's defaults.

Setting Chart Color

You can control the color used to display text in the graph, and also the colors used to display the lines, bars, or symbols for each data range, as the following Quick Steps describe.

Q **Set the Color Used to Display Graph Elements**

1. Select Chart Options Colors.

   The Chart Options Colors dialog box is displayed (Figure 11.17).

2. Use the Chart Title drop-down box to select the color of the main title text.

3. Use the Subtitle, Axis Titles, Legend drop-down box to select the color used for these elements.

4. Use the Labels, Notes, Name of Units drop-down box to select the color used for these elements.

5. Under Data Range Colors, use the corresponding drop-down box to set the colors for data ranges A-F. For clarity, make sure all the data ranges have a different color.

6. Select OK.

   The graph is displayed with the selected colors. □

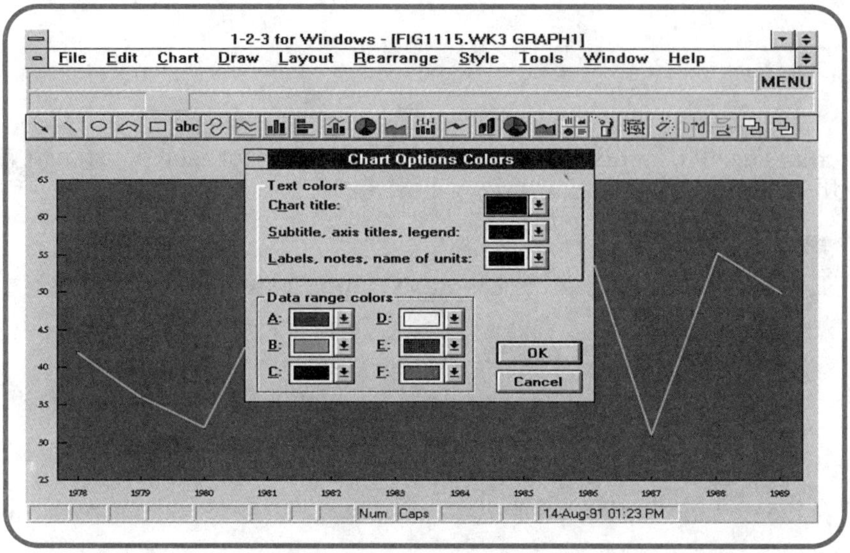

Figure 11.17   The Chart Options Colors dialog box.

226

> **Tip:** To hide a graph element without removing it from the graph, set its color to the same as the background.

Setting Chart Hatch Patterns

Hatches are patterns that can be used instead of or along with colors to differentiate data ranges on your graphs. Hatch patterns are used in the bars of bar, mixed, and HLCO graphs; in the slices of pie charts; and between the lines of area and mixed graphs. Using hatch patterns is particularly helpful when you have a color display and a monochrome printer. When you print a graph, the patterns make the data ranges look more distinct.

Assigning Hatch Patterns to Graph Data Ranges

1. Select Chart Options Hatches.   The Chart Options Hatches
                                         dialog box is displayed
                                         (Figure 11.18).

2. Select the drop-down box for the data range you are assigning a hatch to, then select the desired hatch pattern.

3. Repeat Step 2 for each data range you want to set a hatch pattern for.

4. Select OK.

The graph is displayed with the selected hatch patterns (Figure 11.19). □

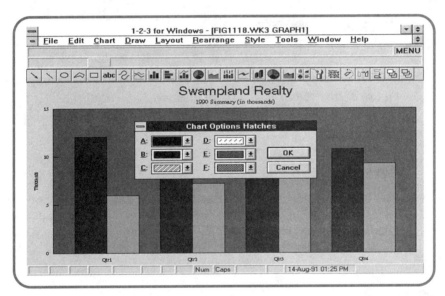

227

Figure 11.18   The Chart Options Hatches dialog box.

▶ **Tip:** To remove the hatch pattern from a data range, use the Chart Options Hatches command and select the solid pattern.

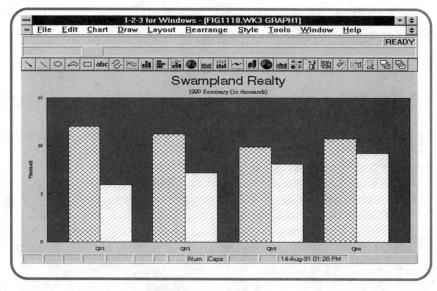

Figure 11.19   *A bar graph displayed with hatch patterns.*

Setting Chart Fonts

A *font* is a style and size of type used for text in a chart. You can control the font used for various graph text elements. Remember, the fonts you have available depend on your printer and Windows installation, and may differ from those shown here. Use these Quick Steps to change graph text fonts.

 Changing the Fonts Used for Text Graph Elements

1. Select Chart Options Font.

   The Chart Options Fonts dialog box is displayed (Figure 11.20).

2. Use the Chart Title drop-down box to select the font used for the main title.

3. Use the Subtitle, Axis Titles, Legend drop-down box to select the font used for these elements.

4. Use the Labels, Notes, Name of Units drop-down box to select the font used for these elements.

5. Select OK.   The graph is displayed with the selected fonts.   □

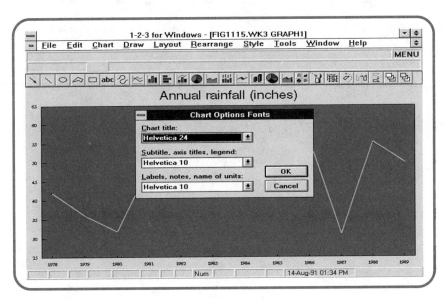

Figure 11.20   The Chart Options Font dialog box.

229

Setting Line Display Options

Line options affect the way lines are displayed for individual data ranges in Line, Mixed, XY, and HLCO graphs. You have three options, which can be applied alone or in combination:

Connectors displays lines connecting each data point in the series.

Symbols displays a symbol at each data point in the series.

Area fill fills the area between one data series and the next with the color and hatch assigned to that data series.

For example, in the graph in Figure 11.21, there are 3 data series. One is displayed with Connectors and Symbols, one with Connectors only, and one with Symbols only.

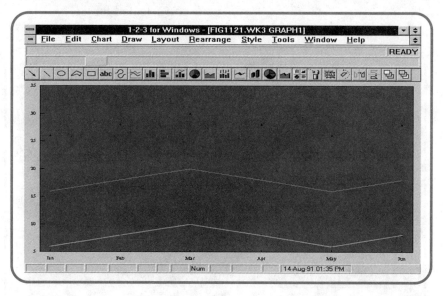

Figure 11.21   A line graph with three different line display options.

Use these Quick Steps to select a line display option.

 Changing Line Display Options

1. Select Chart Options Lines.

   The Chart Options Lines dialog box is displayed (Figure 11.22).

2. For each data range, select the combination of display options desired: Connectors, Symbols, and/or Area Fill.

3. Select OK.

   The graph is displayed with the selected line options. □

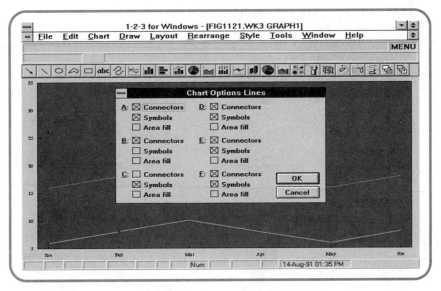

Figure 11.22   The Chart Options Lines dialog box.

231

Clearing Chart Settings

You can reset all or selected chart settings to the defaults, if you don't like any changes you have made. The following Quick Steps describe this procedure.

 Resetting Chart Settings to the Defaults

1. Select Chart Clear.

   The Chart Clear dialog box is displayed (Figure 11.23).

2. Under Data Ranges, select the data series ranges and data label settings to clear. You can select All or individual data ranges.

3. Select Chart Settings to clear data label, heading, legend, axis, color, hatch, font, and line settings from the graph.

4. Select Entire Chart to clear all settings (combination of steps 2 and 3).

5. Select OK.

The graph is displayed with the default settings. If you cleared all settings, an empty graph window is displayed. □

232

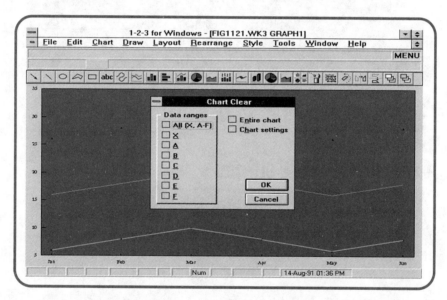

Figure 11.23   The Chart Clear dialog box.

What You Have Learned

▶ Graph enhancements are used to improve the appearance and clarity of a graph.

▶ Explanatory text can be added to a graph as titles, footnotes, legends, or data labels.

► You can modify the scale, type, and units of your graph axes to suit your data.

► A graph can be displayed with or without borders and grid lines.

► The Chart Options command is used to modify colors, fonts, hatch patterns, and lines used in a graph.

233

Adding Text and Drawings to Graphs

In This Chapter

▶ *Adding Text and Objects to a Graph*
▶ *Modifying Graph Objects*
▶ *Changing Graph Window Display*

Adding Objects to a Graph

When a graph window is active, you can add a variety of objects to a graph. Objects include text, arrows, rectangles, and lines. You have complete control over objects added to a graph—you can specify their position, size, and orientation.

Adding Text

You can place explanatory text or labels at any location in your graph. When used in conjunction with arrows (discussed later in this chapter), added text can identify salient features of your data. Figure 12.1 shows a graph with added text. The Quick Steps that follow give the procedure for enhancing your graphs with text.

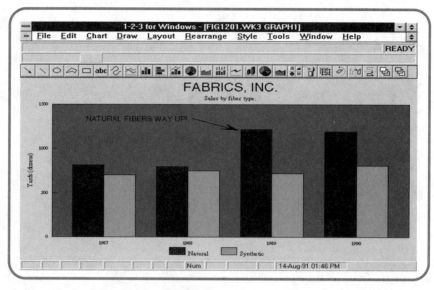

Figure 12.1   A graph with text added to it.

Q Adding Text to a Graph

1. Select Draw Text.

   The Draw Text dialog box is displayed.

2. In the New text text box, enter the desired text (maximum length 512 characters). You can also enter a backslash followed by the address or range name of a worksheet cell containing a label.

3. Select OK.

   The dialog box disappears and the mouse pointer changes to a black crosshair.

4. Use the mouse or the arrow keys to move the crosshair to the location for the text, then click the mouse or press Enter.

   The graph is displayed with the added text.

   □

Adding an Arrow or Line

You can add arrows and straight lines to a graph. Arrows, for example, can be used to point out important features of your data. Figure 12.1 also shows an added arrow. The Quick Steps below give the procedure for adding an arrow. For adding a line, the procedure is the same except you select Draw Line or click the Draw Line SmartIcon.

Q **Adding an Arrow to a Graph**

1. Select Draw Arrow or click the Draw Arrow Smart-Icon.

   The pointer changes to a crosshair.

2. Use the mouse or arrow keys to move the crosshair to the position for the nonhead end of the arrow.

3a. *Using the Mouse:*

   Click to anchor the crosshair, then move the mouse to stretch the other end to its position and double-click.

3b. *Using the Keyboard:*

   Press the space bar to anchor the arrow, then use the arrow keys to move the other end to its position and press Enter.

   The graph is displayed with the arrow.

   □

237

Adding a Polygon or a Multiple-Segment Line

You can add a *polygon* to your graph. (A polygon is a closed figure comprised of three or more straight line segments.) You can also add a *multiple-segment* line. To draw a polygon, use the Draw Polygon command (or click the Draw Polygon SmartIcon). For a line, use the Draw Line command or SmartIcon. The procedures for both are identical. The only difference is that when drawing a polygon, 1-2-3 will (if necessary) automatically draw a final line to connect your start and stop points to create a closed figure. Figure 12.2 illustrates a polygon and a multiple segment line. Use the Quick Steps that follow to add a polygon to a graph.

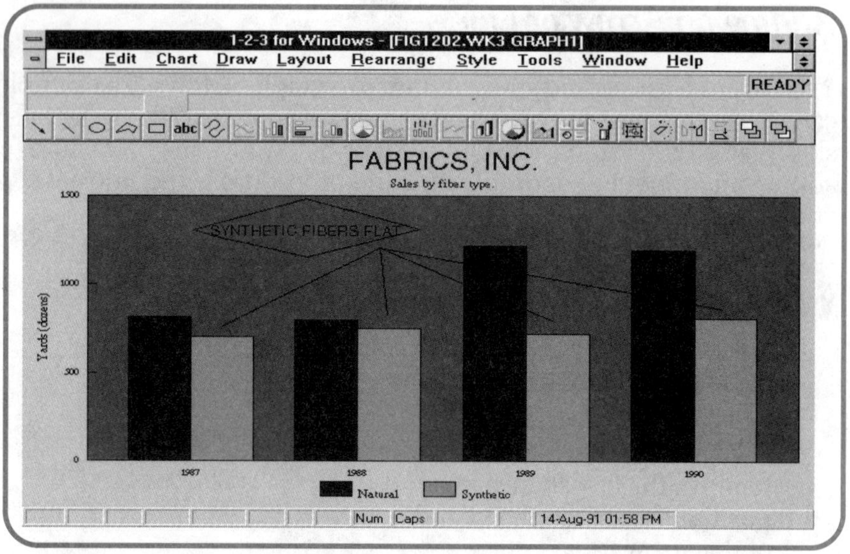

Figure 12.2   A graph with an added polygon and multiple-segment line.

238

 Adding a Polygon to a Graph

1. Select Draw Polygon, or click the Draw Polygon SmartIcon.

   The pointer changes to a crosshair.

2a. *Using the Mouse:*

   Move the crosshair to the start position and click to anchor the first line segment.

2b. *Using the Keyboard:*

   Use the arrow keys to move the crosshair to the start position and press the space bar to anchor the first line segment.

3. Move the crosshair to the next anchor point and click or press the space bar.

4. Repeat until the figure is drawn, then double-click or press Enter.

   The graph is displayed with the polygon.   □

Adding a Rectangle or Ellipse

To add a rectangle, you first anchor one corner in position, then move the diagonally opposite corner to stretch the rectangle to the desired size. Drawing an ellipse is similar; you draw a rectangle to the desired ellipse size, then 1-2-3 erases the rectangle and draws the ellipse. The Quick Steps that follow give instructions for a rectangle. For an ellipse, simply select the Draw Ellipse command or SmartIcon.

 Adding a Rectangle to a Graph

1. Select Draw Rectangle or click the Draw Rectangle SmartIcon.

   The pointer changes to a crosshair.

2a. *Using the Mouse:*

   Move the pointer to one corner of the rectangle, then click to anchor it.

2b. *Using the Keyboard:*

   Use the arrow keys to move the pointer to one corner of the rectangle, then press the space bar to anchor it.

3. Stretch the rectangle to the desired size, then double-click or press Enter.

   The graph is displayed with the rectangle.

   □

239

Drawing Freehand

Freehand drawing lets you add any sort of line you want. Depending on your skill as an artist, you can enhance your graphs in various ways, as the following Quick Steps demonstrate.

 Adding Freehand Drawing to a Graph

1. Select Draw Freehand or click the Draw Freehand SmartIcon.

   The pointer changes to a crosshair.

2a. *Using the Mouse:*

Move the pointer to the start position, and press and hold the mouse button. | The pointer changes to a pencil.

2b. *Using the Keyboard:*

Use the arrow keys to move the pointer to the start position, then press the space bar.

3. Move the mouse or use the arrow keys to move the pencil. | As the pencil moves, it draws a line on the graph.

4. When done, release the mouse button or press Enter.

□

Selecting Graph Objects

To work with objects in a graph, you must first select one or more objects. You can select objects that you added to a graph with the Draw commands covered earlier in this chapter. You can also select the *chart* itself. In this context, the term chart refers to the data plots, axes, titles, legend, data labels, and so on—the components created with the commands covered in the previous chapter.

You can have a single object or multiple objects selected at a time. A selected object is indicated by having small black rectangles, or handles, displayed around its boundary. For example, in Figure 12.3 the rectangle is selected. When you first add an object, it is the selected object.

Here are the procedures for selecting objects with the mouse:

► To select one object, click it.

► To select multiple objects, select the first object, then press and hold the Shift key and click one or more additional objects.

► To deselect all objects, click a graph location not near an object.

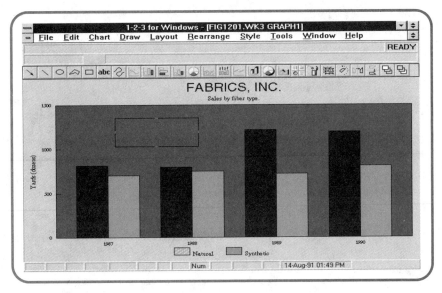

*Figure 12.3   The rectangle is selected, as indicated by the small
black handles around it.*

241

To select objects using the keyboard, use the following procedure:

1. Select Edit Select. The Edit Select cascade menu is displayed
   (Figure 12.4).
2. In the dialog box, select:

   ▶ *All* to select all added objects (but not the graph itself).

   ▶ *Chart* to select the graph.

   ▶ *None* to deselect all objects.

   ▶ *Cycle* to select individual objects.

   ▶ *Next* or *Previous* to move between objects (the current object
   has small, open rectangles around it).

   ▶ *Select* to select the current object.

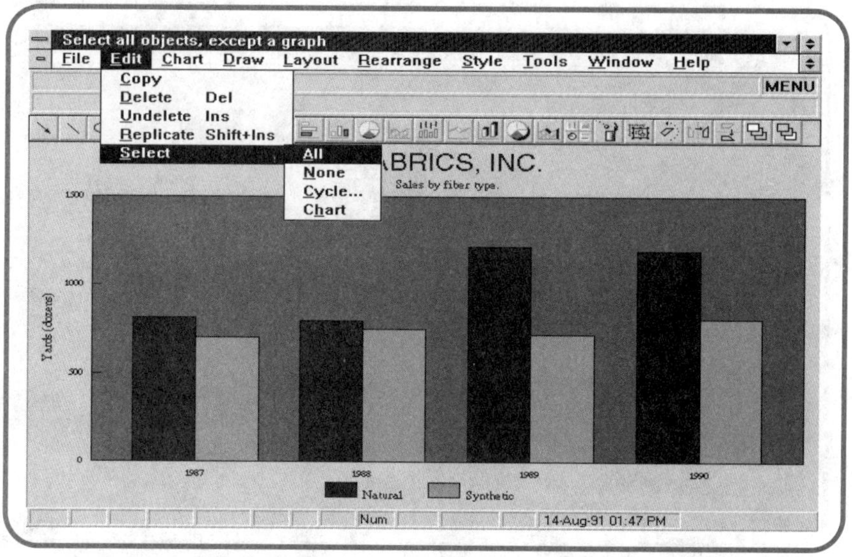

Figure 12.4   The Edit Select cascade menu.

Rearranging Graph Objects

You rearrange graph objects with the commands on the Rearrange Pulldown menu, shown in Figure 12.5. To rearrange a graph object, you must first select it so 1-2-3 knows which object you are changing.

Deleting Objects

To delete the selected object or objects, press Del, click the Delete SmartIcon, or select Edit Delete. To restore, or undelete, the object(s), select Edit Undelete or press Ins.

Replicating Objects

To make a copy of a selected object, select Edit Replicate or press the Shift-Ins key combination. A copy of the object is created adjacent to the original. Use Replicate to make multiple objects that are exactly the same size. You can then move the copy to the desired position.

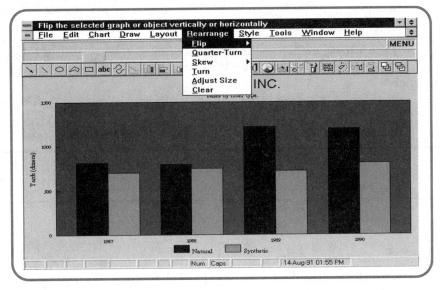

Figure 12.5   The Rearrange pulldown menu.

Moving an Object

To move an object (including added text) with the mouse, point at it and drag it to the new location. You cannot move a graph object with the keyboard.

Changing Object Size

To change an object's size, select Rearrange Adjust Size. A box appears around the object. Next, use the mouse or arrow keys to adjust the object to the desired size. When finished, click the mouse or press Enter.

Changing Object Orientation

You have several options for changing the orientation of graph objects:

> *Rearrange Flip* flips the object either vertically
> (top-to-bottom) or horizontally (left-to-right).

Rearrange Quarter-turn rotates the object one-quarter of a turn (90 degrees).

Rearrange Turn lets you rotate the object by any amount. Use the mouse or keyboard to turn the object, then click or press Enter

Rearrange Skew lets you adjust the skew, or slant, of an object. You can skew an object either vertically or horizontally. Use the mouse or arrow keys to set the desired skew, then click or press Enter.

Editing Graph Text

You can edit any text that was added to the graph with the Draw Text command. To do so, select the text to edit, then press F2 (EDIT). The existing text will be displayed in a dialog box, where you can edit it. When finished editing the text, press Enter and the graph will be displayed with the edited text.

Changing Object Style

Changes in object style are accomplished with commands on the Style pulldown menu, shown in Figure 12.6. You must first select the object(s) whose style you are changing. Not all styles are applicable to every type of graph object. For example, color is applicable to all objects, but it makes no sense to change the font of a rectangle, or the line type of text.

Changing Font

You can change the font used to display text you added with the Draw Text command. The fonts you have available depend on your printer. The next set of Quick Steps describes how to change the font used for added text.

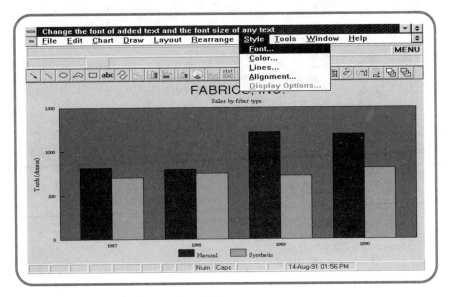

Figure 12.6   The Style pulldown menu.

 Changing Text Fonts

1. Select the text object(s) to change.

   The text object is displayed with handles.

2. Select Style Font.

   The Style Font dialog box is displayed (Figure 12.7).

3. Select the desired font from the list box.

4. To change the size of all text in the graph by a fixed amount, enter a percentage value between 1 and 1000 in the Magnify All Fonts text box. For example, to double the size of all text, enter 200.

5. Select OK.

   The graph is displayed with the selected font and font size. □

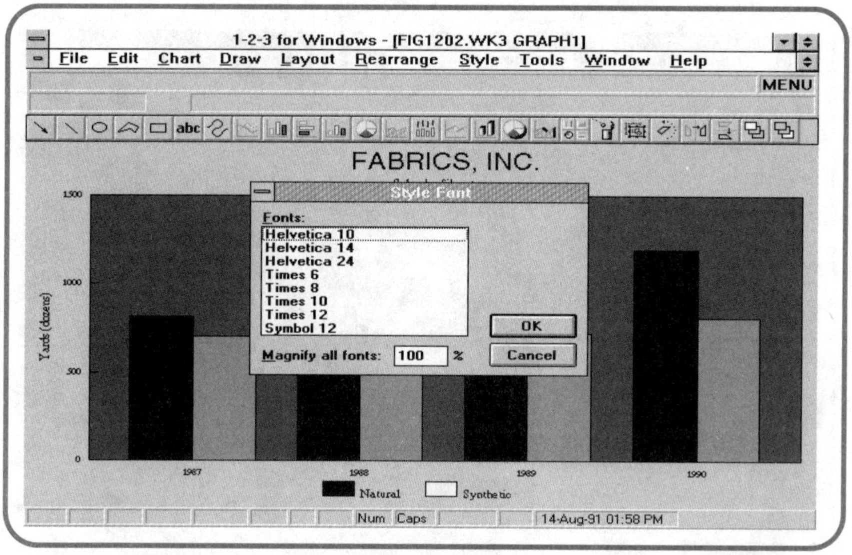

Figure 12.7   The Style Fonts dialog box.

▶ **Tip:** To change the font of text used for headings, axis titles, and so on, use the Chart Options Font command.

Changing Color

To change the color of graph objects, use the Style Color command. You have four options when setting color:

Text sets the color for text added with the Draw Text command.

Line sets the color used for lines, arrows, outlines of shapes, and freehand drawing.

Interior Fill sets the color used for the interior of objects such as rectangles.

Background sets the color used for the graph background (no matter what object is selected).

The following Quick Steps describe how to choose colors for the objects you add to your graphs.

Setting the Color of Graph Objects

1.	Select the object to change.	The object is displayed with handles.
2.	Select Style Color.	The Style Color dialog box is displayed (Figure 12.8).
3.	Select the desired option, as explained earlier.	The option's color palette is displayed. For example, Figure 12.9 shows the Style Color Lines palette.
4.	Select the desired color. Select H to hide the object.	
5.	Repeat steps 3 and 4 as many times as needed.	
6.	Select OK.	The graph is displayed with the selected colors. □

247

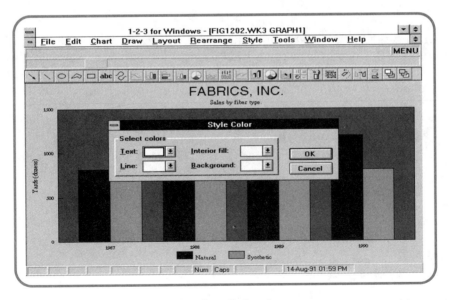

Figure 12.8   The Style Color dialog box.

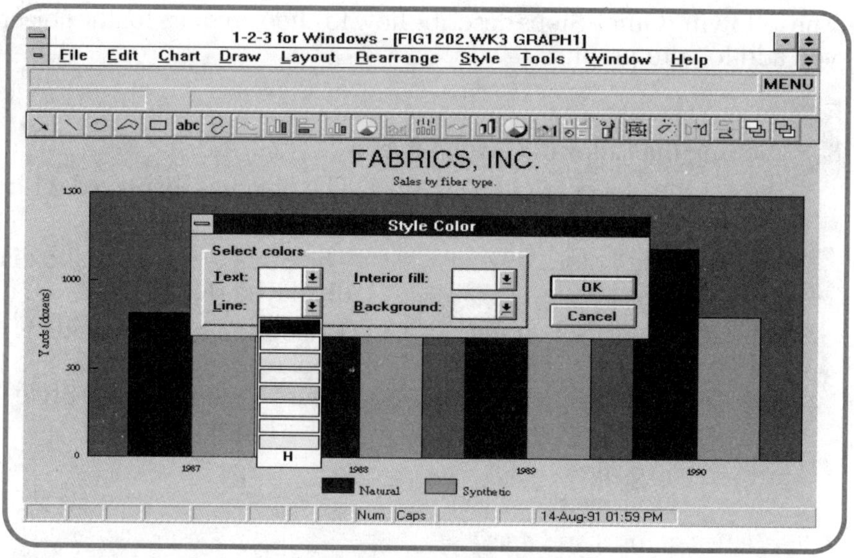

Figure 12.9   The Style Color Lines color palette.

Changing Line Type

You can change the style and thickness of lines that are part of graph objects (for example, arrows and borders of rectangles). You can also add and remove arrowheads from lines, and control the smoothing of corners. The following Quick Steps describe how to change line style.

Changing Line Style

1. Select the object to change.

   The object is displayed with handles.

2. Select Style Lines.

   The Style Lines dialog box is displayed (Figure 12.10).

3. Under Line, use the Style and Width drop-down boxes to select the style and thickness of the lines.

4. Under smoothing, select the extent to which the object's corners are to be rounded.

5. Use the check boxes under Add Arrowheads to place arrowheads at either or both ends of a line.

6. Select OK.

The graph is displayed with the new line styles. □

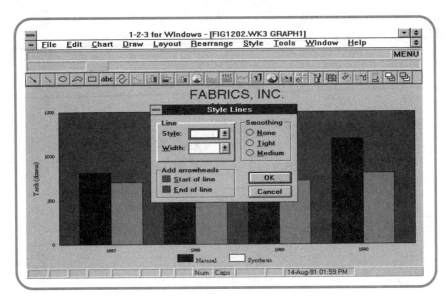

Figure 12.10   The Style Lines dialog box.

Changing Text Alignment

You can change the alignment of text you added to the graph with the Draw Text command. The alignment is relative to the text's center point at the time it was added. Use the following Quick Steps when you want to modify text alignment.

 **Aligning Text in a Graph**

1. Select the text object to align.

The text is displayed with handles.

2. Select Style Alignment.

The Style Alignment dialog box is displayed (Figure 12.11).

249

3. Select Left, Right, or Center
   alignment.

4. Select OK.

The graph is displayed with
text aligned as specified. ☐

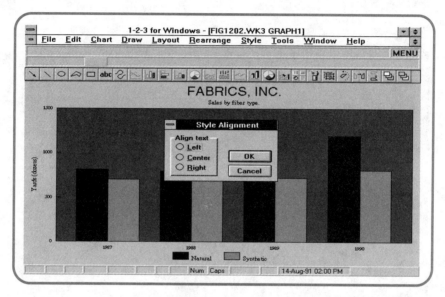

Figure 12.11   The Style Alignment dialog box.

Changing Display Options

The Style Display Options command modifies the way a graph is
displayed when it has been added to a worksheet with the Graph Add
to Sheet command (on the worksheet main menu). These commands
have no effect on the way a graph is displayed in the graph window. The
options are:

A *transparent* graph lets worksheet data behind it show
through. A nontransparent graph (the default) hides
worksheet data behind it.

A *hidden* graph displays in the worksheet as a gray rectangle.
A hidden graph prints normally, however, if you print a
worksheet range that contains the graph.

Updated automatically means that a graph in the worksheet is updated whenever the data it is based on changes. The default is for manual update, done with the Graph Refresh command (on the worksheet main menu).

To change display options for a graph that is inserted in a worksheet, use the following Quick Steps.

Setting Graph Display Options

1. Make the graph window current.

2. Select Style Display Options.

   The Style Display Options dialog box is displayed.

3. Select Transparent, Hidden, and/or Updated Automatically as described above.

4. Select Show Grid Lines to have the worksheet cell grid lines (but not the data) display through the graph when it is inserted in the worksheet.

251

5. Select OK.

   When you make the worksheet that contains the graph active, it is displayed with the selected options. □

The Layout Commands

The commands on the Layout pulldown menu (Figure 12.12) are used to place objects in front of or behind other objects, and to protect objects from modification. As with other graph commands, these commands operate only on the selected object(s).

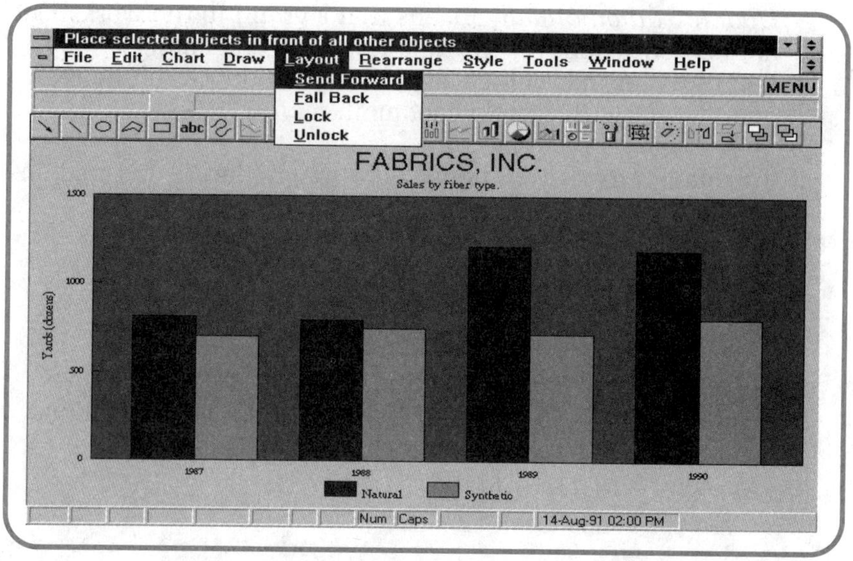

Figure 12.12   *The Layout pulldown menu.*

252

The commands on this menu are as follows:

Send Forward moves the selected object in front of other objects. Such an object may hide objects that are behind it.

Fall Back moves an object behind other objects. An object may be hidden by objects that are in front of it.

Lock protects an object from changes. A locked object's selection handles display as diamonds rather than squares. When an object is locked and you try to change it, 1-2-3 for Windows simply does not perform the task—it does not display a message to inform you that the object is locked.

Unlock removes protection from a locked object.

Changing Graph Window Display

When a graph window is active, you can use the commands on the Window pulldown menu to control window display. This menu is shown in Figure 12.13.

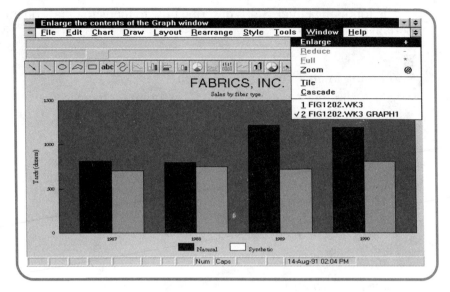

Figure 12.13   The graph Window pulldown menu.

253

Zooming a Graph

The first four commands on the Window menu control how the graph is displayed in its window.

Enlarge enlarges the graph by approximately 100 percent, keeping the window centered on the graph. The window does not change size, but shows only a portion of the enlarged graph. You can select Enlarge one or more times. You can also use the plus key (+) on the numeric keypad to accomplish the same task.

Reduce reduces the graph by approximately 50%, reversing the effect of a single Enlarge command. You cannot reduce a graph smaller than full size (the default, with the entire graph visible in the window). You can also use the minus key (−) on the numeric keypad to accomplish the same task.

Full reduces the graph to its minimum default size. You can also use the asterisk (*) to accomplish the same task.

Zoom lets you zoom in on a selected portion of the graph. You can also use the @ sign to accomplish the same task.

The following Quick Steps describe how to focus the view on an important graph section.

Q Zooming In on a Portion of a Graph

1. Select Window Zoom.

The pointer changes to a crosshair.

2a. *Using the Mouse:*

Point at one corner of the rectangular area you want to view. Press and hold the mouse button, and stretch the rectangle to cover the desired area. Then, release the mouse button.

2b. *Using the Keyboard:*

Use the arrow keys to move the crosshair to one corner of the rectangular area you want to view. Press space bar, and use the arrow keys to stretch the rectangle to cover the desired area. Finally, press Enter.

The graph enlarges to show the selected area in the graph window.

☐

254

All graph commands can be used while a graph is enlarged or zoomed. Figure 12.14 shows a graph window that has been zoomed to show the legend and a portion of the X axis.

Tiling and Cascading Windows

The last two commands on the Window pulldown menu control the way that graph and worksheet windows are displayed in the work area.

Tile arranges all graph and worksheet windows so they do not overlap. Each window has its own, same-size area (Figure 12.15).

Cascade arranges all windows in a partially overlapping stack, much like you might hold a hand of playing cards. The active window is on top, and the title bar of each of the other windows is visible (Figure 12.16).

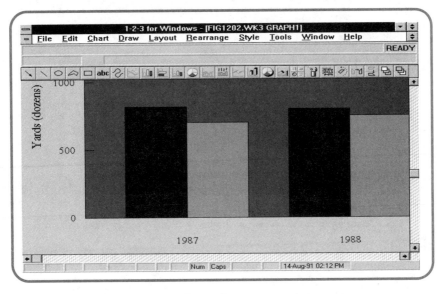

Figure 12.14   *A zoomed graph.*

255

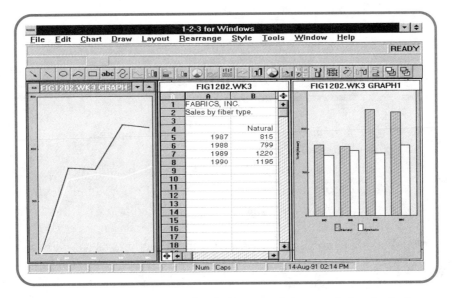

Figure 12.15   *Two graph windows and one worksheet window arranged with Window Tile.*

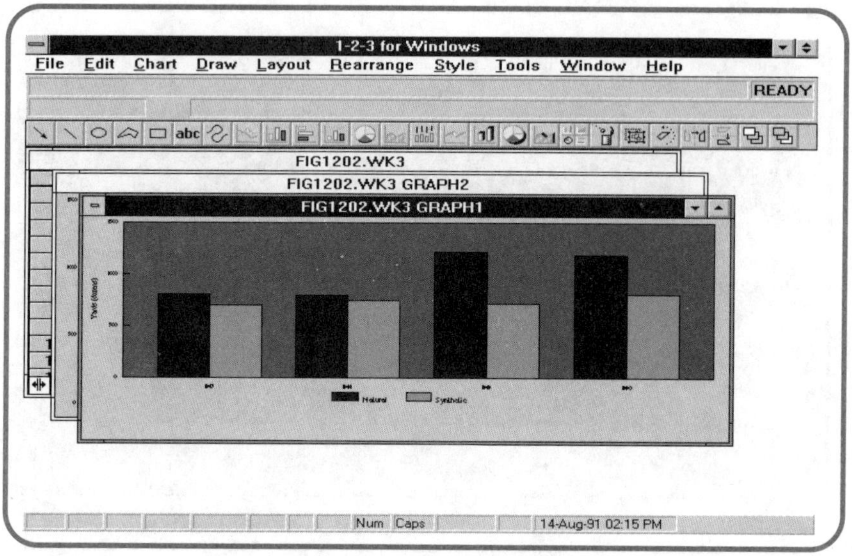

Figure 12.16   *Two graph windows and one worksheet window arranged with Window Cascade.*

What You Have Learned

▶ Once you have created a graph, you can enhance it by adding text and other objects.

▶ The objects you have added to a graph can be modified.

▶ You can zoom in on a portion of a graph to view small details.

▶ The display of graphs that have been added to a worksheet can be modified.

▶ Worksheet and graph windows can be tiled or cascaded in the work area.

File Operations

In This Chapter

▶ *Opening a worksheet file*

▶ *Saving a worksheet file*

▶ *Working with multiple worksheet files*

▶ *Extracting and combining portions of worksheets*

▶ *Exchanging data with other programs*

Worksheet Files

The basic unit of disk storage in 1-2-3 for Windows is the *worksheet file*, which corresponds to the contents of a worksheet window. While you are working on a worksheet in 1-2-3, the worksheet file contents are stored in your computer's random access memory (RAM). RAM is erased when you turn the computer off, so you must save the worksheet file on disk if you want to use it again. You can retrieve it during a future work session. Worksheet files have a WK3 extension, and contain all the information in your worksheet: data, range names, graph definitions, and so on. Named styles and font sets from a worksheet are stored in a separate file with the same name as the worksheet and the FM3 extension.

Opening a Worksheet File

To open an existing worksheet file on disk and read it into a window, use the File Open command. In addition to WK3 files, you can open worksheet files created with Lotus 1-2-3 version 1.1 (WKS extension), 2.x (WK1 extension), and Symphony (WR1 and WRK extensions). Use the following Quick Steps to open a worksheet file.

 Opening an Existing Worksheet File

1. Select File Open, or click the File Open icon.

   The File Open dialog box is displayed (Figure 13.1). The File Name text box contains the name of the current disk, current path, and file name template.

2. In the Directories list box and the Drives drop-down box, select another drive and/or directory if necessary.

   The Files list box lists the names of the files in the current directory that match the file name template.

3. Select the desired file name from the Files List box.

4. Select OK.

   1-2-3 opens a new window and displays the specified worksheet in it. □

 Note: 1-2-3 for Windows can read Microsoft Excel spreadsheet files.

Saving a Worksheet File

To save a worksheet file under its current name (the name in the window title bar), select File Save or click the File Save icon (see Figure 13.1). The file is saved to disk in the current directory using that name with a WK3 extension. The previous version of the file on disk is replaced with the new one. While working on a worksheet, it's a good idea to issue the File Save command once in a while, so your recent changes will be saved. This practice minimizes the chances of serious data loss in the event of a power failure or other system problem.

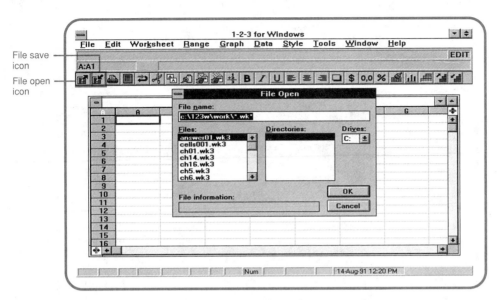

File save icon

File open icon

Figure 13.1   The File Open dialog box.

If the worksheet was originally opened from a WK1, WKS, WRK, or WR1 file, the File Save command will save it with its original name and extension. To save such a file with the WK3 extension, or to make other changes to a file name before saving it, use the File Save As command, as the following Quick Steps describe.

 Saving a Worksheet File Under a New Name

1. Select File Save As.

   The File Save As dialog box is displayed (Figure 13.2). It contains a File Name text box which lists the current disk, directory, and file name.

2. Edit the file name in the File Name text box to give the file the desired name and/or extension.

3. If desired, use the Directories list box and the Drives drop-down box to change to another drive and directory.

4. Select OK.	The worksheet is saved under the name you specified. □

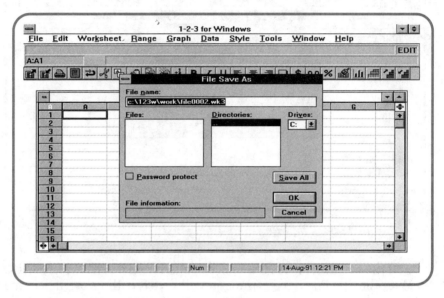

Figure 13.2   The File Save As dialog box.

Saving a File with a Password

You can password protect your worksheet files to provide security for sensitive data. This can be particularly useful when multiple people have access to your system. A file that was saved with a password cannot be retrieved unless the user knows the proper password. Following are the Quick Steps for protecting your worksheet files with a password.

 Saving a Worksheet File with Password Protection

1. Select File Save As.	The File Save As dialog box is displayed (Figure 13.2).
2. If you are saving a new file, type in a file name.	
3. Select the Password protect check box.	

4. Select OK.

    1-2-3 prompts you for a password.

5. Enter a password, then select OK.

    The file is saved with password protection.   □

▶ **Tip:** Use a password you are sure to remember, or keep a written record in a safe place. If you forget your password, you will not be able to access your data.

Using Multiple Worksheet Files

1-2-3 lets you have more than one worksheet file open at the same time. Each open file is displayed in its own worksheet window. A file that is open is *active*; the one file that contains the cell pointer is *current*. You may have more than one active file, but you can have only a single current file.

Even though a single 1-2-3 worksheet has a huge capacity, it is often wise to keep data in several modest size worksheet files instead of a single huge file. Smaller files are easier to use and keep track of. 1-2-3 gives you complete freedom to move and copy data between worksheet files, and to create links that allow formulas in one file to reference data in another file.

Opening an Additional Worksheet File

When you start 1-2-3, it displays an empty worksheet with Untitled in its title bar. You can enter data in this worksheet and later save it using the File Save or File Save As command. If you do not specify your own file name, 1-2-3 will automatically assign default file names FILE*xxxx*.WK3, where *xxxx* is a sequential number starting at 0001.

To open an additional worksheet window containing an existing worksheet file, use the File Open command as described earlier in this chapter. To open a new, empty worksheet window use File New. When you select this command, 1-2-3 opens a new empty window and assigns it a default sequential file name in the form FILE*xxxx*.WK3.

Viewing Multiple Worksheet Files

When you have more than one active worksheet window, you need to arrange them in the work area so the data you are working with is visible. The commands for manipulating individual windows were covered in Chapter 2. Here's a brief review:

▶ You can maximize a window so it fills the entire work area.

▶ You can minimize a window to an icon. A minimized window remains active.

▶ You can change the size, shape, and position of a window.

The *current window* is the one with the highlighted title bar. When multiple windows are active, you can make any active window current in three ways:

▶ If any part of the window is visible, click it with the mouse.

▶ Press Ctrl-F6 one or more times to cycle between all active windows.

▶ Select Window to display the Window pulldown menu (Figure 13.3). The names of all active files are listed at the bottom of the menu. Select the desired window from this list. The current one has a check mark next to the window name.

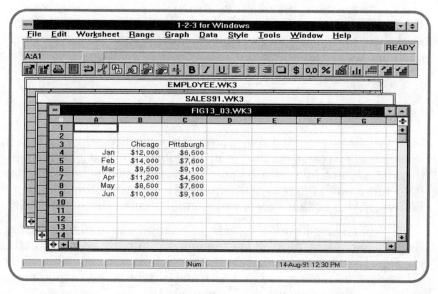

Figure 13.3   The Window pulldown menu lists all active files.

The Window pulldown menu also offers two display options:

Tile arranges all windows, so they do not overlap. Each window has its own, same-size area.

Cascade arranges all windows in a partially overlapping stack, much like you might hold a hand of playing cards. The current window is on top, and the title bar of each of the other windows is visible.

The following special keystroke combinations can be used to move the cell pointer between active files. In all cases, the cell pointer moves to the cell that was last highlighted in the target file.

Keystroke Combination	Result
Ctrl-End Home	Moves the cell pointer to the first active file.
Ctrl-End End	Moves the cell pointer to the last active file.
Ctrl-End Ctrl-PgUp	Moves the cell pointer to the next active file.
Ctrl-End Ctrl-PgDn	Moves the cell pointer to the previous active file.

Saving Multiple Files

When multiple files are active, you save individual files using the File Save and File Save As commands, as described earlier in this chapter. You can also save all active files at one time, as the following Quick Steps describe.

 Saving All Active Files

1. Select File Save As.

   The File Save As dialog box is displayed (Figure 13.2).

2. Select Save All.

   All active files are saved to disk. □

Closing a File

Closing a file means to remove it from memory and close its window. The disk file is not affected. Use the next set of Quick Steps whenever you want to close a worksheet file.

Closing a Worksheet File

1. Make the worksheet window current.

2. Select File Close.

   If the file has been modified since it was last saved, 1-2-3 prompts whether to save it before closing (Figure 13.4).

3. Select Yes to save the file before closing. Select No to close without saving. Select Cancel to cancel the File Close command.

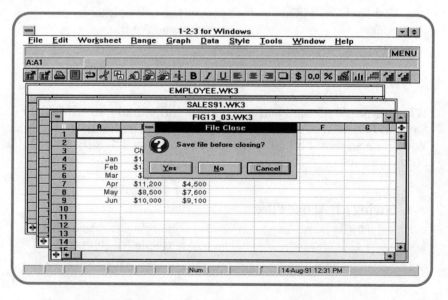

Figure 13.4   The File Close dialog box.

Selecting Data in Another Worksheet File

When using multiple worksheet files, you often need to reference data in one file while working in another. For example, you can copy data from one file to another, and reference one file's data in a formula in another file.

When you specify a range that's in another worksheet, 1-2-3 precedes the range address with the name of the worksheet file enclosed in double angle brackets—for example,

    <<SALES>>A:A1..A:C12.

In addition to using POINT mode (as will be described in the following Quick Steps), you can type the file/range directly. You can specify the range as addresses or as a named range. For the latter, the range must have been named in the source worksheet. For example, the formula @SUM(<<SALES>>WIDGETS) calculates the sum of the values in the range named WIDGETS in the worksheet file SALES.WK3. (Notice that you did not need the WK3 extension in the formula.)

265

Note that there are two types of data transfers between worksheets. If you copy or move data from one worksheet to another, it is a one-time operation. After the copy or move, changes to the data in the source worksheet have no effect on the target worksheet. For a copy or move operation, both the source and target worksheets must be active.

In contrast, referring to a range in another worksheet in a formula or graph data range creates a *link*. Links are updated every time you open the worksheet containing the reference or choose File Administration Update Links. Changes in the source worksheet will be reflected in the target worksheet. To create or update a link, the source worksheet need not be active (but it must be available on disk).

Links are a very powerful feature of 1-2-3. Using links, you can create interconnected worksheet files that refer to each other's data. For example, your retail sales firm may have stores in several cities. You could keep each store's sales data in its own worksheet file, then create a summary worksheet file that uses links to access the data for each store. Each time you retrieve the summary worksheet file, the links will be updated automatically.

A simple link is illustrated in Figure 13.5. Cell B2 in worksheet file SUMMARY.WK3 contains the formula @SUM(<<NEWYORK.WK3>>SALES). In worksheet file NEWYORK.WK3, the range A3..A10 has been assigned the name SALES. Note that the file NEWYORK.WK3 need not be active for this link to work.

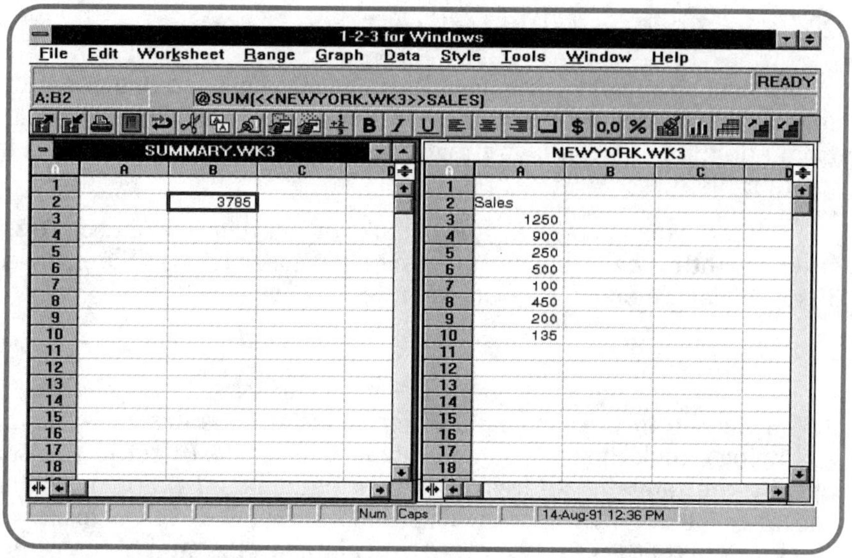

Figure 13.5   Cell B2 in SUMMARY.WK3 is linked to NEWYORK.WK3.

Following are Quick Steps giving general procedures for selecting a range of data in another worksheet file.

Selecting Data in Another Worksheet

Using the Mouse:

1. In the original worksheet, enter a command or a formula to the point where you need to specify a data range.	The formula appears on the input line.
2. Click the title bar of the other worksheet window.	The second worksheet becomes current.
3. Move the mouse pointer to one corner of the data range. If necessary, use the scroll bars to bring the range in view.	
4. Press and hold the mouse button and drag the highlight over the data range.	The range becomes highlighted.

5. Release the mouse button.

6. Click the title bar of the first worksheet window.

7. Continue entering the command or formula.

Using the Keyboard:

1. In the original worksheet, enter a command or a formula to the point where you need to specify a data range.

    The formula appears on the input line.

2. Press Ctrl-F6 one or more times to make the other worksheet current.

3. Move the cell pointer to one corner of the range.

4. Press . (period) to anchor the range, then use the arrow keys to expand the highlight over the data range. Do NOT press Enter.

    The range becomes high-lighted.

5. Press Ctrl-F6 one or more times to make the first worksheet current.

6. Continue entering the command or formula.

    □

267

Extracting and Combining Portions of Worksheets

The File Combine From and Fine Extract To commands are used to copy data between the active worksheet file and a file on disk. These commands are leftovers from earlier versions of Lotus 1-2-3 that did not have the multiple worksheet file capabilities of 1-2-3 for Windows. You'll find that most of the tasks accomplished with File Combine From and File Extract To are more easily done with 1-2-3's three-dimensional and multiple worksheet features.

File Combine From

File Combine From reads data from a worksheet file on disk into the current worksheet. You can read the entire disk worksheet or only a portion of it. With all Combine operations, data from the source worksheet is combined with the active worksheet starting at the current cell. There are three File Combine From options.

Copy copies values from the disk worksheet to cells in the current worksheet, beginning at the curent cell pointer position.

Add adds values from the disk worksheet to values in the corresponding cells of the current worksheet. The result is that each cell in the current worksheet contains a value (not a formula) that is the sum of its original value and the corresponding value in the disk worksheet.

Subtract subtracts values in the disk worksheet from values in the current worksheet.

268

> **Caution:** When using File Combine with the Add or Subtract option, be sure the cells in the two worksheet files line up exactly, or you will get erroneous results.

Combine works with values only. Table 13.1 lists possible Combine results.

Table 13.1   Results of Combine Operations

Source cell	Target cell	Action
Value	Value	Combine occurs
Any	Label, formula	No effect
Label or blank	Any	No effect
Value	Blank	Combine occurs with target cell treated as 0.

> ⊘ **Caution:** Because a File Combine From operation can destroy data in the target worksheet, it's a good idea to save the worksheet first in case you make a mistake.

Following are Quick Steps that explain how to combine all or part of a worksheet file on disk with the current worksheet.

 Combining Worksheets

1. Position the cell pointer in the active specific cell in the worksheet where you want the Combine to occur.

2. Select File Combine From.
   The File Combine From dialog box is displayed (Figure 13.6).

3. Enter the name of the source file in the File Name text box, list box. If necessary, use the Directories list box and the Drives drop-down box to select a different drive and directory.

4. Under Action, select Copy, Add, or Subtract.

5. Under Source, select Entire File or Range. If you select Range, enter the range address or name in the Range text box.

6. Select OK.
   The specified source range is combined with the current worksheet. □

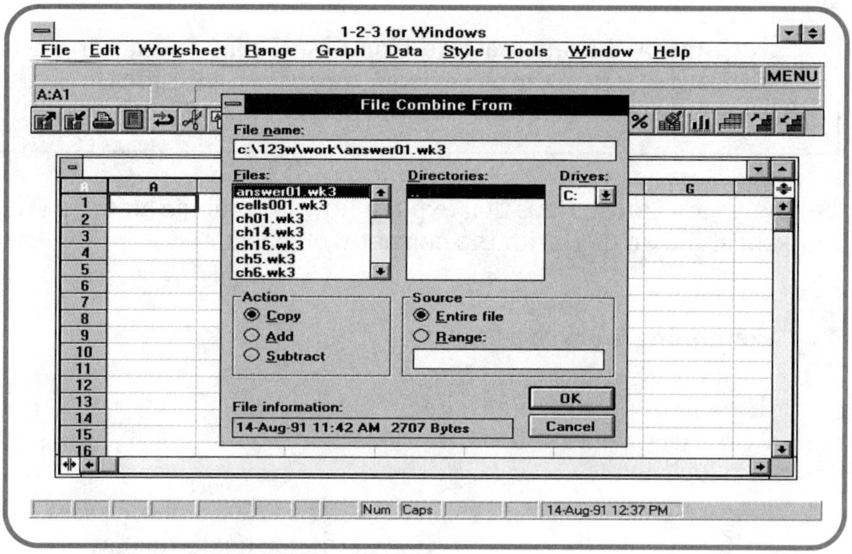

Figure 13.6   File Combine From dialog box.

File Extract To

File Extract saves a portion of the active worksheet to disk in a worksheet file or in an ASCII text file. You can Extract to a new or an existing worksheet file. The extracted data is placed in the target worksheet starting at cell A:A1. If Group mode is on (see Chapter 7), 1-2-3 extracts data from the same range in all worksheets in the current file.

Extracting always copies labels and values to the target file. There are three Extract options:

Formulas extracts formulas to the target worksheet file.

Values converts formulas to values before extracting.

Text extracts to an ASCII text file.

> ▶ **Tip:** An ASCII text file can be read by word processing, database, and other programs. You can use the Text options to transfer data from 1-2-3 to another program. If the other program is a Windows program, however, it is easier to use the Windows clipboard to move data between applications.

The following Quick steps explain how to extract part of the current worksheet file to a disk file.

 Extracting Data to a Disk File

1. Select the range to be extracted from the current worksheet.

   The range is highlighted.

2. Select File Extract To.

   The File Extract To dialog box is displayed (Figure 13.7).

3. Enter the name of the target file in the File Name text box.

4. If necessary, use the Directories list box and the Drives drop-down box to select a different drive and directory.

5. Under Save As, select the extraction method: values, formulas, or text.

6. Select OK.

   The selected range is extracted to the target file. The current worksheet is not affected. □

271

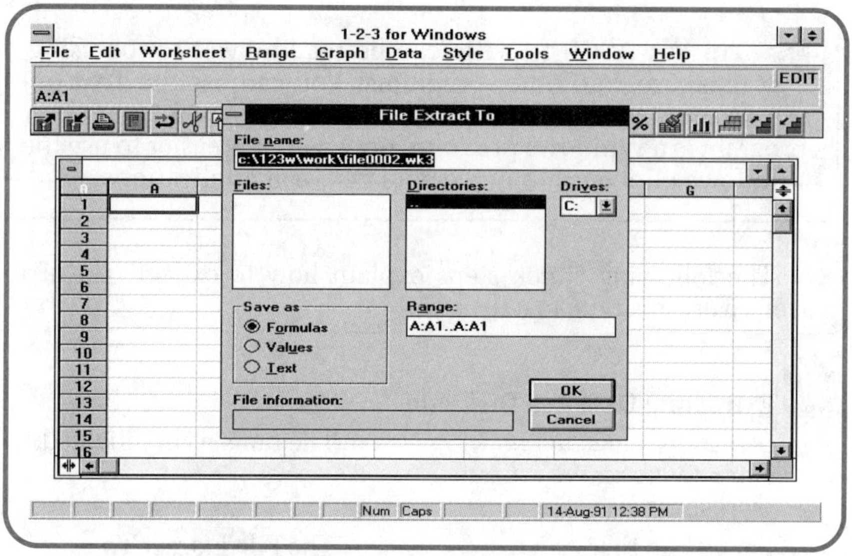

Figure 13.7   The File Extract To dialog box.

Importing Data from Other Programs

To import data from an ASCII text file on disk into a worksheet, use the File Import From command. Since most word processing, database, and other programs can save data in an ASCII text file, you can use File Import From to transfer data from those programs into a worksheet. If the other program is a Windows program, however, it is easier to transfer data using the Windows clipboard. The File Import From command offers two options.

> *File Import From Numbers* analyzes each line in the ASCII file and separates it into labels and values. Each number is placed, as a value, in a separate cell in the worksheet row. Each sequence of characters enclosed in quotation marks ("") is placed in a separate cell as a label. Numbers can be separated by spaces or commas. Characters not recognized as numbers and not enclosed in quotation marks are ignored. Each line of the input file is placed in a separate worksheet row.

File Import From Text reads each line of the ASCII file into a single worksheet cell as a long label. Labels are placed in successive rows of one worksheet column. The maximum line length is 512 characters.

> ▶ **Note:** The Styles option to the File Import From command is used to import styles from another worksheet. See your 1-2-3 documentation for details.

Use the following Quick Steps to import data into a worksheet from an ASCII file.

Ⓠ Importing ASCII Data

1. Move the cell pointer to the first cell to receive imported data.

2. Select File Import From, then select Text or Numbers from the cascade menu.

   The File Import From Text or File Import From Numbers dialog box is displayed. These dialog boxes are identical except for the title (Figure 13.8).

3. If necessary, use the Directories list box and the Drives drop-down box to select another drive and directory.

4. Select the import file name from the Files list box, or enter it into the File Name text box. If the ASCII file you are working with does not have a PRN extension, change the file name to *.* to show all files. In our example, that would be C:\WIN123*.*.

5. Select OK.

   Data from the file is imported into the current worksheet starting at the current cell. □

273

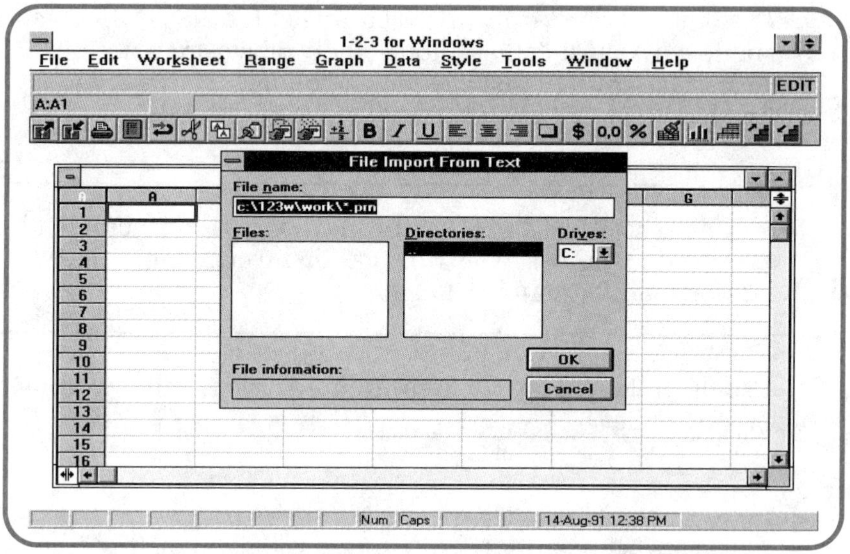

Figure 13.8   The File Import From Text dialog box.

274

When the file is imported, it will overwrite existing data. The number of worksheet rows required is equal to the number of lines in the file. File Import From Text always uses one column. The number of columns used by File Import From Numbers depends on the contents of the file. If you're unsure of the file size, import it into a blank worksheet and then, once you see how much space is required, move the data to its final destination.

File Import Text puts each imported line in a single cell. Often, each imported label will contain several items of numeric and/or text information that should each be in a separate worksheet cell. 1-2-3 can separate, or parse, long labels into individual data items using the Data Parse command. See your 1-2-3 documentation for further information on using Data Parse.

What You Have Learned

- ▶ Worksheet files can be stored on disk for later retrieval.
- ▶ A worksheet file can be password-protected to prevent unauthorized access.

► You can have multiple worksheet files active at one time.

► You can copy and move data between worksheet files, and extablish links between files that are updated automatically.

► Worksheet data can be exported to, or imported from, an ASCII text file.

► Portions of worksheets can be transferred to and from disk.

275

Database Operations

In This Chapter

- ▶ *Structure of a database table*
- ▶ *Creating a database table*
- ▶ *Sorting and searching*
- ▶ *Database statistical calculations*
- ▶ *Data fill commands*

Database Fundamentals

A *database* is a collection of data items that have the same structure but contain different information. Common database examples are a mailing list, parts inventory, or address list. In the following example address list database, each entry, or item, has the same structure: first name, last name, street address, city, and state:

First	Last	Address	City	State
John	Jones	15 Main Street	Baltimore	MD
Wendy	Alexander	101 Alamo Court	Dallas	TX
Pat	Smith	99 Bernardo Dr.	Los Angeles	CA

There are a few terms you need to know to understand 1-2-3 for Windows databases. A *record* is one complete database entry. In the previous example, the information about each individual comprises one record. A *field* is an item of information contained in each record. In our example, there are five fields: First (name), Last (name), Address, City, and State.

The structure of a database fits perfectly into the row and column structure of a 1-2-3 for Windows worksheet. Each database field gets its own column, and each database record gets its own row. The top row of a 1-2-3 for Windows database contains the *field names*, which are unique names identifying the database fields. Field names must be labels.

A rectangular range in a single worksheet that contains information organized in this manner is called a *database table*. A 1-2-3 database can consist of one or more database tables in different worksheets. In this chapter, I will limit discussion to single table databases. Figure 14.1 shows a small 1-2-3 for Windows database table.

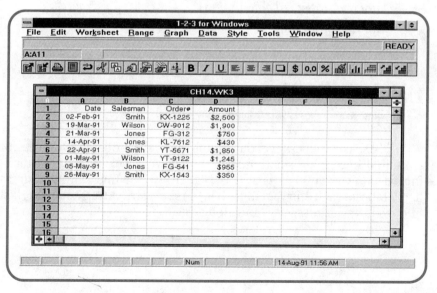

Figure 14.1   A 1-2-3 for Windows database table.

A database table can contain any data you like. The only restriction is that all the entries in a given field should be the same data type: values or labels (or formulas that evaluate to values or labels). While 1-2-3 will not prevent you from entering inconsistent data types in a database field, the inconsistency may result in unexpected results during certain database operations such as searching and sorting.

Creating a Database Table

Before you create a database table, you need to do some planning. Proper planning at this stage will greatly facilitate database operations later. The following points need to be decided:

▶ What information will be included in the database table? For example, does a mailing list need a separate field for "Country" or will it contain only domestic addresses?

▶ How will the information be organized? That is, how will fields be ordered left-to-right in the database table?

▶ What field names will be used? You must use a unique name for each field, and they should be descriptive of the field's contents and also be as short as possible. For example, instead of "FIRST NAME" and "LAST NAME" you could use "FNAME" and "LNAME".

Once the above decisions have been made, creating the database table is quite simple. Use the following steps when you want to create a database table.

1. Use a worksheet region that has enough empty space to hold the table.
2. In the first row of the database table, enter the field names.
3. In the second row of the table, enter the field data for the first record.
4. Enter data for additional records in the third and subsequent rows.
5. If desired, change formatting, label alignment, and column width to best display the data.

279

A database table cannot contain any blank rows. Individual records may contain one or more blank fields, as long as at least one field in the record contains data. To add data to an existing database table, simply move to the first blank row and begin entering the new data.

Data in a database table is different from other worksheet data only because it is organized with a record/field structure. Otherwise it is just like any other worksheet data. You can graph it, print it, edit it, copy it to other worksheets, use it in calculations, and so on. 1-2-3 also has some special capabilities designed specifically for use with database tables. The remainder of this chapter deals with the most frequently used of these capabilities.

Sorting a Database

You may need to sort your database records into a particular order. A mailing list can be sorted into ZIP code order before printing mailing labels, for example, or a customer database can be sorted by "date of last order" to determine active and inactive customers. 1-2-3 for Windows can sort database table records based on the contents on one or more fields. A field used to order records is called a *sort key*.

When sorting a database, you always use a *primary* sort key to order the records. You can also specify a *secondary* sort key, which will be used to order the records when there is a tie in the primary sort key field. *Extra* sort keys may be specified to break ties in the secondary sort key field. Sorts can be in either ascending or descending order. *Ascending order* sorts labels alphabetically A-Z and numbers smallest to largest; *descending order* sorts Z-A and largest to smallest. Use the following Quick Steps to sort the records in a database.

 Sorting a Database Table

1. Select the range that includes all the table records but not the table's field names.

   The range is highlighted.

2. Select Data Sort.

   The Data Sort dialog box is displayed (Figure 14.2).

3. In the Primary Key text box, specify the worksheet column that contains the primary key sort field. You can enter the address of any single cell in that column. Select Ascending or Descending sort order.

4. If you are using a secondary key, enter the address of a cell in the secondary key sort field column under Secondary Key. Select Ascending or Descending order for the secondary key.

5. If you need extra keys, select Extra Keys and specify the extra keys in the dialog box.

6. Select OK.

The database table records are sorted and are placed in the original range. ☐

281

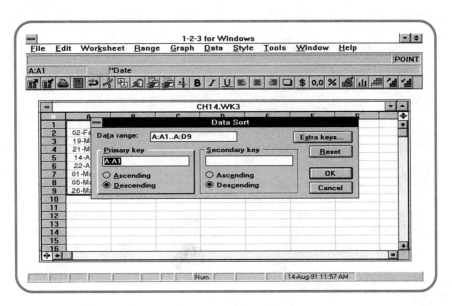

Figure 14.2   The Data Sort dialog box.

Setting Up Criteria

Many database tasks require that you locate certain records in the database. For example:

▶ In a mailing list database, find all addresses in California.

▶ In a sales database, find all sales for amounts less than $500.

▶ In a college student database, find all female freshman who are receiving athletic scholarships.

In 1-2-3, searching a database for specific information is called a *query*. A query locates those database records that meet one or more criteria. In the above examples, "STATE = CA" is a criterion, as is "amount less than 500." To query a database table, you must be able to specify exactly those criteria you are interested in. The next two sections show you how to do this.

Using a Single Criterion

A *criteria range* is a rectangular range of worksheet cells that contains the criteria to be used for searching a database table. A criteria range has the following characteristics:

▶ It may contain as many columns as there are in the database table. At a minimum, it contains one column for each field being matched against criteria.

▶ It contains at least two rows, and may contain more.

▶ It contains the names of the fields being searched in the first row.

▶ It contains search criteria in the second and additional rows.

Look at Figure 14.3, which shows a sample database table and a criteria range containing field names but no criteria. I'll use this table for the following examples. Note that the criteria range need not contain all of the table's field names (although it does no harm), but only the names of the fields being searched.

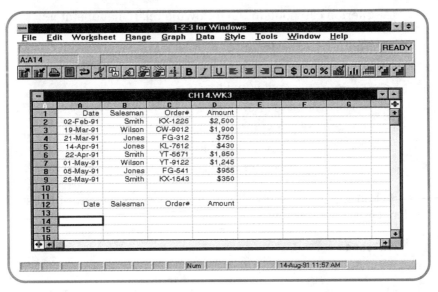

Figure 14.3   The field names in A12..D12 are the first row of a criteria range.

To find an exact match for a label or value field, enter the criterion in the cell directly under the field name in the criteria range. For example, the criteria range:

```
Amount
500
```

would match all records where the Amount field contained the value 500. Likewise, the criteria range:

```
Salesman
Winston
```

would match all records where the Salesman field contained the label "Winston." 1-2-3 normally does not distinguish between upper- and lowercase letters, so "Winston" would match "WINSTON", "wInSTon", and so on. Label prefix characters are ignored in queries.

A criterion can contain the following relational operators:

Symbol	Meaning
=	equal to
<> or ~	not equal to
>	greater than
<	less than
<=	less than or equal to
>=	greater than or equal to

When applied to labels, the relation operators refer to alphabetical order. Thus, the criterion:

```
Salesman
<B
```

would match all records where the label in the Salesman field began with A. Likewise,

```
Amount
<500
```

would match all records with a value less than 500 in the Amount field.

Criteria can contain formulas and @functions. For example, if the database Date field contains date serial numbers, the criterion:

```
Date
>@DATE(91,1,1)
```

will match all entries later than January 1, 1991.

Label criteria can contain the wildcard characters ? and *. A ? in a criterion stands for any single character, and the * stands for any sequence of 0 or more characters. Here are some examples:

Label criterion	Match
pa??	Matches paul, past, and pane, but does not match pad or paper.
pa?er	Matches paper and pacer but not painter.
wa*er	Matches washer, water, wandering traveller, etc.

wa*	Matches anything that starts with "wa".
p*	Matches anything beginning with P.

Using Multiple Criteria

A 1-2-3 database query can find records based on multiple criteria. That means you can set two or more conditions that the search will be based on. In a multiple criteria search, the criteria must be joined by a logical operator. There are two logical operators you need to know:

▶ If two search criteria are joined by the OR operator, a record is considered a match if it matches either one of the criteria (or both of them).

▶ If two search criteria are joined by the AND operator, a record is considered a match only if it matches both of the criteria.

Multiple criteria are entered in the criteria range. The logical relationship between them is determined by their positions within the criteria range:

285

▶ Criteria in the same row of the criteria range are joined by a logical AND.

▶ Criteria in different rows of the criteria range are joined by a logical OR.

Let's look at some examples of multiple criteria. If you wanted to find all records where Amount is greater than or equal to 1000 and Salesman is Smith:

Salesman	Amount
Smith	>=1000

To find all records where the Salesman is Smith or Jones:

Salesman
Smith
Jones

To find all records where Salesman is Smith, and also find those records where Date is later than January 1, 1991 and Amount is less than 500:

```
Salesman            Date                        Amount
Smith

                    >@DATE(91,1,1)              <500
```

In the above examples, a criterion's position in the criteria range determines the database field it is matched against, and also its logical relationship to other criteria in the criteria range. These factors can also be specified by including field names or logical keywords in a criterion:

▶ The #AND# and #OR# keywords are used to specify logical relationships in a criterion.
▶ Field names are used to specify the database field to which a criterion applies.

Here are some examples. To find records where Amount is equal to 1000, you could write:

286

```
Amount
Amount=1000
```

In this case the criterion is under the corresponding field name in the criteria range. This is not necessary, however, as the field name in the criterion has priority. You could as well have written this criterion:

```
Date
Amount=1000
```

and you would get the same result. You could also omit the field name heading altogether.

The logical keywords are used to combine two or more criteria in a single cell. For example, to find records where Salesman is Smith and Amount is greater than 500:

```
Salesman="Smith"#AND#Amount>500
```

Data Query Operations

Remember that the purpose of a criteria range is to find specific records in the database. 1-2-3 has several different query commands that perform different types of query operations. These commands are accessed via the Data Query command, which displays the Data Query dialog box (Figure 14.4).

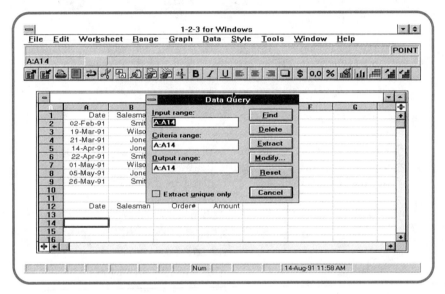

Figure 14.4   The Data Query dialog box.

The three text boxes in the Data Query dialog box are used as follows:

Input range specifies the range containing the database table to be queried. The first row of the input range must contain the database table's field names. You can assign a range name to the database table, if desired, and enter the range name here.

Criteria range specifies the range that contains the query criteria (which are explained earlier in this chapter). The criteria range does not have to be in the same worksheet as the database table; it can be located in another worksheet or worksheet file.

Output range specifies where the results of the query operation are to be placed. The output range is a single row containing the database table's field names. The query results are placed below the field names, and will overwrite any existing data. An output range is needed only for some query operations.

The buttons in the Data Query dialog box select the specific query operation to perform. These are described in the next section.

Data Query Find

Use Data Query Find to locate records for viewing or modification. When you select Find, 1-2-3 highlights the first record in the input range that matches the criteria. You can then use the following keys:

Keys	Action
Left and right arrows	Move between fields in the current record
Up and down arrows	Move to the previous or next matching record
Enter or Esc	Returns you to the Data Query dialog box
F2 (EDIT)	Edit the current cell
Home or End	Move to the first or last matching record in the database table
F7 (Query)	Ends the Data Query Find operation and returns to READY mode

Figure 14.5 shows the sample database table after executing Data Query Find with the given criteria. The highlight is on the first matching record.

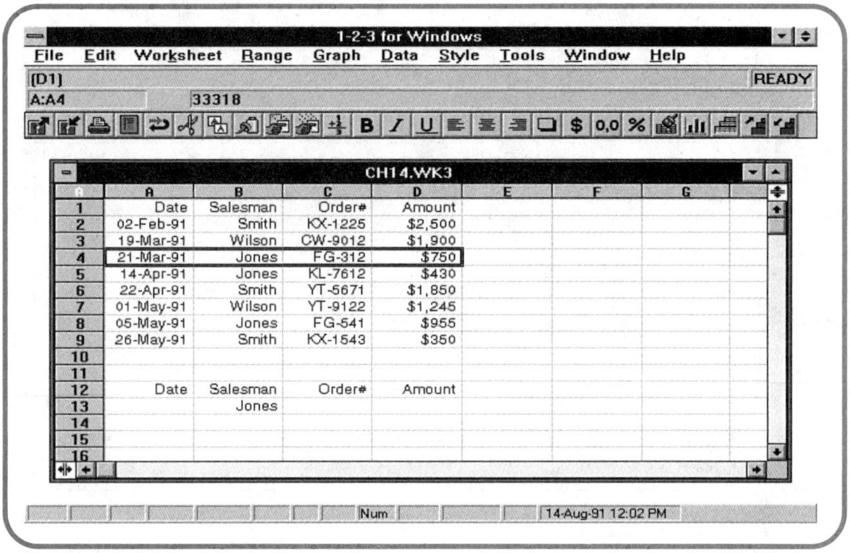

Figure 14.5   The results of executing Data Query Find.

Data Query Extract

Use Data Query Extract to copy matching records from the input range to the output range. All records that match the criteria are copied, including cell attributes. The input range is not modified. If the input range contains formulas, the results of the formulas are copied, not the formulas themselves.

The output range must contain the field names in its first row. You can include only some of the database table field names, and the Extract operation will copy only those fields to the output range. When specifying the output range, you need specify only the row containing the field names. The output range will contain as many columns as there are field names in the output range, and as many rows as there are matching records. All existing data below the output range, to the bottom of the worksheet, will be erased even if extracted records are not placed there. Figure 14.6 shows the result of Data Query Extract using a criteria range of A12..D13 and an output range of A15..D15.

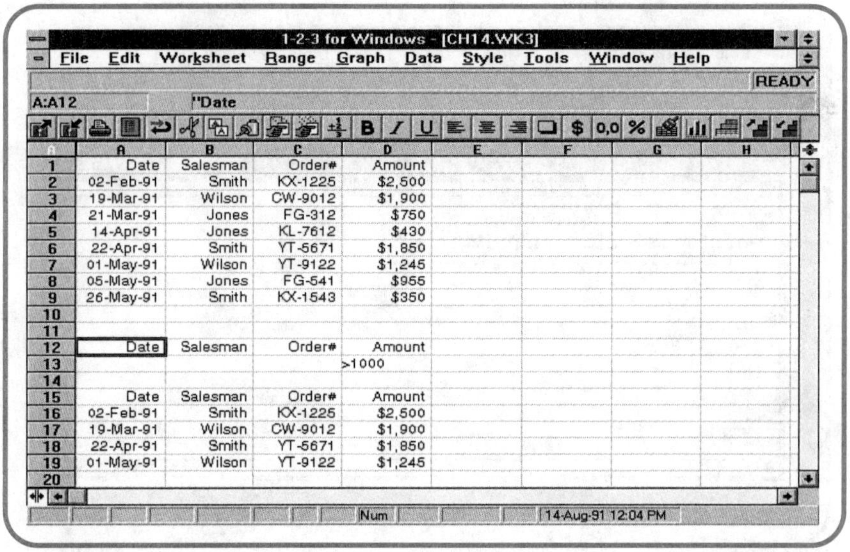

Figure 14.6 Results of a Data Query Extract operation.

> ▶ **Tip:** If you select the Extract Unique Only option in the Data Query dialog box, duplicate records (if any) are eliminated from the output range.

Data Query Delete

Use Data Query Delete command to delete matching records from the database table. Before using Delete, it is a good idea to use Data Query Find to examine the matching records to verify that you will delete the proper ones. 1-2-3 deletes matching records from the database table and moves remaining records up to fill the blank rows. A Data Query Delete operation can be reversed with the Undo command.

Data Query Modify

Use Data Query Modify to modify records in a database table. Data Query Modify first extracts matching records from the database table to the output range. You then edit the extracted records to make necessary changes. 1-2-3 then returns the modified records to the database table. The following Quick Steps explain this procedure.

 Using Data Query Modify

1. Set up a criteria range to match the records you want to modify.

2. Set up an output range containing the database field names.

3. Select Data Query.

   The Data Query dialog box is displayed (Figure 14.4).

4. In the dialog box enter the ranges for the input, criteria, and output ranges.

5. Select Modify.

   The Data Query Modify dialog box is displayed (Figure 14.7).

6. Select Extract, then select Finish.

   Matching records are copied to the output range, and the dialog box is removed.

7. Edit the extracted records as needed. When finished, select Data Query, then select Modify from the Data Query dialog box.

   The Data Query Modify dialog box is displayed again.

8. Select Replace to replace the original database table records with the modified ones. Or, select Insert to add the modified records to the database table while retaining the original versions.

291

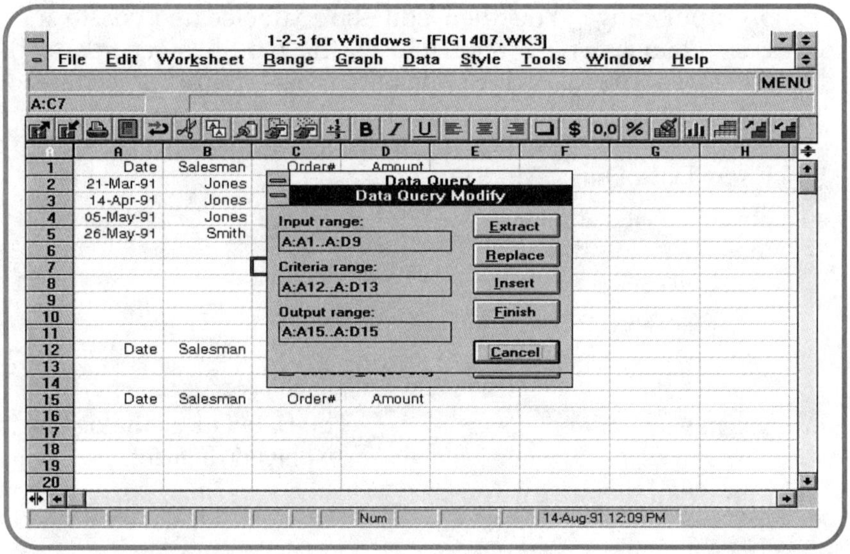

Figure 14.7   The Data Query Modify dialog box.

292

Data Query Reset

The Data Query Reset command erases the contents of the range text boxes in the Data Query dialog box. Select Reset before beginning any new Data Query Operation to be sure you don't accidentally use a range left over from a previous operation.

Performing Database Calculations

1-2-3 for Windows has some specialized @functions that allow you to perform calculations on data contained in a database table. These functions, called database @functions, are very powerful, allowing you to answer questions such as:

▶ In an employee database, what is the average salary of workers over 50 years of age?

▶ In a sales database, what is the total of all sales made in 1990?

▶ In an inventory database, what's the total value of inventory over 60 days old?

All of the database @functions work in the same basic way. Each function takes arguments that specify an input range containing database records, a specific field in the database, and a criteria range. The database @function scans the database table, selecting only those records that meet the criteria and performing its calculation on the contents of the specified field. There are 10 database @functions that perform calculations on worksheet database tables, listed in Table 14.1.

Table 14.1   Database @functions

@function	Description
@DAVG	Calculates the arithmetic average
@DCOUNT	Counts the nonblank cells
@DGET	Returns the cell contents
@DMAX	Returns the maximum value
@DMIN	Returns the minimum value
@DSTD	Calculates the population standard deviation
@DSTDS	Calculates the sample standard deviation
@DSUM	Calculates the sum
@DVAR	Calculates the population variance
@DVARS	Calculates the sample variance

All database @functions take three arguments:

Input specifies the input range containing the database table. This range can be an address or a range name, and must include the field names in the first row of the database table.

Field specifies the database table field on which the @function is to operate. Field can be specified in three ways:

▶ As a field name, enclosed in double quotation marks.

▶ As a numerical offset, giving the column position within the table (the leftmost column is 0).

▶ As an address, specifying a worksheet cell containing either a field name or a column offset.

Criteria is the address of the criteria range. The criteria range for a database @function is the same as a criteria range for a Data Query operation, as explained earlier in this chapter.

An example will help you understand how to use database @functions. Figure 14.8 shows our sales database. We want to calculate, for salesman Smith, the total sales, average sale, and maximum sale. The range A12..A13 contains a criterion that will select records where Salesman="Smith". In cells C15..C17 we enter the following @functions:

`@DSUM(A1..D9,"Amount",A12..A13)` calculates the sum of all of Smith's sales.

`@DAVG(A1..D9,"Amount",A12..A13)` calculates the average of all of Smith's sales.

`@DMAX(A1..D9,"Amount",A12..A13)` returns the largest of Smith's sales.

294

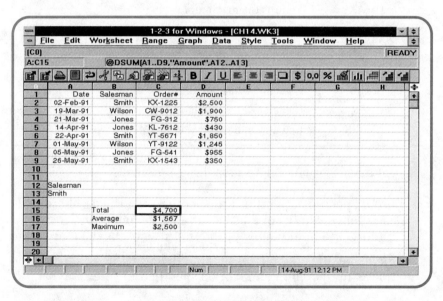

Figure 14.8   Using the database @functions.

Note that by simply changing the criterion in cell A13, we could quickly calculate the same statistics for other salesmen.

Data Fill

The Data Fill command is used to enter a sequence of values in a worksheet range. You can specify the start value, increment, and end value of the sequence. There are many uses for this command, such as:

► Assigning sequential numbers to records in a database table.
► Create a sequence of percentage interest rates when designing a loan payment table.
► Entering weekly dates for the next year in a sales projections worksheet.

When you use Data Fill, you must specify the worksheet range where the sequence of values is to be placed. You must also specify the following:

295

Start specifies the beginning value of the series. The default value is 0.

Step specifies the increment between values in the series. The default is 1.

Stop specifies the fill series terminating value.

When filling a range with values, Data Fill stops when it reaches the end of the specified range or the Stop value, whichever comes first. The following Quick Steps explain how to use Data Fill.

Entering a Sequence of Values

1. Select the range where you want the values.

   The range is highlighted (Figure 14.9).

2. Select Data Fill.

   The Data Fill dialog box is displayed (Figure 14.10).

3. Enter the desired values for Start, Step, and Stop.

4. Select OK.

   The sequence is entered in the worksheet range (Figure 14.11). ☐

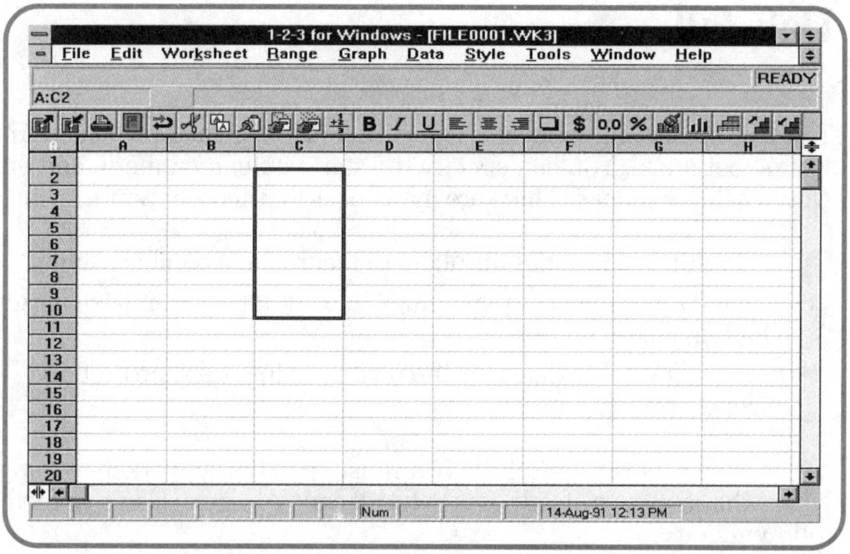

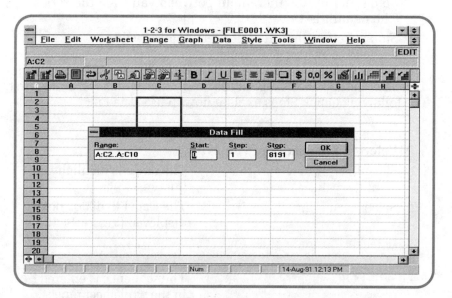

Figure 14.9   To enter a sequence of values, first select the desired range.

Figure 14.10   Display the Data Fill dialog box and enter the desired Start, Step, and Stop values.

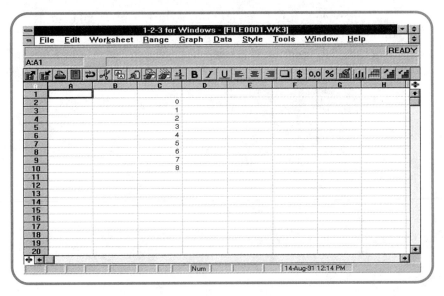

*Figure 14.11   Select OK and the range is filled with the speci-
fied sequence of values.*

297

When using Data Fill to enter a sequence of dates, remember that
1-2-3 stores dates as serial numbers (as covered in Chapter 5). To enter
a sequence of weekly dates, therefore:

▶   The Start value is the serial number of the first date.

▶   The Step value is 7.

What You Have Learned

▶   A 1-2-3 for Windows database table organizes similar data
items in a row and column structure.

▶   Each row in a database table is called a record; each column is
called a field.

▶   You can sort the records in a database table based on the
contents of one or more fields.

▶   You can find, edit, and delete specific records in a database
table.

▶ The database @functions let you perform statistical calculations on data in a database table.

▶ The Data Fill command is used to enter sequences of values in a worksheet.

298

Worksheet Settings

In This Chapter

- ▶ *Changing global settings for a worksheet*
- ▶ *Changing user setup for the 1-2-3 for Windows program*
- ▶ *Using worksheet protection*

Global versus User Settings

1-2-3 for Windows has a variety of settings that control certain aspects of how worksheets appear and how the program operates. Defaults are provided for these settings, but you can change them to suit your preferences. It's easy to become a bit confused about 1-2-3 for Windows' various settings and what they affect. Keep the following distinction in mind.

Worksheet Global settings apply to individual worksheets. The Worksheet Global Settings are saved with a worksheet file and will be in effect when the worksheet file is again opened.

User settings apply to the 1-2-3 for Windows program itself. When you change User Settings, your changes will be in effect for the current work session, and can optionally be saved for future work sessions as well.

Worksheet Global Settings

Use the Worksheet Global Settings command to change Worksheet Global settings. The changes you make here affect the current worksheet, and will be saved with the worksheet and remain in effect the next time you open the file. The Worksheet Global Settings dialog box is displayed in Figure 15.1.

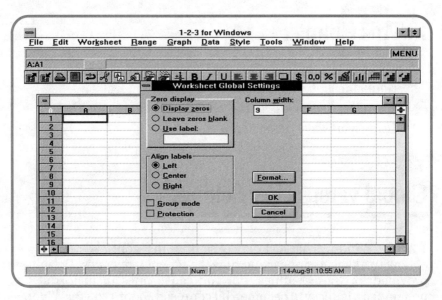

Figure 15.1   The Worksheet Global Settings dialog box.

Under Zero Display, select the way you want worksheet cells containing the value of 0 to display:

Select *Display Zeros* (the default) to display zero values as 0.

Select *Leave Blank* to display 0 cells as empty (although the contents appear in the contents box when the cell pointer is on the cell).

Select *Use Label* to display 0 cells as the specified label (which you enter in the text box).

Under Align Labels, select the default label alignment: Left, Center, or Right. This alignment will be used for all worksheet labels whose alignment hasn't been set with the Style Alignment command.

In the Column Width text box, enter the default column width. This width will be used for all worksheet columns whose width hasn't been set explicitly by the user.

Select the Group Mode check box to enable Group Mode (covered in Chapter 7).

Select Protection to enable worksheet protection (covered later in this chapter).

Select Format to set the default numeric display format. The Worksheet Global Settings Format dialog box is displayed (Figure 15.2). In this box, select the default numeric display format. This format will be used for all value cells that have not been formatted with the Range Format command.

301

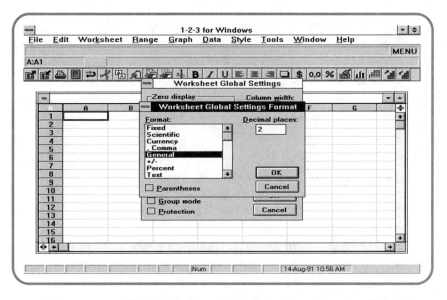

Figure 15.2   The Worksheet Global Settings Format dialog box.

User Settings

Use the Tools User Setup command to change user settings. User settings control certain overall aspects of the 1-2-3 for Windows program, such as whether or not 1-2-3 should "beep" when an error is made. Changes you make will be in effect for the remainder of your work session, and can be saved for future sessions as well (discussed later in this chapter). The Tools User Setup dialog box is shown in Figure 15.3.

302

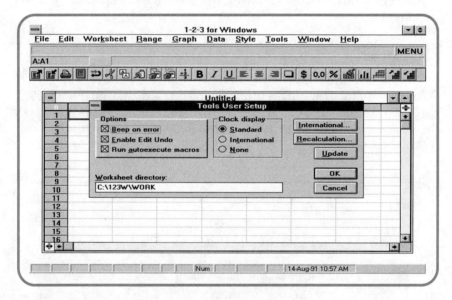

Figure 15.3   The Tools User Setup dialog box.

Under Options, you have the following choices:

Select *Beep on Error* to have 1-2-3 sound a beep whenever an error occurs.

Select *Enable Edit Undo* to enable to Undo feature (discussed in Chapter 5). Because the Undo feature uses some memory, you may need to turn this off when working with large worksheets or multiple Windows applications.

Select *Run Autoexecute Macros* to have 1-2-3 run the autoexecute macro when a worksheet file containing one is opened.

Under Clock Display, select the format of the time displayed in the status bar.

Under Worksheet Directory, specify the disk and/or directory that 1-2-3 will use for saving and retrieving worksheet files.

Select International to display the Tools User Setup International dialog box (Figure 15.4). In this dialog box, you set the way 1-2-3 displays dates, currency amounts, and punctuation.

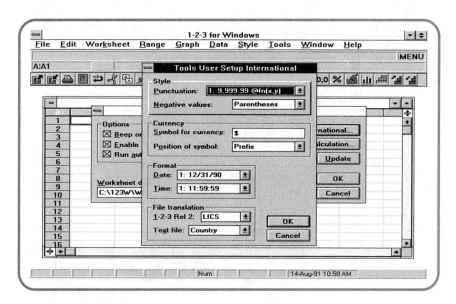

Figure 15.4   The Tools User Setup International dialog box.

Select Recalculation to display the Tools User Setup Recalculation dialog box (Figure 15.5). Settings here determine how and when 1-2-3 recalculates formulas in the worksheet.

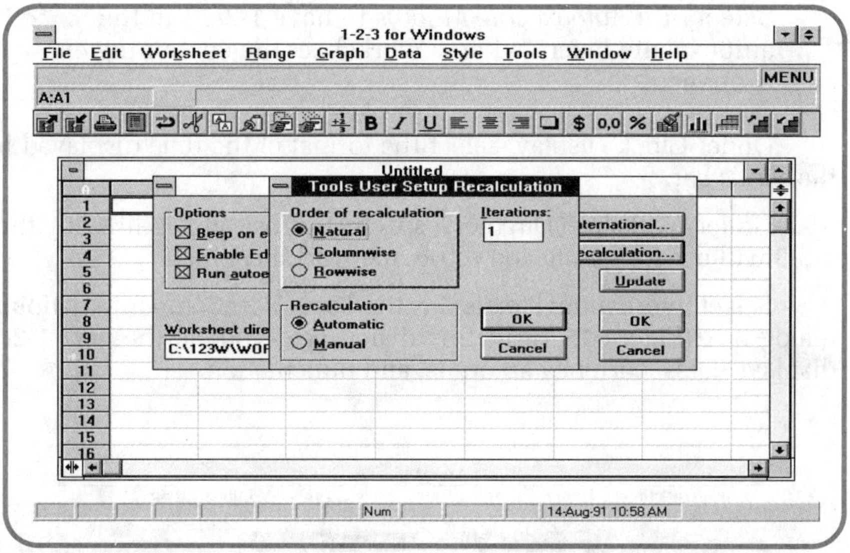

Figure 15.5   The Tools User Setup Recalculation dialog box.

For Recalculation, you have two options:

Automatic is the default setting. Whenever worksheet data changes, 1-2-3 recalculates all worksheet formulas that are affected by the change. Automatic recalculation proceeds in the background so you can continue working while recalculation is being performed.

Manual performs recalculation of formulas only when you press F9 (CALC). Manual recalculation is performed in the foreground so you must wait for it to finish.

For Order of Recalculation, you have three options:

Natural is the default setting. 1-2-3 calculates formulas in the order they depend on each other.

Columnwise starts in cell A:A1 of the first active worksheet file and recalculates on a column-by-column basis.

Rowwise starts in cell A:A1 of the first active worksheet file and recalculates on a row-by-row basis.

Saving User Settings

Changes you make with the Tools User Setup command will remain in effect for the current work session. To save them for future work sessions, select the Update button in the Tools User Setup dialog box (Figure 15.3). Selecting Update saves all user settings except recalculation options, which are saved with the individual worksheet files.

Worksheet Protection

Worksheet protection can be used to prevent accidental changes to important worksheet data. Worksheet protection works at two levels:

305

▶ At the cell level, each individual cell is either protected or unprotected. The 1-2-3 for Windows default is for all cells to be protected when the worksheet protection is turned on. To remove protection from a range, highlight the range and select Range Unprotect. To restore protection to unprotected cells, highlight the range and select Range Protect.

▶ At the worksheet file level, global protection is either on or off, with the default being off. When global protection is on, protected cells cannot be changed; only unprotected cells can be edited, erased, and so on. To turn global protection on or off, select Worksheet Global Settings and select or deselect the Protection check box.

 Note: To remove protection from a range of cells with Range Unprotect, Global Protection must be off.

Here's the general procedure to use for worksheet protection:

1. Create your worksheet with global protection turned off (the default).
2. Decide which cells need to be unprotected. For example, cells where a user will enter data should be unprotected. Formula cells, on the other hand, usually should be protected.

3. Use the Range Unprotect command to remove protection from the appropriate cells.

4. Turn global protection on.

Data in cells that have been unprotected is displayed in a different color, and the indicator line displays a "U" when the cell pointer is on an unprotected cell. When global protection is on and the cell pointer is on a protected cell, the indicator line displays "PR."

What You Have Learned

▶ Worksheet Global settings affect individual worksheets. You can use 1-2-3 for Windows' default settings or change them to suit your needs.

▶ User Settings affect the way the 1-2-3 for Windows program operates. Again, you can use the defaults or change them to suit your needs.

▶ You can use worksheet protection to prevent accidental changes to important data and formulas.

The Solver Utility

In This Chapter

▶ *The types of problems that Solver can analyze*
▶ *Setting up a worksheet model*
▶ *Defining a Solver problem*
▶ *Activating Solver and viewing the answers*
▶ *Generating Solver reports*

Solver Basics

Solver is a utility that provides powerful "what-if" analysis and goal seeking. Solver operates within a worksheet, using a model that you have created. A *model* is nothing more than a worksheet (or part of a worksheet) that uses formulas to calculate results based on the values in one or more input cells. For example, you might create a worksheet model that projects next year's income based on estimates of sales and expenses. With Solver, you specify the results you want from your model. Solver then determines the input values needed to achieve those results.

An Example Problem

To understand the capabilities of Solver, it will help to look at an example problem. Also, it will be helpful to have a real Solver problem to refer to as we work through the chapter. This example problem is relatively simple compared to real-world problems, but it will serve to illustrate how to use Solver.

Imagine that you are opening an automobile rental agency, and you need to decide what proportion of the vehicles will be luxury models and what proportion will be compacts. You want, of course, to maximize your profits. Here are the relevant facts:

▶ Your lot has space for a maximum of 100 vehicles.

▶ Luxury cars cost $15,000 a year to operate and rent for $100 a day.

▶ Compact cars cost $9,000 a year to operate and rent for $55 a day.

▶ From experience you know that, on the average, each compact car will be rented 65% of the time and each luxury car will be rented 50% of the time.

Figure 16.1 shows the worksheet containing our model. Cells B2 and B3 contain the numbers of each type of car, arbitrarily set for the present at 50 luxury and 50 compact. Cells B5 and B6 contain formulas that calculate one year's operating cost for the fleet:

In B5: +B2*9000
In B6: +B3*15000

Cells B8 and B9 calculate the number of days each type of car will be rented per year:

In B8: +B2*365*0.65
In B9: +B3*365*0.5

Cell B11 calculates the Annual Gross Income:

+B8*55+B9*100

Finally, cell B13 calculates Gross Annual Profit by subtracting the cost of operation from the total rental income:

+B11 - (B5+B6)

For the initial values of 50 of each type of car, we see that expected profit is $364,938.

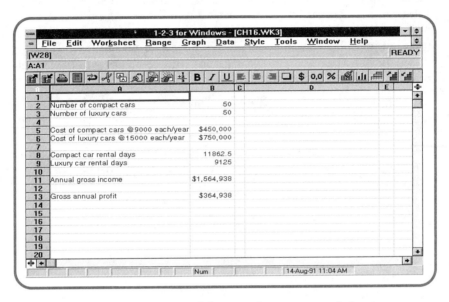

	A	B	C	D	E
1					
2	Number of compact cars	50			
3	Number of luxury cars	50			
4					
5	Cost of compact cars @9000 each/year	$450,000			
6	Cost of luxury cars @15000 each/year	$750,000			
7					
8	Compact car rental days	11862.5			
9	Luxury car rental days	9125			
10					
11	Annual gross income	$1,564,938			
12					
13	Gross annual profit	$364,938			

Figure 16.1   The automobile rental agency worksheet.

The goal is to determine the values required in cells B2 and B3 (the number of each type of car) that will result in the maximum value in cell B13 (annual profit). This is just the type of problem for which Solver was designed. When you use Solver, there are three types of cells you must specify, discussed next.

Adjustable Cells

Adjustable cells are cells that Solver can change, or adjust, as it solves the problem. An adjustable cell can contain only a value, not a label or a formula, and cannot be protected. In our example, the adjustable cells are obvious: B2 and B3. In more complex models, the appropriate adjustable cells may not be so obvious. When deciding on adjustable cells, think of those cells whose contents affect the final result of the model. Remember that an adjustable cell must be used in a formula calculation in your worksheet model.

Some Solver problems involve only a few adjustable cells, while others require many more. There is no limit on the number of adjustable cells you can use.

309

Constraint Cells

Constraint cells tell Solver about conditions that must be met by the solution(s) to the problem. In our example, one constraint is the total number of cars. Your facility will hold a maximum of 100 cars, so there's no point in looking for answers that require a larger number. By setting this constraint we tell Solver "Do not find answers where the total number of cars is greater than 100."

Constraints are entered in the worksheet as logical formulas that depend, either directly or indirectly, on one or more of the adjustable cells. The constraint formula should be written so that it evaluates as TRUE when the constraint is met, and as FALSE when the constraint is not met. For the constraint on total number of cars, we would use the following formula:

```
(B2+B3)<=100
```

Constraint formulas can use only the simple logical comparison operators:

> (greater than)
< (less than)
>= (greater than or equal to)
<= (less than or equal to)
= (equal to)

The <> operator (not equal to) and compound operators (#AND#, #OR#, #NOT#) cannot be used. Constraint formulas can be entered in any unused worksheet area. While not required, it is a good idea to put labels in adjacent cells to identify the constraint cells.

The Optimal Cell

The *optimal cell* is the single worksheet cell for which you want to find the maximum or minimum. Having an optimal cell is optional—you can define a Solver problem without one. In most problems, you will have an optimal cell. Your goal is to find the adjustable cell values that will maximize or minimize a particular worksheet cell. In our example, B13, Gross Annual Profits, is the optimal cell. The optimal cell must contain a formula that depends, either directly or indirectly, on the values in the adjustable cell(s).

If your problem definition includes an optimal cell, Solver will calculate several answers including the optimal answer. If you do not specify an optimal cell, Solver will find several answers that meet the constraints without making any effort to maximize or minimize any cell.

Using Solver

Now that we have covered the basic concepts of Solver, it's time to look at the actual steps involved in using it. I'll continue to use the automobile rental agency example from above.

Setting up the Adjustable Cells

There are no special steps involved in setting up the adjustable cells. You can enter your own "educated guess" at the problem, or any arbitrary figures. Solver will modify these cells, but saves their initial values. For our problem, leave the initial values of 50 and 50 in the cells.

Setting Up the Constraint Cells

I mentioned one constraint previously: that the total number of cars be no more than 100. For that constraint, put the formula **(B2+B3)<=100** in cell E3. There are two other constraints: your franchise agreement requires you to have at least 20 of each type of car. Enter the appropriate formulas in cells E4 and E5 as follows:

In E4: **+B2>=20**
In E5: **+B3>=20**

After you enter identifying labels in D2..D5, the example worksheet will appear as in Figure 16.2. Note that all of the constraint cells evaluate as 1 (TRUE) because the initial values in cells B2 and B3 satisfy all of the constraints. You're now ready to activate Solver.

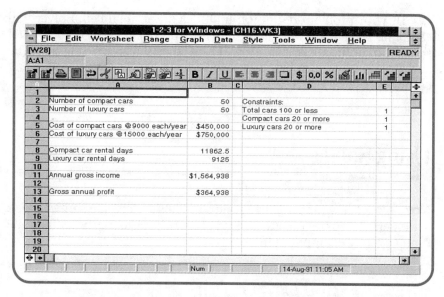

Figure 16.2 *The automobile rental agency worksheet with constraint formulas entered.*

Activating Solver

To activate Solver, select the Tools command on the main worksheet menu, then select Solver from the pulldown menu. The Solver Definition dialog box appears, as shown in Figure 16.3.

Worksheet gives the name of the current worksheet file. You cannot change this information. To tell Solver about your problem, you will need to make entries in all three of the fields in this dialog box.

In Adjustable Cells, enter the problem's adjustable cells. You can enter range names or cell addresses. If the cells are not in a contiguous range, enter their addresses separated by semicolons: A1;B6..B8;F9, for example.

In Constraint Cells, enter the problem's constraint cells. Again, you can enter range names or cell addresses.

In Optimal Cell, enter the address or range name of the problem's optimal cell, if you are using one.

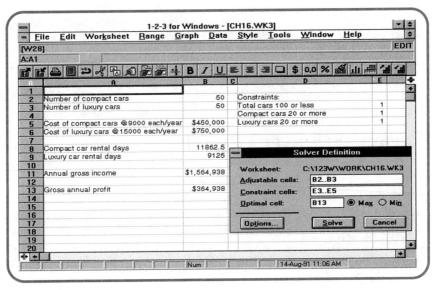

Figure 16.3   The Solver Definition dialog box.

If you are using an optimal cell, select either Max or Min to tell Solver whether to maximize or minimize the optimal cell.

Select the Options button to display the Solver Options dialog box. The one option available is Number of Answers—the number of answers Solver will find for the problem. Enter a number between 1 and 999; the default is 10. The value entered here is only a suggestion. Depending on the nature of the problem, Solver may find more or fewer answers.

For our example, enter `B2..B3` for the adjustable cells, `E3..E5` for the constraint cells, and `B13` for the optimal cell, and choose Max. Figure 16.3 shows the Solver Definition dialog box with the entries made for the example problem.

Once the problem is defined, select Solve to have Solver begin solving the problem. As it is working on the problem, Solver displays a progress report in a window. Our example will take only a few seconds to solve, but complex problems can take much longer. You cannot use your computer for anything else while Solver is calculating, so you may wish to schedule long calculations for lunch hour or evenings. If you need to interrupt Solver, select Cancel in the Solver Progress dialog box.

> ▶ **Tip:** Solver problem definitions are saved with your worksheet.

Reviewing Solver's Results

When the problem has been solved, the Solver Definition dialog box is replaced with the Solver Answer dialog box, as shown for our example in Figure 16.4. This dialog box tells you how many answers were found, and lets you display each answer in the worksheet. At first, answer #1 is displayed. If you requested an optimal cell in your problem definition, this is the optimal answer.

Answers themselves are displayed in the worksheet, in the adjustable cells. In Figure 16.4 the first, or optimal, answer is being displayed. You can see that a mix of 80 compact cars and 20 luxury cars will maximize your profits. The optimal cell shows the expected gross profit for this mix of cars: $388,900.

The buttons in the Solver Answer dialog box let you review other, nonoptimal answers.

Select *Next* to view the next answer.

Select *First* to view the optimal answer again.

Select *Original* to view the original values that were in the worksheet before you activated Solver.

Select *Report* to generate Solver reports (discussed later in this chapter).

Select *Solve* to have Solver generate more answers, if the number of answers found is less than the number requested in the Solver Options dialog box. If you select Solve and Solver cannot find any more answers, it displays a message to that effect.

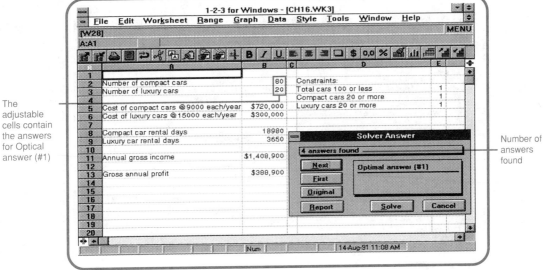

The adjustable cells contain the answers for Optical answer (#1)

Number of answers found

Figure 16.4   The Solver Answer dialog box. Three answers have been found, and answer #1, the optimal answer, is being displayed in the worksheet.

315

For example, Figure 16.5 shows the worksheet after selecting Next. This answer tells you that if you have a mix of 50 compact cars and 50 luxury cars, you can expect a gross profit of $364,938.

Solver does not automatically save its answers. You must do so by displaying the desired answers in the worksheet, then saving the worksheet file. To save several different answers, you must display each one and save the file under different names using the File Save As command. The Solver problem definition is also saved with the worksheet file.

Solver Reports

Solver can generate a variety of reports that contain information on the answers that were found or, if no answers could be found, the attempts. To generate reports, select the Report button in the Solver Answer dialog box. The Solver Report dialog box will be displayed (Figure 16.6).

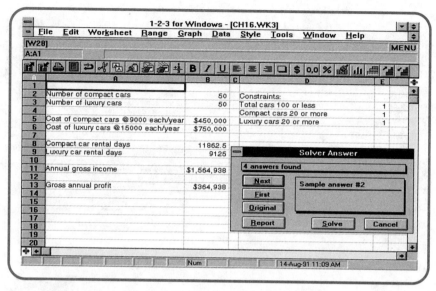

Figure 16.5   The automobile rental agency worksheet with Solver answer #2 displayed.

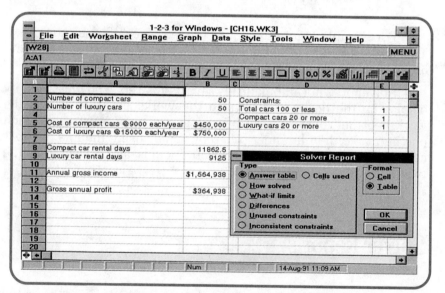

Figure 16.6   The Solver Report dialog box.

Report Formats

Solver reports are available in two formats. *Cell format reports* provide information about a single cell in the worksheet model. When you request a single cell report, Solver displays a dialog box containing the requested information about one worksheet cell, and highlights that cell in the worksheet. For example, Figure 16.7 shows a cell format What-If Limits report for our auto rental model. This report tells you that in solving the problem, Solver tried values between 20 and 80 for adjustable cell B2. In the report dialog box, select Next to display information about the next cell; select Cancel to close the report window and return to the Solver Report dialog box.

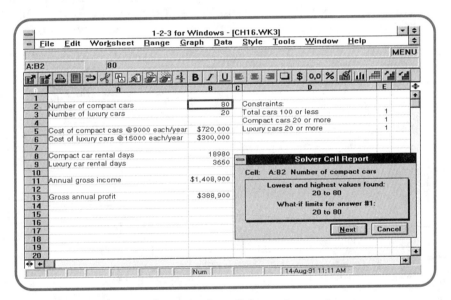

Figure 16.7   A Solver single cell format report.

Table format reports provide detailed information about the various aspects of the current problem. When you request a table report, Solver creates a new worksheet file and places the report in the file. The file is assigned a name similar to the report name. You can modify or accept the default name. This new worksheet file can be used like any other worksheet file: saved, graphed, printed, and so on. You'll see examples of table format reports later in the chapter.

In both report formats, Solver lists both the addresses and range names for cells. If you have not assigned a range name to a cell being reported on, Solver creates a name consisting of the first label found to the left of the cell combined with the first label it finds above the cell.

Types of Reports

Solver offers seven different types of reports. All report types are available in table format, and all types except Answer Table and How Solved reports are also available in cell format.

Answer Table Report

An Answer Table report lists all of the answers that Solver found for the just-solved problem. If no answers were found, attempts are listed. Answer Table report is available only in table format. The Answer Table report for our auto rental agency example is shown in Figure 16.8.

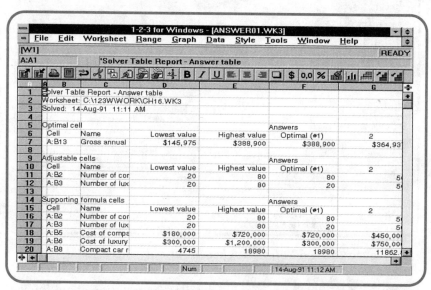

Figure 16.8 *The Answer Table report for the auto rental agency problem. Only part of the report is visible because it is too wide for the window.*

The Answer Table report lists the lowest and highest values used for each cell, plus the optimal value for each cell (if an optimal cell was included in the problem definition) and the value corresponding to each answer. The report has the following sections:

Optimal Cell reports values for the problem's optimal cell, if one was included in the problem definition. Otherwise this report section is not included.

Adjustable Cells reports values for each adjustable cell in the problem.

Supporting Formula Cells reports values for all other worksheet cells that Solver used to solve the problem.

Looking at the report in Figure 16.8, you can see, for example, that the range of Gross Annual Profit figures found by Solver ranged from a low of $145,975 to the optimal value of $388,900.

Cells Used Report

The Cells Used report provides information about which cells Solver used to solve the problem. This report is available in both single cell and table formats. In single cell format, the report window lists the name and address of the cell, plus information about the cell: whether it's an adjustable cell, constraint cell, and so on. A Cells Used report window is shown in Figure 16.9.

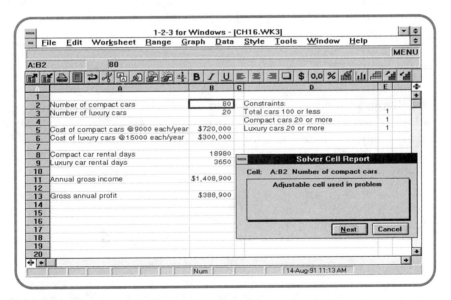

Figure 16.9   A Cells Used report in single cell format.

If you display a Cells Used report in table format, information about all cells in the problem is placed in a table in a worksheet file. This type of report for our auto rental store example is shown in Figure 16.10.

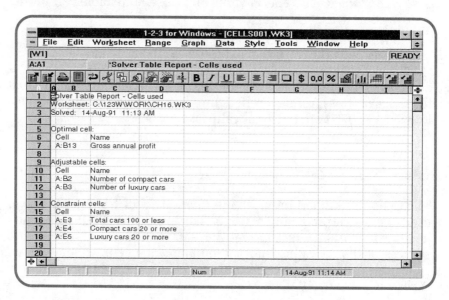

Figure 16.10   A Cells Used report in table format.

Differences Report

A Differences report displays the differences between two answers or attempts, both as an amount and as a percentage. This report is available in both single cell and table formats. Whichever format you select you must first specify which answers to compare, using the Solver Report Differences dialog box shown in Figure 16.11.

Under Compare Answers, enter the numbers of the two answers to be compared. Under For Differences >=, specify the minimum difference for which a comparison will be made. If you selected a table format report, this dialog box will also display a Create Report in File text box.

The Solver Cell Report text box shown in Figure 16.12 shows a single cell format Differences report. This report compares answers 1 and 2 for cell B2, Number of Compact Cars. Figure 16.13 shows a table format report comparing the same two answers for all cells used in the report.

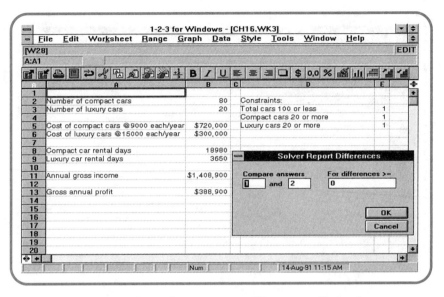

Figure 16.11   The Solver Report Differences dialog box.

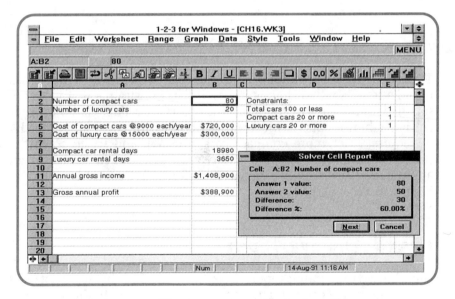

Figure 16.12   A Differences report in single cell format.

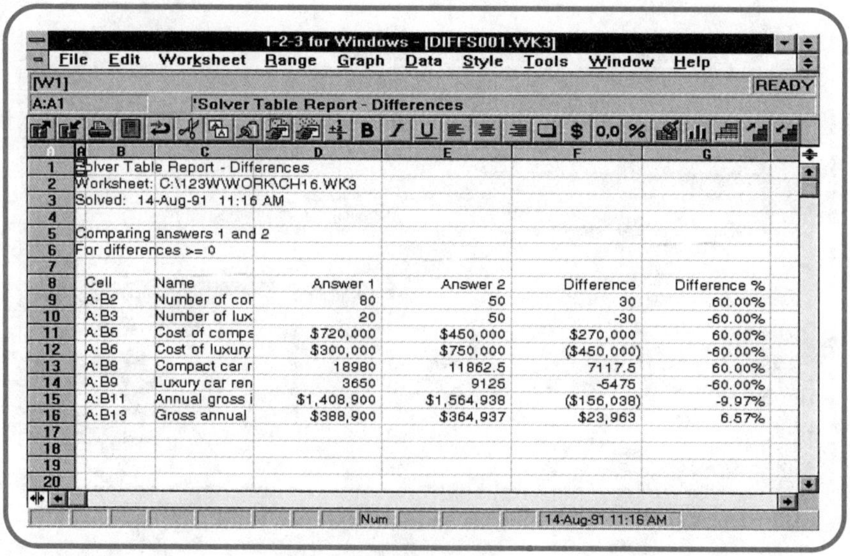

1-2-3 for Windows - [DIFFS001.WK3]

File Edit Worksheet Range Graph Data Style Tools Window Help

[W1] READY

A:A1 'Solver Table Report - Differences

Solver Table Report - Differences
Worksheet: C:\123W\WORK\CH16.WK3
Solved: 14-Aug-91 11:16 AM

Comparing answers 1 and 2
For differences >= 0

Cell	Name	Answer 1	Answer 2	Difference	Difference %
A:B2	Number of cor	80	50	30	60.00%
A:B3	Number of lux	20	50	-30	-60.00%
A:B5	Cost of compa	$720,000	$450,000	$270,000	60.00%
A:B6	Cost of luxury	$300,000	$750,000	($450,000)	-60.00%
A:B8	Compact car r	18980	11862.5	7117.5	60.00%
A:B9	Luxury car ren	3650	9125	-5475	-60.00%
A:B11	Annual gross i	$1,408,900	$1,564,938	($156,038)	-9.97%
A:B13	Gross annual	$388,900	$364,937	$23,963	6.57%

Num 14-Aug-91 11:16 AM

322

Figure 16.13 A Differences report in table format.

Inconsistent Constraints Report

The Inconsistent Constraints report can be generated only if Solver has found attempts rather than answers. It lists constraints that were not satisfied for the current attempt. This report is available in both single cell and table formats. To illustrate this, change the constraint in cell E4 to require 90 or more compact cars (+B2>90), and try to solve the problem. Since Solver cannot solve this problem, it generates an attempt, and the resulting Inconsistent Restraints report is shown in Figure 16.14.

Unused Constraints Report

The Unused Constraints report lists any constraints that were not used to find the current answer. This report is available in both single cell and table formats, but only if unused constraints exist. The report lists the cell address, name, and formula for each unused constraint. It also lists Becomes Binding if Written As, which shows how the constraint could be modified so it would be binding on the current answer.

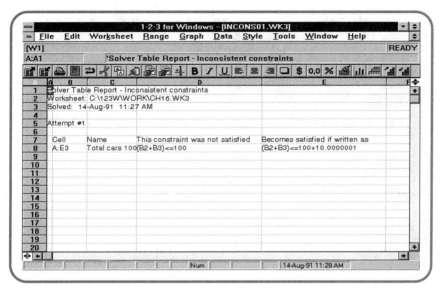

Figure 16.14   An Inconsistent Constraints report in table format.

323

An unused constraint can result from various conditions, and it does not mean there is an error in the problem. For example, if a problem includes the constraints +G5<20 and +G5<30, the second constraint will be unused because any answer that meets the first constraint will also meet the second constraint. Figure 16.15 shows the Unused Constraints report for our auto rental agency example in table format. This report tells you that the constraint in cell E4 was not used in the current solution.

What-if Limits Report

The What-if Limits report shows the range of values that could be used in each adjustable cell while still satisfying all of the problem's constraints. This report is available in both single cell and table formats. A What-if Limits report can be obtained only when an answer is being displayed in the worksheet.

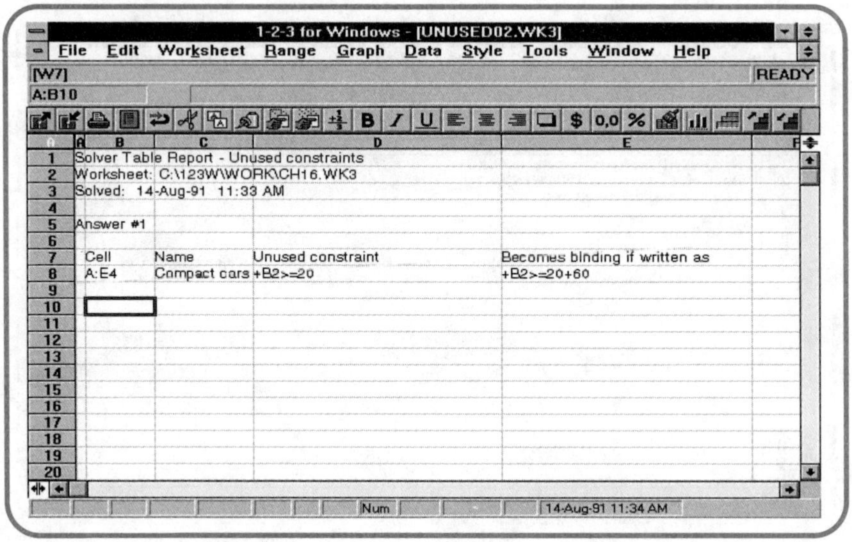

Figure 16.15   *The Unused Constraints report for the auto rental*
agency problem.

For each adjustable cell, the What-if Limits report lists the highest and lowest values found for all answers, plus the highest and lowest values found for the currently displayed answer. Figure 16.16 shows a table format What-if Limits report for answer #1 of the auto rental agency problem.

How Solved Report

The How Solved report gives information about how the current problem was solved. This report is available only in table format. Figure 16.17 shows the How Solved report for our auto rental agency example.

The How Solved report lists the values, names, and addresses of all cells used in the problem. The values listed are for the currently displayed answer or attempt. Binding constraint cells are listed also, along with the logical formula of each constraint. Depending on the specific problem, the How Solved report may also list additional information.

If one or more constraints were not used to find the current answer, those cells are listed under Unused Constraints. For such cells, Becomes Binding if Written As shows how you could modify the unused constraint's logical formula to make it binding (that is, used) for the current answer.

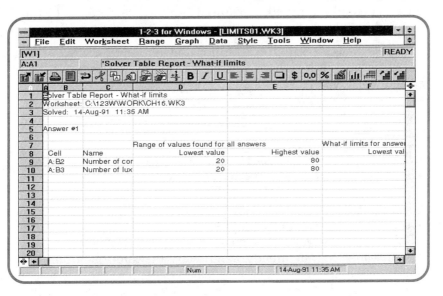

Figure 16.16   A What-if Limits report on the auto rental agency example problem.

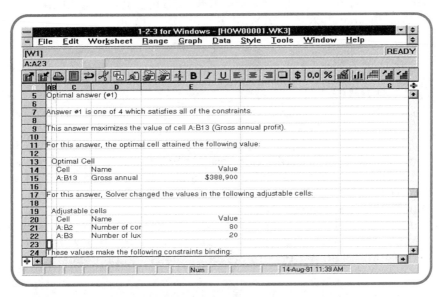

Figure 16.17   The How Solved report for our auto rental agency problem. Only a portion of the report is visible in the worksheet window.

If Solver is reporting on an attempt rather than an answer, Unsatisfied Constraints lists the addresses, names, and logical formulas of the unsatisfied constraints. Becomes Satisfied if Written As shows how you could modify the constraint cell's logical formula to make it satisfied (that is, display as 1).

If Solver is reporting on a solution that required guesses, Guessable Cells lists the cells for which guesses were required, showing initial and current guess values.

Using @functions in Solver Problems

Because of the way Solver operates, there are limitations on using @functions in Solver problems. Certain @functions cannot be used in a Solver problem cell. In this context, a problem cell is any cell whose contents affect, either directly or indirectly, the value of the optimal cell or any constraint cell. Generally speaking, the unallowed @functions are the string, date, time, database, and some special @functions.

Your 1-2-3 for Windows documentation contains a list of @functions that are allowed in problem cells. If you're not sure about a particular @function, try solving the problem. If Solver detects an @function that it can't deal with, it will inform you.

A Warning

Solver is a very powerful worksheet tool. It allows you to do things in your worksheets that were not possible before. Nevertheless, Solver cannot think for you. Before you make an important decision based on a Solver answer, it's important to check that your worksheet model is valid and that the Solver problem was set up properly. The *1-2-3 Solver Guide* included with your 1-2-3 for Windows package contains a number of sample problems. I recommend going though these to increase your familiarity with Solver methods and problems.

What You Have Learned

- ► The Solver can provide answers to complex "what-if" problems in your worksheets.
- ► Solver works with a worksheet model that calculates results based on values in the worksheet.
- ► Solver can find the optimal answer to your problem, or calculate a range of possible answers.
- ► In addition to answers, Solver can create detailed reports on how it found the answer.

Using the Icon Palette

In This Chapter

▶ *What is special about SmartIcons?*

▶ *Changing the icon palette position*

▶ *Hiding the icon palette*

▶ *Changing the SmartIcons on the Icon Palette*

▶ *Using SmartIcons to run macros*

What are SmartIcons?

You've been introduced to SmartIcons earlier in the book. A *SmartIcon* is a small graphic symbol, or button, that is displayed on the 1-2-3 for Windows screen in the *Icon Palette*. Each SmartIcon is associated with an important worksheet command or task; when you click the SmartIcon the task or command is executed immediately. Figure 17.1 shows the Icon Palette with the default SmartIcons. Your screen may show a different set of SmartIcons on the Icon Palette.

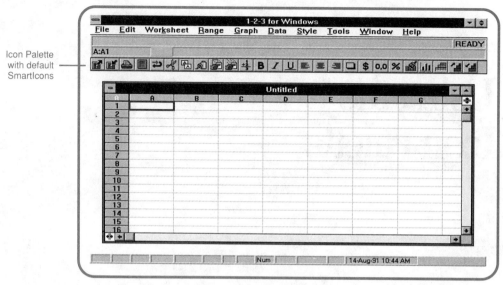

Icon Palette
with default
SmartIcons

Figure 17.1   *SmartIcons are displayed on the Icon Palette.*

SmartIcons are handy timesaving shortcuts, but they are more than that as well. (That's why they are called Smart!) You can:

▶   Change the screen position of the Icon Palette, or hide it altogether, to suit your preferences.

▶   Select from over 60 standard, predefined SmartIcons, displaying on the Icon Palette only those that you use frequently.

▶   Assign your own macros to SmartIcons so that clicking the SmartIcon executes the macro.

 Tip: You must have a mouse to use SmartIcons; you cannot select a SmartIcon using the keyboard.

Moving and Hiding the Icon Palette

The default Icon Palette position is near the top of the 1-2-3 screen, as shown in Figure 17.1. You can change the position of the Icon Palette, or hide it altogether, as follows:

▶ *Left, Right, Top,* or *Bottom* displays the Icon Palette at the indicated position on the 1-2-3 screen.

▶ The *Floating* choice places the Icon Palette in a window you can move to any screen location by dragging it with the mouse. You can also resize the floating Icon Palette by grabbing one of the borders with the mouse and dragging to the new size.

▶ If you select the *Hide Palette* option box, the Icon Palette is not displayed.

The Quick Steps for changing the Icon Palette display follow.

Moving or Hiding the Icon Palette

1. Select Tools Smart Icons.

   The Tools Icon Palette dialog box is displayed (Figure 17.2).

2. Select the desired palette position, or select Hide palette, as described above.

331

3. Select OK.

   1-2-3 displays or hides the Icon palette as specified. □

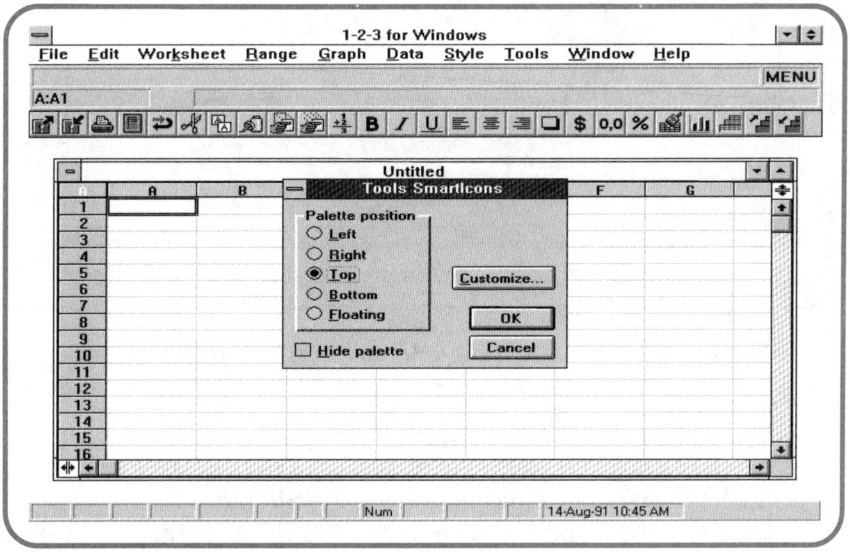

Figure 17.2   *The Tools SmartIcons dialog box.*

Adding and Removing Standard SmartIcons

A *Standard* SmartIcon is one whose function is predefined by 1-2-3. There are over 60 standard SmartIcons available. Only some of them are displayed on the Icon Palette when 1-2-3 is first installed. You can add, delete, and move SmartIcons to customize the Icon Palette to best suit your specific needs.

The first step in customizing the Icon Palette is to select Tools Smart Icons to display the Tools Smart Icons dialog box (Figure 17.2). In this dialog box select Customize to display the Tools Smart Icons Customize dialog box (Figure 17.3). Then, use one of the procedures that follow:

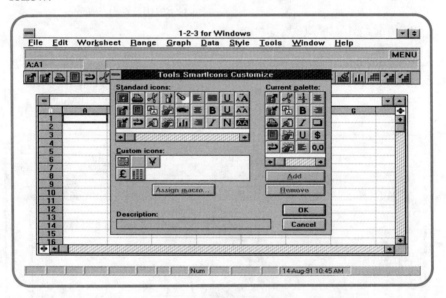

Figure 17.3   The Tools SmartIcons Customize dialog box.

To add a SmartIcon at the end of the existing Icon Palette:

1. Select the desired SmartIcon from the Standard icons box. When a SmartIcon is selected, its description is displayed at the bottom of the dialog box.
2. Select Add.

To add a SmartIcon at a specific location on the Icon Palette:

1. Under Current palette (which shows the SmartIcons currently on the Icon palette), select a SmartIcon. The new SmartIcon will be displayed immediately before the selected SmartIcon.
2. Under Standard icons, select the SmartIcon to be added to the Icon Palette.
3. Select Add.

To remove a SmartIcon from the Icon Palette:

1. Under Current palette, select the SmartIcon to remove.
2. Select Remove.

Repeat the appropriate steps as many times as needed to add and remove the desired SmartIcons. Select OK to redisplay the Tools Smart Icons dialog box, then select OK again. The Icon Palette is displayed with the new selection of SmartIcons.

333

> ▶ **Tip:** The Icon Palette can contain more SmartIcons than can be displayed using the Left, Right, Top, or Bottom position options. If this happens, select a Floating Icon Palette. You will then be able to resize the Icon Palette so that all of the SmartIcons are displayed.

Attaching Macros to SmartIcons

You learned in Chapter 8 that you can write your own macros to automate complex and repetitive worksheet tasks. If you have a macro that you use frequently, you can assign it to a custom SmartIcon. Then, clicking that SmartIcon will execute your macro.

The first step is to write and debug your macro. There are a few special considerations that you must take into account when writing a macro that will be attached to a SmartIcon. To review these items, activate the 1-2-3 for Windows Help system and display the topic *Writing Macros for Custom SmartIcons*.

Q Assigning a Macro to a Custom SmartIcon

1. Select Tools Smart Icons Customize.

   The Tools Smart Icons Customize dialog box is displayed (Figure 17.3).

2. Under Custom icons, select one of the sample SmartIcons or select the blank SmartIcon.

3. Select Assign Macro.

   The Tools Smart Icons Customize Assign Macro dialog box is displayed (Figure 17.4).

4. In the Range text box enter the address of the work sheet range that contains the macro. This must be the range of the entire macro, not just the first cell.

5. Select Get macro.

   The macro is copied from the worksheet to the Macro text box.

6. Select OK three times.

   The macro is assigned to the SmartIcon.   □

> ▶ **Tip:** If desired, change the graphic on the custom SmartIcon (or add a graphic to the blank SmartIcon) using the techniques described in the 1-2-3 for Windows Help system.

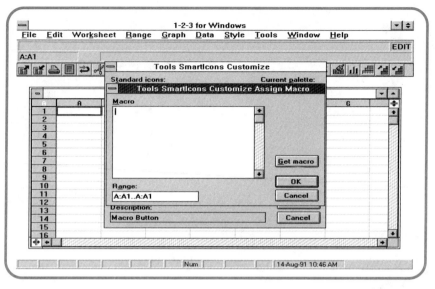

Figure 17.4   The Tools SmartIcons Customize Assign Macro
dialog box.

335

Assigning a macro to a custom SmartIcon does not automatically add the SmartIcon to the Icon Palette. To do so you must follow the steps already described for adding one of the standard SmartIcons to the Icon Palette, selecting the custom icon before selecting Add.

What You Have Learned

▶ SmartIcons are graphic symbols on the 1-2-3 screen that you can click to accomplish frequently needed worksheet tasks.

▶ You can customize the position and contents of the Icon Palette to suit your needs.

▶ User-written macros can be assigned to custom SmartIcons.

Index

Symbols

+/- numeric format, 116
1-2-3 Classic menus, 31
1-2-3 for Windows
   exiting, 31
   installing, 3
   starting, 2-5
3-D area graph, 188
3-D bar graph, 189
3-D line graph, 186
3-D pie graphs, 190

A

About 1-2-3 (Help)
   command, 37
ABS (F4) function key, 152
absolute cell references,
   108-110
activating Solver utility,
   312-314
addition (+) mathematical
   operator, 99

address boxes, 17, 70
adjustable cells, 309-311
aligning text in graphs, 249
{ALT} macro command, 149
ampersand (&) string
   operator, 102
anchoring, 56-59
#AND# logical operator,
   101-102
area graphs, 187
arrows, 2
   in graphs, 237
ASCII data (importing), 273
assigning range names, 61
autoexecute macro, 155-156
automatic
   graphs, 199
   numeric format, 116
AVG @function, 104
axes, 216
   numeric, 218
   scaling, 217

axis scale, 216
axis titles, 221
axis units, 220

B

Back (Help) button, 34
background shading (adding to
  worksheets), 134-136
backward quotes (") label
  prefix character, 72
bar graphs, 188
basic graphs, 182-184
Bookmark (Help) option, 33
borders, 174, 222
  adding to worksheets, 131-
  132
Browse Backward (Help)
  button, 34
Browse Forward (Help)
  button, 34
built-in formulas, 103

C

CALC (F9) function key, 152
canceling dialog boxes, 15
caret (^) label prefix
  character, 72
Cascade (Windows)
  command, 254
cascade menus, 10-13
cell addresses, 40
Cell Contents (Edit Clear
  Special) option, 85
cell pointer, 4
  moving in worksheets,
  48-49
cell references
  absolute, 108-110
  relative, 108-110

cells
  absolute references, 108-110
  adjustable, 309-311
  anchoring, 56-59
  changing fonts for cell
    range, 126-128
  clearing, 85
  constraint, 311-312
  constraint cells, 310
  editing, 90-91
  entering formulas, 98
  erasing, 84-85
  finding and replacing
    entries, 91-94
  height modification, 119,
    123-125
  label alignment
    modification, 128-130
  optimal cells, 310-311
  relative references, 108-110
  width modification, 119-122
changing
  axis scaling, 217
  colors in graphs, 246-247
  display options in graphs,
    250-251
  displaying format for
    numeric axes, 218
  graph types, 196
  object orientation in graphs,
    243
  page setup for a print
    job, 171
Chart Axis Y Options dialog
  box, 222-223
Chart Borders/Grids dialog
  box, 223
Chart Clear dialog box, 231
Chart Data Labels dialog
  box, 215

Chart Headings dialog
    box, 209
Chart Legend dialog box, 211
Chart Legend Group Range
    dialog box, 212
Chart Options Colors dialog
    box, 225-226
Chart Options Fonts dialog
    box, 228-229
Chart Options Lines dialog
    box, 230
Chart Ranges dialog box, 200
Chart Ranges Group Range
    dialog box, 202
Chart Type dialog box, 196
check boxes, 13
Classic menus, 31
clearing cell information, 85
clearing chart settings in
    graphs, 231-232
clicking, 2
closing
    windows, 28
    worksheet files, 264
color in graphs, 224-226,
    246-247
color, changing in worksheet
    display, 133
columns
    deleting, 87-90
    of numbers, 165-166
Combine From (File)
    command, 267-268
combining worksheets, 269
comma numeric format, 115
commands buttons, 13
compressing printouts, 173
concatenation, 102
confirm box, 70
constraint cells, 310-312

constraint formulas, 310
contents boxes, 17, 70
context-sensitive help, 33
control line, 4
controlling minimized
    windows, 22-23
Convert to Values (Edit Quick
    Copy) option, 77
copying
    data, 76-80
    objects in graphs, 242
    with Edit Quick Copy
        command, 76
criteria ranges, 282-284, 288
currency numeric format, 115

D

data
    copying, 76-80
    editing, 90-91
    entering in worksheets, 6
    erasing, 84-85
    labels, 70
    moving, 80-84
    values, 70
Data Fill command, 295-296
Data Fill dialog box, 296
data labels, 213-215
Data Query Delete
    command, 290
Data Query dialog box,
    287-292
Data Query Extract
    command, 289
Data Query Find dialog
    box, 288
Data Query Modify command,
    290-291
data ranges, 198

339

Data Sort dialog box, 280-282
data storage, 69
data types, 69
database @functions, 103
database tables, 279
databases, 277-279
  criteria ranges, 282-284
  data query operations, 287
  deleting data, 290
  entering sequences into
    worksheet ranges, 295-296
  extracting data, 289
  @functions, 293
  modifying data, 290-291
  multiple criteria, 285-286
  performing calculations, 292
  searching, 288
  sorting, 280
DATE @function, 76
date and time @functions, 103
dates, 74-75
DAVG @function, 293
DCOUNT @function, 293
debugging macros, 162-164
deleting
  columns, 87-90
  data from databases, 290
  objects from graphs, 242
  range names, 65, 66
  rows, 87-90
  worksheets, 87-90
descending order, 280
DGET @function, 293
dialog boxes, 13
  anchoring, 56-59
  canceling, 15
  Chart Axis Y Options,
    222-223
  Chart Borders/Grids, 223
  Chart Clear, 231

Chart Data Labels, 215
Chart Headings, 209
Chart Legend, 211
Chart Legend Group
  Range, 212
Chart Options Colors,
  225-226
Chart Options Fonts,
  228-229
Chart Options Lines, 230
Chart Ranges, 200
Chart Ranges Group
  Range, 202
Chart Type, 196
check boxes, 13
command buttons, 13
Data Fill, 296
Data Query, 287, 292
Data Query Find, 288
Data Sort, 280-282
dotted lines, 13
Draw Freehand, 239
Draw Polygon, 238
Draw Rectangle, 239
Draw Text, 236
drop-down boxes, 13
Edit Clear Special, 86
Edit Move Cells, 82
File Close, 29, 264
File Import From Text, 274
File Open, 259
File Page Setup, 171
File Page Setup Named
  Save, 175
File Preview, 170
File Print, 168
File Save As, 259
Graph Add to Sheet, 203
Graph New, 183
Graph View, 203

340

highlighting characters, 16
information boxes, 13
list boxes, 13
moving within, 14-16
option buttons, 13
Range Name Delete, 66
Range Name Label
    Create, 64
Solver Definition, 313-316
Solver Report, 317
Solver Report
    Differences, 322
Style Color, 247
Style Display Options,
    250-251
Style Fonts, 246
text boxes, 13
title bar, 13
Tools Icon Palette, 331
Tools Icon Palette
    Customize, 332
Tools Macro Debug, 164
Tools Macro Run, 151
Tools User Setup, 156
Tools User Setup
    International, 303
Window Split, 43
Worksheet Delete, 89
Worksheet Global
    Settings, 300
Worksheet Global Settings
    Format, 301
Worksheet Insert, 42
Worksheet Page Break, 177
displaying
    Classic menus, 31
    different parts of same
        worksheet, 44
    graphs, 7
    multiple worksheets, 42

pulldown menus, 12
    Window Control menu, 23
    WYSIWYG menu, 31
division (/) mathematical
    operator, 100
DMAX @function, 293
DMIN @function, 293
documents, inserting page
    breaks, 177
double-clicking, 2
dragging, 2
draft mode (printing
    worksheets), 143
Draw Freehand dialog box, 239
Draw Polygon dialog box, 238
Draw Rectangle dialog box, 239
Draw Text dialog box, 236
drop shadows (adding to
    worksheets), 131-132
drop-down boxes, 13
DSTD @function, 293
DSTDS @function, 293
DSUM @function, 293
dual Y-axes graphs, 197
DVAR @function, 293
DVARS @function, 293

341

E

EDIT (F2) function key, 152
Edit (Help) option, 33
Edit Clear command, 84
Edit Clear Special command,
    84, 141
Edit Clear Special dialog
    box, 86
Edit Copy command, 80
Edit Cut command, 83-84
EDIT mode, 90-91
Edit Move Cells command,
    81-82

Edit Move Cells dialog box, 82
Edit Quick Copy command, 76
Edit Undo command, 95
editing
    cells, 90-91
    data, 90-91
    data in databases, 290-291
    graph text, 244-245
ellipses in graphs, 239
End key, 49
Enlarge (Window)
    command, 253
entering
    columns of numbers into
        worksheets, 165-166
    data in worksheets, 6
    dates, 74-75
    formulas into cells, 98
    labels, 72
    sequence of values into
        databases, 295
    time, 74-76
    values, 70
    equal to (=) logical
        operator, 101
erasing
    data, 84-85
    graphics, 85
    ranges of cells, 84-85
ERR indicator, 111
errors, 162
    undoing, 95
executing macros, 150
exiting 1-2-3 for Windows, 31
exponential notation, 115
exponentiation (^)
    mathematical operator, 100
Extract To (File) command,
    267-271

extracting data
    from databases, 289
    from worksheets, 270-271
    to disk files, 271-272

F

Fall Back (Layout)
    command, 252
File (Help) option, 33
File Close dialog box, 29, 264
File Import From Text dialog
    box, 274
File Open dialog box, 259
File Page Setup dialog
    box, 171
File Page Setup Named Save
    dialog box, 175
File Preview dialog box, 170
File Save As dialog box, 259
Fill (Data) command, 295-296
financial @functions, 103
finding and replacing entries,
    91-94
fixed numeric format, 114
fonts, 125, 228-229
    changing for cell ranges,
        126-128
footers, printing, 171-172
footnotes, 208-209
For Upgraders (Help)
    command, 37
formats, 113
    numeric, 114-117
        +/-, 116
        automatic, 116
        changing display, 118
        comma, 115
        currency, 115
        hidden, 116

label, 116
parentheses, 116
percent, 115
removing from range,
141-142
scientific, 115
text, 116
formulas
@functions, 103
automatically
recalculating, 111
constraint, 310
referencing, 104-107
writing, 98
forward slash (\) label prefix
character, 72
freehand drawings in graphs,
239-240
Full (Window) command, 253
function keys
as macro commands, 152
GoTo (F5), 50, 152
Help (F1), 33
@functions, 103-104, 293
DATE, 76
DAVG, 293
DCOUNT, 293
DGET, 293
DMAX, 293
DMIN, 293
DSTD, 293
DSTDS, 293
DSUM, 293
DVAR, 293
DVARS, 293
in Solver utility, 327-328
@function (Help)
command, 37

G

general numeric format, 114
Global Settings (Worksheet)
command, 118, 300-301
GoTo (F5) function key,
50, 152
grabbing, 2
Graph (Edit Clear Special)
option, 85
Graph Add to Sheet dialog
box, 203
Graph New command, 184
Graph View dialog box, 203
graph windows, 181
graphics, erasing, 84-85
graphs, 180-181
3-D area, 188
3-D bar, 189
3-D line, 186
3-D pie, 190
adding
arrows and lines, 237
axis titles, 221
data labels, 215
ellipses, 239
footnotes, 208-209
freehand drawings,
239-240
legends, 210-211
multiple-segment
lines, 237
polygons, 237-238
rectangles, 239
text, 235-236
titles, 208-209
aligning text, 249
area, 187
automatic, 199
axes, 216

344

axis scaling, 218-219
bar, 188
borders, 222
changing
    colors, 246-247
    display options, 250-251
    line styles, 248-249
    object orientation, 243
    types, 196
    window displays, 252
chart fonts, 228-229
chart hatch patterns, 226
clearing chart settings,
    231-232
copying objects, 242
creating, 182-184
data labels, 213-214
deleting objects, 242
displaying, 7
dual Y axes, 197
editing text, 244-245
grids, 222
HLCO (High-Low-Close-
    Open), 192-194
inserting into worksheets,
    203-204
line, 185-186
line display options,
    229-230
mixed, 194-195
moving, 204
    objects, 243
pie, 190
plotting values, 192
printing, 176
resetting defaults, 231-232
saving, 202
selecting
    objects, 240-242
    types, 196

setting chart options,
    224-226
viewing, 202
XY, 192
zooming, 253-254
grayed text, 11
greater than (>) logical
    operator, 101
greater than or equal to (>=)
    logical operator, 101
grids, 222
Group Mode, 140
group ranges, 201-202

H

headers, 171-172
help, context-sensitive, 33
Help (F1) function key, 33, 152
Help (Help) option, 36
Help Index, 33-34
Help pulldown menu, 36
Help system, 32
Help window, 33-34
hidden numeric format, 116
hiding Icon Palette, 330-331
HLCO (High-Low-Close-Open)
    graphs, 192-194
horizontal page breaks, 177
Horizontal Pane, 46
horizontal window panes, 45
hourglass, 2
How Do I (Help) command, 37

I

indicator line, 141
Icon Palette, 16-17, 329
    adding SmartIcons, 332-333
    hiding, 330-331
    moving, 330-331

icon palette, 4
Import From (File)
   command, 273
importing
   ASCII data, 273
   data from other programs,
      272-273
Index (Help) button, 34
Index (Help) command, 37
indicate box, 70
information boxes, 13
input ranges, 287
inserting
   graphs into worksheets,
      203-204
   horizontal/vertical page
      breaks, 177
   worksheets into worksheet
      files, 41
installing 1-2-3 for Windows, 3

K

Keyboard (Help) command, 37
keyboard commands, 49-50
keystroke macros, 151-153

L

label criteria, 284
label numeric format, 116
label prefix characters, 72
labels, 69, 74, 128
   assigning as range names,
      62-63
   data, 213-215
   entering, 72
      dates, 74-75
      time, 74-75
   modifying alignment,
      128-130

landscape orientation, 173-174
Layout Fall Back command, 252
Layout Lock command, 252
Layout Send Forward
   command, 252
Layout Unlock command, 252
legends, 210-211
less than (<) logical
   operator, 101
less than or equal to (<=)
   logical operator, 101
line graphs, 185-186
lines in graphs, 248-249
list boxes, 13
Lock (Layout) command, 252
logical @functions, 103
logical operators, 101-102

M

macro commands, 154-155
   {ALT}, 149
macros, 148-149
   as navigation keys, 152
   attaching to SmartIcons,
      333-335
   autoexecute, 155-156
   debugging, 162-164
   errors, 162
   executing, 150
   keystroke, 151-153
   naming, 150
      backslash names, 150
      multiple character
         names, 150
   playing back, 161
   recording, 157-161
   stopping, 150
   storing, 149
Macros (Help) command, 37
Main 1-2-3 Window, 29-30

345

346

mantissa, 115
manual range selection, 199-200
margins, 172
mathematical @functions, 103
mathematical operators, 99
maximize window boxes, 17
maximizing windows, 20-21, 24
menu bar, 4, 10, 17
MENU (F10) function key, 152
menu pointer, 11
menus, 10
  cascade, 10
  Classic, 31
  Data, 290
  Edit, 84
  Graph, 184
  grayed text, 11
  Help, 33
  Layout, 251
  pulldown, 10
    displaying, 12
    Help, 36
  Range, 61
  selecting commands, 12
  Style, 246
  Tools, 302
  Window, 253
  Window Control, 20
  Worksheet, 300
  WYSIWYG, 31
MIN @function, 104
minimize window boxes, 17
minimizing windows, 20-23
mixed graphs, 194-195
modes
  EDIT, 90-91
  Group, 140
  POINT, 56-59, 104-107

STEP, 162-164
TRACE, 162-164
mouse, 1-2
mouse pointer, 1
moving
  between worksheets, 49-50
  cell pointer between active worksheet files, 263
  cell pointers in worksheets, 48-49
  data, 80-84
  Icon Palette, 330-331
  in worksheets (keyboard commands), 49-50
  inserted graphs, 204
  objects in graphs, 243
  windows, 24
  within dialog boxes, 14-16
multiple criteria, 285-286
multiple worksheet files, 261
multiple worksheets, 42
multiplication (*)
  mathematical operator, 100

N

NAME (F3) function key, 152
naming
  macros, 150
  ranges, 60-61
    assigning labels as names, 62-63
navigating in worksheet files, 47-48
navigation keys, 152
not equal to (<>) logical operator, 101
#NOT# logical operator, 101-102

Number Format (Edit Clear Special) option, 85
numeric axes, 218
numeric formats, 114-117
    changing display, 118
    removing from range, 141-142

O

object orientation in graphs, 243
objects in graphs, 240-242
opening
    worksheet files, 258
        windows, 3
operator precedence, 99
operators, 99
    logical, 101-102
    mathematical, 99-100
    order of precedence, 100
    string, 102
optimal cells, 310-311
option buttons, 13
#OR# logical operator, 101-102
order of precedence, 100
orientation, 173-174
output ranges, 288

P

page breaks, 176
    horizontal, 177
    vertical, 177
page layout library file, 175
Page Setup dialog box, 171-172
PANE (F6) function key, 152

parentheses numeric format, 116
password protection, 260, 305-306
percent numeric format, 115
period (.) character, 56-59
Perspective View, 46
pie graphs, 190
playing back macros, 161
plotting values on graphs, 192
PMT @function, 104
POINT mode, 56-59, 104-107
pointing, 2
points, 126
polygons in graphs, 237-238
portrait orientation, 173-174
previewing before printing, 169-170
primary sort key, 280
Print File dialog box, 168
Print Preview window, 170
printing
    adjusting margins, 172
    borders, 174
    changing page setup, 171
    compressing printouts, 173
    controlling page breaks, 176
    graphs, 176
    headers, 171-172
    orientations, 173-174
    previewing, 169-170
    reports, 167-168
    worksheets, 167-168
        in draft mode, 143
protection, 305-306
pulldown menus, 10
    displaying, 12
    Help, 36
    selecting commands, 12-13

Q

QUERY (F7) function key, 152
Query Delete (Data)
  command, 290
Query Modify (Data)
  command, 290-291
querying databases, 288

R

Range Format command, 114
Range Name Create
  command, 61
Range Name Delete
  command, 65-66
Range Name Delete dialog
  box, 66
Range Name Label Create
  command, 150
Range Name Label Create
  dialog box, 64
Range Name Past Table
  command, 66
ranges, 53
  assigning labels as names,
    62-63
  creating tables of names, 66
  criteria, 282-284
  data, 198-200
  deleting names, 65-66
  entering into a formula in
    POINT mode, 104-107
  erasing, 84-85
  group, 201-202
  naming, 60-61
  removing styles/numeric
    formatting from, 141-142
  selecting, 55-59
  three-dimensional, 59-60
  two-dimensional, 54-55
  using in legends, 212

recalculating worksheets, 304
recording, 156-161
rectangles in graphs, 239
Reduce (Window)
  command, 253
referencing formulas, 104-107
relative cell references,
  108-110
reports
  Answer Table, 320
  Cells Used, 319-320
  Differences report, 321
  generating from the Solver
    Utility, 317-318
    Answer Table Report,
      319-320
    Cells Used, 319-320
    Differences, 320
    How Solved, 326-327
    Inconsistent Restraints, 323
    Unused Constraints, 324
    What-if Limits, 325
  How Solved, 326-327
  Inconsistent Constraint, 323
  printing, 167-168
  Unused Constraints, 324
  What-if Limits, 325
repositioning windows, 25-27
resizing windows, 24-25
restoring
  page setups, 174
  windows, 23

S

saving
  current page setup, 175
  graphs, 202
  multiple worksheet
    files, 263
  page setups, 174

user settings for
worksheets, 305
worksheet files, 165,
258-260
scattergrams, 192
scientific numeric format, 115
screens, 4
scroll bars, 48
Search (Help) button, 34
searching databases, 288
secondary sort key, 280
selecting
axis units, 220
data in other worksheet
files, 265-267
data ranges, 198-200
graph objects, 240-242
graph types, 196
menu commands, 12-13
numeric axis scale type, 220
ranges, 55-59
Send Forward (Layout)
command, 252
serial numbers, 75
setting
axis scale types, 219
chart fonts in graphs,
228-229
chart hatch patterns, 226
chart options for graphs,
224-226
line display options for
graphs, 229-230
pages, 171
single backward quote (') label
prefix character, 72
SmartIcons, 16, 329
adding macros, 333-335
Solver Answer Table Report,
319-320

Solver Definition dialog box,
313-316
Solver Differences report, 321
Solver How Solved report,
326-327
Solver Inconsistent Restraints
report, 323
Solver Report dialog box, 317
Solver Report Differences
dialog box, 322
Solver Unused Constraints
report, 324
Solver utility, 307-316
activating, 312-314
adjustable cells, 309-311
Cells Used report, 320
constraint cells, 310-312
generating reports, 317-318
optimal cells, 310-311
reports, 319-324
using @functions, 327-328
What-if Limits report, 325
sorting databases, 280
special @functions, 103
splitting windows into panes, 44
SQRT @function, 104
standard SmartIcons, 332-333
starting 1-2-3 for Windows, 2-5
statistical @functions, 103
status line, 4, 17
STEP mode, 162-164
stopping macros, 150
storing macros, 149
string @functions, 103
string operators, 102
strings, 98
style, 113
creating named style for
worksheets, 136-137
removing from range,
141-142

349

Style Alignment command, 128
Style (Edit Clear Special)
    option, 85
Style Color command, 246-247
Style Color dialog box, 247
Style Display Options dialog
    box, 250-251
Style Fonts dialog box, 246
Styles Only (Edit Quick Copy)
    option, 77
Style Shading command, 134
SUM @function, 104
Synchronization (Window
    Split) button, 46
synchronizing worksheets, 46

T

TABLE (F8) function key, 152
text boxes, 13
text in graphs, 235-236,
    244-245, 249
text numeric format, 116
three-dimensional
    ranges, 59-60
    worksheet, 39
Tile (Windows) command, 254
time, 74-76
title bar, 4, 13, 17
titles, adding to graphs,
    208-209
toggling, 14
Tools Icon Palette Customize
    dialog box, 332
Tools Icon Palette dialob
    box, 331
Tools Macro Debug dialog
    box, 164
Tools Macro Run dialog
    box, 151

Tools User Setup command,
    302-303
Tools User Setup dialog
    box, 156
Tools User Setup International
    dialog box, 303
TRACE mode, 162-164
Transcript window, 156
TRUE/FALSE answers, 101
two-dimensional ranges, 54-55

U

undefining range names, 65
undoing errors, 95
Unlock (Layout)
    command, 252
unsplitting windows, 44
User Setup (Tools) command,
    302-303
Using Help (Help)
    command, 37

V

values, 69, 295
    entering, 70
        dates/times, 74-75
    plotting, 192
vertical page breaks, 177
Vertical Pane, 47
vertical window panes, 45
viewing
    graphs, 202
    multiple worksheet files,
        262-263

W

Window Control menu, 20-23
window control menu box, 17
window panes, 44

350

windows, 17
  address box, 17
  changing displays, 252
  closing, 28
  contents boxes, 17
  graph, 181
  Help, 33
  Main 1-2-3, 29-30
  maximize windows box, 17
  maximizing, 20-21, 24
  minimize windows box, 17
  minimizing, 20
  moving, 24
  opening, 3
  Print Preview, 170
  repositioning, 25-27
  resizing, 24-25
  restoring, 23
  splitting panes, 44-45
  status indicator, 17
  status line, 17
  title bar, 17
  unsplitting, 44
  windows control menu
    box, 17
  work area, 17
  worksheet, 18-19
Windows Cascade command, 254
Windows Enlarge
  command, 253
Windows Full command, 253
Windows Program Manager, 4
Windows Reduce
  command, 253
Windows Split dialog box, 43
Windows Tile command, 254
Windows Zoom command, 253
work area, 17
Worksheet Delete dialog
  box, 89

worksheet files, 39, 258
  adding worksheets, 41
  cell addresses, 40
  closing, 264
  inserting worksheets, 41
  moving cell pointer, 263
  multiple, 261
  navigating in, 47-48
  opening, 258
  saving, 165, 258-259, 263
    with passwords, 260
  selecting data from other
    files, 265-267
  viewing, 262-263
Worksheet Global Settings
  command, 300-301
Worksheet Global Settings
  dialog box, 300
Worksheet Global Settings
  Format dialog box, 301
Worksheet Insert dialog
  box, 42
Worksheet Page Break dialog
  box, 177
Worksheet Titles command,
  143
worksheets, 39
  adding
    background shading,
      134-136
    borders/drop shadow,
      131-132
    to worksheet files, 41
  assigning labels as range
    names, 62-63
  automating tasks with
    macros, 148-149
  borders, 174
  combining, 269
  copying data, 76, 80

351

deleting, 87-90
displaying, 42-44
entering
    columns of numbers,
        165-166
    data, 6
    time, 75-76
    values into cells, 70
erasing ranges of cells, 84
extracting data, 270-271
extracting/combining data,
    267-268
formats, 113-118
frame, 39
freezing titles on screen,
    143-144
global settings, 300-301
Group Mode utilization, 140
Horizontal Pane, 46
inserting graphs, 203-204
modifying
    cell height, 119, 123-125
    cell width, 119-122
    color displayed, 133
    fonts for cell range,
        126-128
    label alignment, 128-130
    settings, 302-303

moving
    between, 49-50
    cell pointers, 48-49
    inserted graphs, 204
Perspective View, 46
printing, 167-168
    in draft mode, 143
protecting, 305-306
ranges in legends, 212
recalculating, 304
removing styles/numeric
    formatting from range,
    141-142
storing macros, 149
style, 113
    creating named style for,
        136-137
synchronizing, 46
three-dimensional, 39
Vertical Pane, 47
windows, 4, 18-19
writing formulas, 98
WYSIWYG menu, 31

X-Z

XY graphs, 192
YEAR @function, 104
Zoom (Window) command, 253
zooming graphs, 253-254